How To Be A Smart
MONEY
MANAGER

...without being a Wall Street wizard

ETHAN POPE

A
JANET
THOMA
BOOK

THOMAS NELSON PUBLISHERS

Nashville • Atlanta • London • Vancouver

For speaking and conference information, write:

Ethan Pope
Financial Foundations for Living
P.O. Box 15356
Hattiesburg, MS 39404

Published in Nashville, Tennessee, by Thomas Nelson, Inc., Publishers, and distributed in Canada by Word Communications, Ltd., Richmond, British Columbia.

Unless otherwise indicated, the Bible version used in this publication is THE NEW KING JAMES VERSION. Copyright © 1979, 1980, 1982, 1990, Thomas Nelson, Inc., Publishers. Scripture verses indicated TLB are from *The Living Bible* (Wheaton, Illinois: Tyndale House Publishers, 1971) and are used by permission. Scripture verses indicated NAS are from the NEW AMERICAN STANDARD BIBLE, copyright © 1960, 1962, 1963, 1968, 1971, 1972, 1973, 1975, 1977 by The Lockman Foundation and are used by permission.

NOTE: This book is not intended to give SPECIFIC legal, tax, or investment counsel. Its purpose is to give general insight in the area of personal financial planning while simplifying and clarifying financial issues from both a biblical and practical perspective. All principles taught are general in nature and are not to be taken as specific recommendations for any individual or business. Every attempt has been made to verify the information in financial tables, charts, and planning worksheets in this volume; however, the reader is urged to seek independent verification before basing decisions on these figures. Neither the author nor the publisher can take responsibility for readers' decisions based on this data. Finally, every financial decision needs to be evaluated in light of current tax laws. Changes in the tax laws may decrease the relevancy of some of the illustrations used in this book.

All illustrations and stories included in this book are composites and summaries of the author's work in financial counseling. Illustrations have been pieced together from bits of counseling sessions and from conversations with hundreds of individuals at conferences, seminars, and lectures. Some of the illustrations or stories are not based upon actual events, but are a combination of lessons learned.

Certified Financial Planner is a federally registered mark of the Certified Financial Board of Standards, Inc.

Library of Congress Cataloging-in-Publication Data

Pope, Ethan.
   How to be a smart money manager—without being a Wall Street wizard / Ethan Pope.
     p. cm.
    ISBN 0-8407-7709-4
    1. Finance, Personal—Moral and ethical aspects. 2. Investments—Moral and ethical aspects. I. Title
HG179.P558 1995
332.024—dc20

94-37272
CIP

Printed in the United States of America.
1 2 3 4 5 6 — 00 99 98 97 96 95

Thanks to . . .

Janet, for being my *best* friend.
Natalie, for bringing so much *joy* in my life.
Austin, for being my *faithful* buddy.
Janet Thoma, for *helping* to make
this book the best it could be.
Thomas Nelson Publishers for taking me on as an author.
I am indeed *thankful*.

CONTENTS

How To Be A Smart
MONEY
MANAGER
...without being a Wall Street wizard

TEN HABITS THAT COULD CHANGE YOUR LIFE:

How to Be a Smart Money Manager

1

Vince Lombardi, the great football coach of the world champion Green Bay Packers, on occasion would hold up a football and say, "This is a football." Every year, year after year, Coach Lombardi would teach his players the basics . . . the fundamentals of football.

Every discipline in life has certain fundamentals or basics that must never be forgotten. In football it is how to tackle. In baseball it is how to throw a baseball. In tennis it is the swing. In speaking it is communication techniques. Whether it is football, baseball, or money management, we *must* know and understand the basics! Financial planning is no exception. There are fundamental principles that we must never forget.

During the past ten years of my life, I have had the privilege of teaching and interacting with thousands of individuals concerning their financial lives. Some could not be happier with their personal circumstances, while others would end their story with tears streaming down their faces. However, if you are like most of the people I have talked with, you are somewhere in between those sparkling eyes and the tear-filled ones.

People seek me out because of two major reasons: stress and disorganization.

The Two Most Common Reasons for Seeking Help

Stress

Usually at the end of my first session with a couple or a single person, I will ask the question, "What motivated you to pick up the telephone and call me?" Most responses include the word *stress*. The pain level had risen so high they had to seek relief.

Stress can be caused by a number of factors: A little disorganization. Uncertainty of the future. Lack of communication. Lack of knowledge.

I remember a telephone call from a retired couple in Arizona who were both in their seventies. "We are very concerned that our money is going to run out before we die," they said. I could sense their tension and frustration as I talked to both of them on the telephone. The wife even said she was getting more depressed every day. After several minutes of gathering data and a few quick calculations, I was able to estimate that they could continue to make their present monthly withdrawals for the next twenty years or more. In their case, stress was caused by lack of knowledge about their financial condition. Several days later, I received one of the kindest notes from this couple.

Not every counseling appointment has such a happy ending, however. I have to inform some people that they will be suffering the consequences of their financial mistakes for years to come. Yes, you do, indeed, reap the consequences of what you sow.

Stress relief is very possible for anyone who seeks it. It will take some work, but it is well worth your effort. Life is like a pressure cooker; we all need a pressure-relief valve. This book should help relieve some financial pressure from your life!

Disorganization

I am no longer amazed at how many families fail to organize their financial lives. One couple walked into my office with a manila file folder. Unfortunately (for both of us) that one folder was about six inches wide and stuffed full of past-due bills, bank statements, payment stubs, booklets, notes—everything but the kitchen sink!

Others will have their valuables in an old shoe box. It is ironic that a person will spend six hours working in the yard and only six *minutes* working on his or her financial matters, and then wonder why the finances are always a mess.

Now before we place too much blame on these people, though, think about their financial training—and your own. How many years were you in the formal education system? Your answers probably range from twelve years to sixteen or even twenty years. Next question: How many classes did you have on personal money management during all those school years?

If you are like most people, your answer is, Not one! Did anyone prepare you for some of the most basic aspects of financial management such as using credit cards, buying a house or car, preparing a budget, balancing a checkbook? In fact, most people never once heard the words *money management* during their formal education. Our educational system never took the time to teach us the basics of one of the most important aspects of our lives: how to manage our money.

Now don't read me wrong. I believe in the disciplines of science, mathematics, English, and history. These are all very worthwhile subjects. But let's be realistic. During this week, how much did you use the knowledge you learned in history? How many checks did you write? How many credit card transactions did you make? How many purchases did you make? Ten, twenty, fifty, or even a hundred?

Money is one aspect of our lives that will not just go away. It does not matter if you are a doctor, truck driver, teacher, mechanic, preacher, or rocket scientist . . . you deal with financial issues in some way every day of your life!

Are you absolutely worn out from being financially disorganized? Do you get the impression that your financial life could be compared to a three-ring circus? Well, help is on the way. There are solutions to your problems. This book can help you organize your financial life!

Let Me Be Your Coach

I cannot become everyone's personal financial planner. It's literally impossible, especially through a book. But let me coach you through the process and instruct you in the basics of financial planning.

In the world of finance everything seems to be so complex . . . but it doesn't have to be that way. I have found that most financial principles are, in reality, very simple. Individuals either write to me or come up to me after a seminar and say things like, "I never knew finances could be so simple," or "This is the first time I have ever understood how to manage my money."

As in any area of instruction, the teacher or coach is very important. Remember the first time you learned how to add numbers as a young child? Something just clicked inside your head. You thought,

Wow, this is how it really works! Chances are the teacher simplified the concept so it was easily understandable.

By spending a little time in training in my systems, you will be able to quickly answer the questions on the following quiz. But just for fun, see how well our educational system has prepared you to answer them now. (The answers follow the quiz.)

FINANCIAL QUICK QUIZ

1. What will the total cost be for a $100,000 mortgage for thirty years at 10 percent? (Go ahead and guess, even if you don't know.) $_____

2. If you saved $2,000 every year and it earned 9 percent interest, how much would you have in forty-five years? $_____

3. How many years will it take for your money to double if it earns 8 percent interest? _____ years

4. What is the number one cause of most financial problems?

    _____

5. You have just purchased a $10,000 car. The car dealer says your monthly payments will be $253.63 for the next forty-eight months. How much is that $10,000 car really going to cost you? $_____

QUICK QUIZ ANSWERS

Now let's take a look at the answers to these questions, and the way you can easily calculate them.

1. **$315,925.20.** Without doing any calculations, I have learned that any amount of debt spread out over thirty years will cost about three times the original loan: $100,000 × 3 = $300,000. (Time needed for a trained individual to answer this kind of question: five seconds.)

The actual cost would be: $877.57 monthly payment × 12 months × 30 years = $315,925.20.

2. **$1,051,717.47.** To answer this question, you need a very basic understanding of a concept called the "time value of money," which we will discuss in Chapter 3. The charts given in this book can help you calculate the answer to questions just like this one in less than one minute.

3. **Nine years.** For this question, you only need to know the rule of 72 (which I will explain completely in Chapter 9). The rule of 72 says that if you take 72 and divide it by the interest rate you project to earn, you will find out how many years it will take for your money to double.

Example: 72 divided by 8 = 9 years. Time needed to answer this question: 5 seconds.

4. **Lack of setting financial goals and having a plan.** Most people don't plan to fail, they just fail to plan.

5. **$12,174.24.** Multiply the monthly payment of $253.63 × 48 months = $12,174.24. This means you will be paying $2,174.24 in interest for your $10,000 car.

Get the picture? I hope you're starting to see that anyone can understand the practical concepts and tips that can improve his or her financial outlook. But before we begin our journey toward smart money management, let's get just a little more personal. Tell me, how are you doing in your financial life? One way to find out is to take a financial checkup.

The Financial Checkup

Just as many people go to a medical doctor for an annual physical checkup, we also need to give ourselves an annual financial checkup to help identify any problems.

Several years ago I designed a financial checkup that I give to people on my first appointment with them. I always explain that this checkup is designed to help me quickly determine where their problems are and what our immediate plan of action needs to be; it's not intended to embarrass them or cause them to feel guilty. Within a few minutes, I can determine how serious the situation is, why they are having problems, and what areas need to be worked on.

Take a few minutes now to take this financial checkup. Write your score for each answer in the blank space in front of the question.

FINANCIAL CHECKUP

_____ I have the equivalent of one month's salary in savings available for a crisis. (10 points for more, 5 points for one month, and 0 points for no savings)

_____ I have no outstanding *past-due* bills. (5 points for a yes)

_____ I save money each month to pay for major expenses like Christmas or car insurance. (5 points for a yes)

_____ I have written financial goals for my life. (5 points for a yes)

_____ I am prepaying on my mortgage to quickly reduce the debt and save on interest. Or my house is completely debt free. (5 points for a yes)

_____ I have insurance on my car(s). (5 points for a yes)

_____ I have insurance on my home or apartment. (5 points for a yes)

_____ I have health insurance. (5 points for a yes)

_____ I have disability insurance. (5 points for a yes)

_____ If you are earning income, do you have life insurance coverage equivalent to at least five times your annual income? (5 points for a yes)

_____ I have filled out a personal balance sheet within the last twelve months. (5 points for a yes)

_____ I have a written budget that I use every week/month. (5 points for a yes)

_____ There is no tension or stress in our family over money issues. (5 points for a yes, 3 points for some, 0 points for much tension)

_____ I have a legal will. (If married, both the husband and wife have wills.) (5 points for a yes)

_____ I have a regular savings plan for salary income. Do not consider company pension plans in answering this question. (1 point for each percent of salary saved, with a maximum of 10 points)

_____ I am involved and take advantage of my company pension savings plan. (5 for yes or company offers no plan, 3 for one spouse involved, 0 for no involvement in an offered plan)

_____ I make charitable contributions. (5 points for 10 percent, 2 points for 5 percent, 0 points for less)

_____ I pay all my credit card bills in full every month. (5 points for a yes, 0 points for a no)

_____ Write your total here, then mark your score below:

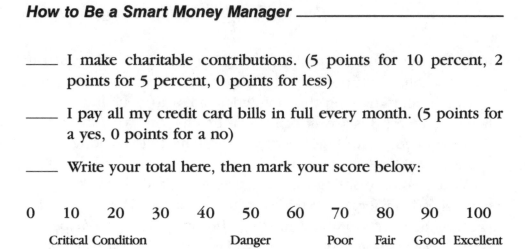

0	10	20	30	40	50	60	70	80	90	100
Critical Condition					Danger		Poor	Fair	Good	Excellent

How did you do? The following analysis will help you assess your situation.

Excellent: Keep up the good work. Your financial life appears to be in good shape. No one is perfect, but you appear to have a well-rounded approach to maximizing your personal financial plan. We can all improve, but you are definitely on the right track. Remember, though, that pride comes before the fall (see Prov. 16:18). Be careful not to let down your guard and fall prey to some very costly mistakes. Give yourself a big pat on the back; you are definitely to be commended for your efforts.

Good: Once again, keep up the good work. It appears you have one or two areas that you either have overlooked in your financial plan or in which you just need to exhibit some self-discipline. Take a few minutes to determine where you are falling short. Make some written action points and begin to improve your plan. You have covered most of the basics; now why not try to score a home run within the next six to twelve months? Hang in there.

Fair: You are probably doing enough to keep yourself out of major trouble, but stress points are beginning to appear. If you are married, financial arguments are probably a regular aspect of your marriage. You probably could not handle a major medical bill or car repair at this time, and knowing this only adds stress to your life. There is hope, however; this aspect of life can be changed with some work. Don't settle for a life of mediocrity. Spend some time working on your financial life!

Poor: You are sitting on the fence. Make a definite decision to move ahead in your financial life before it is too late. Don't be discouraged about your score and give up. However, you *should* be concerned. Start making changes today! The decisions you make during the next few months could change the destiny of your financial life. Seeking financial counsel is recommended for you.

Danger: The warning horn is sounding, and red lights are flashing. You are probably experiencing occasional wind gusts of up to one hundred miles per hour in your financial life, and you are wondering if you will be able to survive the storm. Danger is imminent if problems have not already arrived. One major expense, one car accident, one major medical bill could affect your financial life for the next ten to twenty years. Don't delay one day seeking financial counsel and help.

Critical Condition: All vital signs are fading fast. Unfortunately, there appears to be no financial plan at all. If you are not already living in complete financial bondage, it's an absolute miracle. Seek financial counsel fast. Your number one priority must be to get your financial house in order!

No matter what the results of your checkup, you will begin to find many answers to your financial questions in the following pages. Use this book as your personal financial adviser.

After years of study, I have compiled a list of ten habits of smart money managers.

The Ten Habits of Smart Money Managers

Smart money managers:

1. Have a plan. Set financial goals.
2. Control their debt.
3. Have a consistent savings program.
4. Live within their means.
5. Plan for a crisis.
6. Are generous givers.
7. Understand money myths.
8. Have a MAP (a budget, but one that is quite unique).
9. Have an eternal perspective.
10. Take charge of their finances.

Many of these habits seem very basic. It's my methods of implementing them that will change your life.

In Chapter 2 we will talk about financial goals. Did you know that most people will earn over one million dollars during their working lives? Yet few will plan to use that money effectively.

In Chapter 3 we will talk about the time value of money. I have developed quick, easy-to-use tables to answer questions such as:

- How much money do I need to save each month in order to have ——————————— dollars?

- How much will my investment be worth in thirty years?

- How much do I need in a fund today to accumulate a ——————————— dollar goal in the future?

In Chapters 4, 5, 6, and 7 we will discuss the dangerous lure of debt. I will show how you can make wise decisions in three major areas that often lead to debt: credit card usage, home mortgage commitments, and car purchases. Did you know you can buy four cars and get the fifth one free? (We'll talk about that in Chapter 6.)

Then in Chapter 8 we will look at the prevalent misconception that "more money will solve my financial problems." I've found that people need to learn how to live within their means. Did you know you can reduce your spending during your working life and save yourself between $62,000 and $700,000?

Once you get control of your spending you will be able to develop a consistent savings program, which is the topic of Chapter 9. I will show you how to save more than one million dollars in a lifetime! In fact you can end up with 100 percent of your lifetime earnings by saving just 10 percent per year!

Yet a smart money manager must always plan for a crisis, which is the topic of Chapter 10. We will discuss the possibilities of reducing your insurance in small ways so you can have adequate amounts of health, life, and home insurance.

And a smart money manager is a generous giver. We'll discuss that in Chapter 11 and then look at typical money myths in Chapter 12. Does the "I can write it off on my taxes" philosophy really work?

Finally, in the last chapters in the book I will present my money allocation plan, a unique but simple budgeting system, and help you to develop your own personal financial plan.

As you can already tell, you need to have a sharp pencil and a recharged calculator to obtain the maximum benefit from this book. Highlight the important concepts for future study. Wear it out from cover to cover!

Money . . . either you will master it, or it will master you. Either it will become your friend, or it will become your enemy. Either it will help you to accomplish your goals in life, or it will destroy your ambitions.

In the spirit of Vince Lombardi, "This is money." Turn the page and we'll start with the basics of smart money management.

FINANCIAL GOALS:
You Can Save over One Million Dollars in a Lifetime!

2

It was one of the most awesome sights I have ever seen in my life. The setting was the opening ceremony of the Winter Olympics in 1992. The Olympic torch, which had traveled from Greece, entered the stadium; the runner carried it proudly in his hand as he circled the stadium. The crowd was on its feet, cheering wildly.

The lights went out when the runner stopped in the middle of the stadium. An archer stepped forward and lit an arrow from the runner's torch. Then the archer took one step forward, cocked the bow, aimed, and shot the flaming arrow into the dark midnight sky, high over the spectators' heads. The arrow fell perfectly, igniting the large Olympic torch high above the last row of seats. This was the torch that would burn during the coming days of Olympic competition.

As the crowd cheered, all I could think was, *That's incredible!* In my opinion, a potentially boring opening ceremony had become one of the most spectacular events in Olympic history.

Of course, this didn't just happen by accident. I later learned that three archers had been practicing for hours every day for several months. Only minutes before the opening ceremony one was selected to light the Olympic torch—and he hit the bull's eye! But success came only after hours and hours of disciplined practice.

The Importance of Planning

Planning is important to any task. Even a slight mistake can sometimes lead to disastrous results. What if the Olympic archer had aimed a few degrees too high? More important, what if he had aimed too low? The flaming arrow could have landed in the fortieth row of spectators, causing a horrible disaster.

Planning is the key to every successful adventure. Playing a football game, fighting a war, running a business, lighting the Olympic torch, or developing your personal financial plan. Smart money managers always have a financial plan.

Take Mike Armstrong, for example. When he finished college, he was determined to make some good financial decisions. He knew that unless he established goals and a plan, he would never achieve his full potential. One of those goals was to become totally debt free before he reached age forty.

Mike secured a good job, worked hard, and managed his money wisely. At age twenty-five he bought a house, and within a few years began prepaying on his mortgage. Mike accomplished his goal five years ahead of schedule. He was debt free at age thirty-five! Mike's goal didn't just happen. He made it happen through wise planning.

We all need to know what our goals are and begin to plot a course of action. If we don't, we can end up in a disaster. Consider that if a cruise ship leaves Miami, headed for the Virgin Islands, and only veers off course by five degrees, it will never reach its destination! The captain must plot the course and make minor corrections along the way to reach the Virgin Islands. Similarly, in financial planning, we must establish our goals and continually make adjustments as we go through life.

Financial planning is not a once in a lifetime event!

Unfortunately, a lot of American families suffer because they don't have a plan to reach their financial goals.

Primary Symptoms of a Family Without Goals

Five primary and numerous secondary symptoms plague a family without goals:

A Feeling of Aimlessness in Life

There never seems to be any real direction for the family. They go to work. They buy groceries. They watch a little television, and then they go to bed. They have the same routine day after day.

We all need to have direction and a purpose in life; having goals gives us more motivation and energy. If you don't have a vision or a dream for your life, get one! Life with a purpose becomes meaningful. What do you want to accomplish in this life?

Start your own business?
Work for yourself?
Become debt free?
Finish college?
Earn a master's or doctorate degree?
Plan for retirement?
Give more to God's kingdom?

The possibilities are unlimited! But don't go through life looking for success to be handed to you on a silver platter. You must have a plan and work for it.

Daily Worry

A family without goals must deal daily with financial worry. They never know if they are going to make it to the next paycheck. They worry about paying for car repairs and medical bills. They worry about mounting credit card debt. Financial stress and worry begin to affect every other area of life. They become less productive at work. There is more tension in the marriage. The kids are affected, and so is their spiritual life.

Goals will not solve your problems, but they will give you a plan to solve your problems and help keep you out of trouble.

Frequent Arguments over Money

Without a plan, couples will frequently argue about money. Everyone is fighting for his or her fair share, whatever that is! Everyone thinks he or she is getting the least amount of money to spend. Mutually agreed-upon goals help direct how the money is going to be spent and thus help reduce arguing.

Limited or No Savings

Very few couples will ever save money unless they *plan* to save it. It just does not happen magically. Limited savings can become the source of stress and arguments and can translate into enormous pressure to meet unexpected financial demands.

Financial Destruction

The ultimate outcome and consequence of a family without goals is financial destruction. Marriages end in divorce. Bankruptcy courts take over your personal affairs. Families are torn apart, and children suffer the consequences for the rest of their lives.

Families without financial goals also suffer from numerous secondary symptoms. Read through this list to see if you or your family is suffering from any of these problems:

1. Selfishness in protecting money for your wants.
2. Being unaware of spouse's financial desires in life.
3. Feeling the need to hide money from spouse.
4. Frustration when things don't go your way.
5. Feelings of not getting ahead in life.
6. Problems with having unexpected bills arrive in your mailbox.
7. Little or no savings.
8. Insignificant giving.
9. No real freedom in spending money.
10. Financially tired and worn out!

What Goals Can Do for You

If you do not have written financial goals for your life, most of the above will be true of you. Surveys reveal that only 10 percent of individuals set written goals for their lives. That means that 90 percent go through life without specific direction in their finances (see graph on page 23). Developing and implementing a simple plan can have astronomical consequences. For example, let's say Peter recently finished college and obtained his first job. He decided that one of his basic financial goals would be to save $1,000 every year during his working life of forty-five years. If he only earned a return of 7 percent, his annual savings of $1,000 each year would be worth $285,749. There is a good chance this would not meet all his needs during later years in life, but it would be a great help.

Most people will earn more than one million dollars during their working lives!

Most people go through life consuming all their income. Did you realize that if you earn an average of $22,222.23 each year during your forty-five-year working life, *more than one million dollars* will pass through your checking account ($22,222.23 × 45 years = $1,000,000)?

At the end of your working life, what will you have to show for it? How much will you have saved? How much will you have wasted? How much will you have used wisely? How much will you have given?

The following chart shows how much your *total earnings* will be at various levels of average earnings. (This chart assumes you will earn income for forty-five years.)

TOTAL AMOUNT ACCUMULATED
FROM 10 PERCENT SAVINGS

(1)	(2)	(3)	(4)	(5)
		Save 10% Each Year		Total Worth of Fund in
Annual Earnings	Total Earnings	During 45 Years	Total Saved	45 Years If Earning 8.5%
$ 10,000	$ 450,000	$ 1,000	$ 45,000	$ 450,530
25,000	1,125,000	2,500	112,500	1,126,325
50,000	2,250,000	5,000	225,000	2,252,651
75,000	3,375,000	7,500	337,500	3,378,977
100,000	4,500,000	10,000	450,000	4,505,303

Column (1) = Annual earnings
Column (2) = Annual earnings (1) × 45 Years
Column (3) = Annual earnings (1) × 10 percent
Column (4) = 10 percent savings each year (3) × 45 years
Column (5) = Total worth of annual savings (3) earning 8.5 percent each year

Look at this amazing analysis again. If you save 10 percent of your income each year and can earn 8.5 percent on your savings, in forty-five years you will have an investment fund equal to all the money you earned during your working life.

Just to be sure you understood what I said, let me repeat it. If you save 10 percent of your income each year, and you can earn 8.5 percent on your savings, in forty-five years you will have an investment fund equal to *all the money you earned during your working life.*

It's as if you worked your entire life, and still have every penny you earned in your savings!

It's as if you worked your entire life, and still have every penny you earned in your savings!

Now here comes the great part. Not only would you have every penny you earned, but if your investment continued earning 8.5 percent, *you could withdraw from your account almost four times what you were earning* and still have 100 percent of your earnings—even after thirty years of withdrawals!

Withdraw Four Times Your Average Annual Earnings Each Year!

Let's assume you will earn $25,000 each year during your working life. If you save 10 percent of your income each year, you will be saving $2,500 ($25,000 × 10 percent) each year. If you save $2,500 each year for forty-five years and your savings earns 8.5 percent each year, your savings will be worth $1,126,325. Starting at age sixty-five you will now be able to withdraw $95,737 *every year* for thirty years and *still have* your original investment of $1,126,325 in your investment account at age ninety-five!

This is even more spectacular than the archer's shooting the flaming arrow to light the Olympic torch! The following chart shows this calculation for differing amounts of savings.

TOTAL AMOUNT SAVED EVEN WITH WITHDRAWALS

Annual Savings	Total Worth of Fund in 45 Years If Earning 8.5%	Annual Withdrawals for 30 Years	Total Worth of Fund Even After 30 Years of Withdrawals
$ 1,000	$ 450,530	$ 38,295	$ 450,530
2,500	1,126,325	95,737	1,126,325
5,000	2,252,651	191,475	2,252,651
7,500	3,378,977	287,213	3,378,977
10,000	4,505,303	382,950	4,505,303

It really takes so little sacrifice on our part to fulfill long-range financial needs. And no, I have not overlooked inflation!

SETTING GOALS

Percentage of People Who Set Goals

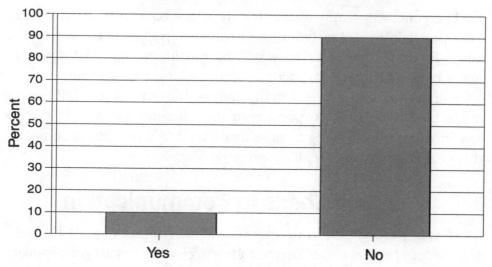

The Added Factor of Inflation

Now, before all my financial planning friends start accusing me of overlooking the consequences and impact of inflation, let me continue my scenario and add the following assumptions and concepts:

1. It is my assumption that no one will earn exactly the same salary, for example $25,000, every year for forty-five years.
2. It is my assumption that as income increases each year, so will savings. In other words, an individual might earn $25,000 the first year and save $2,500. In the second year the earnings might be $27,000 and he or she would save $2,700. In year three the earnings might be $28,000 and the saved amount would be $2,800.
3. Due to increasing salary, you will be able to withdraw more income when you turn age sixty-five. This will help account for inflation.
4. Also, during your withdrawal years you may withdraw some of the principal if needed due to inflation.
5. If you execute this plan, you will have accomplished more than 99.99 percent of all people have accomplished.

Everyone will surely agree that this very basic plan should meet most people's needs for their retirement. Most people in the workforce know for forty-five years they will be retiring at age sixty-five. Yet many ignore planning for income needs in later years of life.

I understand that it is literally impossible for some families and single parents to save 10 percent of their income every year due to low income or just trying to raise a family. But if you can accomplish this goal during your life, it's a great plan.

Planning Leads to Communication

If you were to ask your spouse, "What are your goals in life?" what would he or she say? Do the following exercise with your spouse.

This will help you to begin to understand what is important to each other. Two forms have been provided. Do not let your spouse see your answers until you both have finished. Once you finish, compare your lists. If you are single, do this exercise for yourself.

HUSBAND'S GOAL-SETTING EXERCISE

Establish your priorities (from 1 to 17) on the following list, making your highest priority number 1. You cannot use a number more than once. You must rank all 17!

1. _____ Pay for college expenses for our children.

2. _____ Pay off all credit card debt.

3. _____ Pay off home mortgage.

4. _____ Pay off business debt.

5. _____ Leave our children an inheritance.

6. _____ Plan for retirement financial needs.

7. _____ Increase our giving.

8. _____ Major purchase of _____ (home, furniture, etc.).

9. _____ Buy a car or van.

10. _____ Send our children to Christian school.

11. _____ Move to a new home.

12. _____ Start a new business.

13. _____ Have more children.

14. _____ Operate our family finances on a budget.

15. ____ Accumulate a specific amount of money.

16. ____ Take annual family vacations.

17. ____ Enjoy an annual getaway as a couple.

WIFE'S GOAL-SETTING EXERCISE

Establish your priorities (from 1 to 17) on the following list, making your highest priority number 1. You cannot use a number more than once. You must rank all 17!

1. ____ Pay for college expenses for our children.

2. ____ Pay off all credit card debt.

3. ____ Pay off home mortgage.

4. ____ Pay off business debt.

5. ____ Leave our children an inheritance.

6. ____ Plan for retirement financial needs.

7. ____ Increase our giving.

8. ____ Major purchase of _____ (home, furniture, etc.).

9. ____ Buy a car or van.

10. ____ Send our children to Christian school.

11. ____ Move to a new home.

12. ____ Start a new business.

13. ____ Have more children.

14. ____ Operate our family finances on a budget.

15. _____ Accumulate a specific amount of money.

16. _____ Take annual family vacations.

17. _____ Enjoy an annual getaway as a couple.

Now look at your answer sheets together. Do you have the same priorities? Yes _____ No _____

What did you learn from this exercise? _____
_____
_____
_____
_____
_____
_____
_____
_____
_____

The Consequences of Not Communicating About Goals

A lack of communication and commitment to the same goals can lead to unhappiness—even divorce! Without clear goals for a family, the husband has his "hidden" agenda for the money, and off he goes. The wife has her "hidden" agenda for the money, and off she goes. The word *hidden* is in quotations because in most cases, neither the husband nor wife is deliberately hiding anything. They simply have not discussed their goals and dreams with their spouse.

Proverbs 21:5 says, "The plans of the diligent lead surely to advantage, / But everyone who is hasty comes surely to poverty" (NAS). I like to view this verse as a biblical formula for success.

Plans + Diligence = Advantage

It takes a combination of planning and hard work to equal your advantage. Notice that it is not just planning that equals advantage, nor is it just hard work. It is when we put them together that we see advantage! Yet some of us refuse to plan. We do so because of three primary reasons.

Three Primary Reasons People Don't Set Goals

1. We don't know what we want!

Many people just don't know what they want in life. Thankfully, this has never been my problem. Soon after graduating from college I sat down and roughly planned out the next fifteen years. I knew where I wanted to be and what I wanted to be doing. However, God had different plans for my life and my direction changed. It is a comforting thought that God gives us the freedom to set goals while knowing that He has the freedom to change them.

Don't just sit there and do nothing. Establish a plan and move in that direction. God can open and close the doors of opportunity for you.

2. We don't believe goal setting works.

Have you ever set goals and failed to accomplish them? If the answer is yes, you probably don't believe goal setting really works. Let me assure you, setting goals and even accomplishing them can work in *your* life, which leads us to our next point.

3. We don't know how to set goals.

The primary reason most people do not set or accomplish their goals is that they don't know how to write them. For that reason, I'd like to take a little time now to talk about goal setting. Even if you've already been through this process, you might want to glance through the following material as a review for future goal-setting sessions.

How to Set Goals

I suggest you work through a six-step process:

1. Seek counsel.

The first step in setting successful goals is to seek the counsel of someone who can help you in the planning process. This could be a friend, a parent, a professional financial planner or adviser—or this book. Not everyone needs professional help with their planning. However, the more complex your financial situation, the more help you will need.

Ask God to give you wisdom. James 1:5 says, "If any of you lacks wisdom, let him ask of God, who gives to all liberally and without reproach, and it will be given to him." When you pray, expect supernatural wisdom from God. I continually find myself praying for this when I am giving a couple advice.

2. Write your goals on paper.

Be sure to write your goals on paper. Our minds are incredible, but many details get put away in the storage compartment in the brain, never to be recovered. Writing your goals on paper helps you to visualize your goals as well as remember them.

I recommend that you consider setting goals in the following areas:

1. Eliminate all credit card debt.
2. Accelerate or prepay mortgage payment.
3. Set aside college expenses for children.
4. Purchase a car.
5. Buy a home.
6. Save for retirement.
7. Save for home repair or expansion.
8. Fund a business venture.
9. Save a specific amount of money.
10. Contribute a sum of money to your church or a charity.
11. Fund personal educational goals (graduate school, etc.).
12. Obtain certain lifestyle goals for your family.

Of course, not every family will need to have goals for all the areas listed here.

3. Make your goals challenging but possible.

One of the most common mistakes is setting unrealistic goals. It is far better to set challenging, realistic goals and achieve them, and then set more goals in the future than to set unattainable goals at the beginning.

For example, it is unrealistic for a couple earning $40,000 in annual salary to invest or save $20,000 a year. It is more realistic for a couple earning $40,000 a year to invest $4,000 annually.

4. Set a deadline.

When was the last time you had to give a speech or complete a project? When did you do it? If you are like most people, you pulled it together the week or the night before. Unless you set deadlines for meeting each goal, you will never be motivated to accomplish them. It is also good to be accountable to a friend, preferably someone else who wants to set goals and be accountable to you also. This accountability will help you both be successful.

Here are two examples of good deadlines:

- My goal is to save $100 by the end of each month.
- My goal is to accumulate $5,000 by December 31.

5. Make your goals measurable.

Exactly what are you trying to accomplish? A poorly written goal would read, "I would like to help with my children's college expenses." A better goal would be, "I need $25,000 in ten years to help with my children's college expenses." Or, "I need $12,000 in five years to purchase a new car for my family."

6. Continually review your goals.

Reviewing your goals is the key to success; if you never review them, they are unlikely to be accomplished. Yet don't be afraid to fail. Many times success comes out of successful failures. Think about Thomas Edison, who invented the light bulb. It is reported that he suffered ten thousand failures before he succeeded.

Or consider Babe Ruth, the legendary baseball player. He is known for his 714 home runs but hardly anyone talks about the 1,330 times he struck out.

Never give up! Just because you have failed to accomplish a project in the past does not mean you will never be successful. The only way you will fail is if you don't get up and try again.

Be all that God wants you to be. Do all that God wants you to do. When you are knocked down, get up and try again.

Once you have identified your goals, you need to develop a clear understanding of the time value of money, which we will discuss in Chapter 3. I have found this concept to be essential to clear decision making.

THE TIME VALUE OF MONEY:
Quick Answers to Hard Financial Questions

3

I was speaking at a conference in Montgomery, Alabama, and had just finished discussing the time value of money, a concept financial planners use to help project the future worth of a dollar in relationship to its present "dollar" value. For example, one dollar invested "today" with a growth rate of 9 percent per year for thirty years will have a "future" dollar value of $13.27. It is upon this concept that the true essence of financial planning is built.

During the break, a young lady walked up with a great big smile on her face. "I can't believe it," she said. "I just can't believe it."

"You can't believe what?"

"For years I have been looking for a way to figure out how much my savings will be worth in the future, and now I know how! Thank you!" She went on to explain that various financial advisers could answer her question, but they would never teach her how to do it herself.

Knowing how to calculate the time value of money helps to answer questions such as:

- "How much money do I need to save each month in order to have a certain amount of money?"

- "What will $30,000 in today's dollars be worth in thirty years?"

- "How much money do I need in a fund in order to have an annual outflow of _____ dollars for _____ years?"

- "How much will my investment be worth in thirty years?"

- "I'm saving _____ dollars annually. What will this money be worth at _____ percent in _____ years?"

Smart money managers find themselves asking these types of questions on a regular basis. But where do they find the answers without seeking the help of a professional?

On the following pages I will answer these questions through a series of examples, sharing the exercises and tables I used to help solve the problems. (You will find abbreviated tables in this chapter; check the expanded tables in Appendix A for more information.) The tables related to the time value of money proved to be valuable tools in helping these people make good financial decisions.

Don't let all the data in the tables scare you away from learning more about this important principle. Just take the tables slowly, one at a time. Carefully read through each illustration and see how it uses a particular table. Then you will be asked to work through some examples yourself and determine which table you need to answer the particular question.

Let's begin with the first question:

1. How much money do I need to save each month in order to have _____ dollars?

Use the Monthly Savings Table (Table A) on pages 36–37 to determine the dollar amount you need to save each month in order to accomplish a specific dollar goal in the future. The Monthly Savings Table is helpful for determining the following typical savings goals:

1. Buying a car.
2. Planning for retirement.
3. Purchasing new major appliances.
4. Remodeling a home.
5. Planning for college expenses.
6. Starting a business.
7. Saving for a down payment for a home.
8. Saving for personal educational expenses.

Let's look at some examples of how this table is used. I'll compute two of them; then you do the third one:

1. Jon and Susan need $10,000 for various home-remodeling expenses, which they plan to begin in three years. They project they will be earning 6 percent on their investment each year. How much do they need to save each month to accomplish their goal?

$10,000 (Goal) ÷ Factor *39.34* = *$254.19*

2. When Warren and Jennifer evaluate their college education fund they decide they will need an additional $15,000 in ten years. They project they will be earning 12 percent on their investment each year. How much do they need to save each month to accomplish their goal?

$15,000 (Goal) ÷ Factor *230.04* = *$65.21*

3. The Millers have told their son they would buy him a car for his high school graduation in six years. If the car will cost $12,000 and their investment will earn 6 percent, how much will they need to save each month to accomplish this goal?

After you have consulted the Monthly Savings Table and worked the problem, turn the book upside down to check your answer.

$_____ (Goal) ÷ Factor _____ = $_____

Answer:

$12,000 (Goal) ÷ Factor 86.41 = $138.87

TABLE A
MONTHLY SAVINGS TABLE

Let's say you have established a savings goal of $10,000. You need to accomplish your goal in five years. How much would you need to save each month in order to accomplish your goal?

First, find 8 percent and five years on the table. The factor given is 73.32.

Second, divide $10,000 by 73.32, which equals $136.39. Therefore, you need to save $136.39 each month for five years earning 8 percent to accomplish your goal of $10,000.

Note: More monthly savings factors can be found in Table A in Appendix A.

Summary: $ Goal ÷ Factor = Amount Needed to Save Each Month

PROJECTED RATE

Years	2%	4%	6%	8%	9%	10%	12%
1	12.11	12.22	12.34	12.45	12.51	12.56	12.68
2	24.48	24.93	25.43	25.91	26.19	26.44	26.97
3	37.09	38.16	39.34	40.49	41.15	41.76	43.08
4	49.97	51.92	54.10	56.26	57.52	58.67	61.22
5	63.11	66.23	68.77	73.32	75.42	77.36	81.67

Years	2%	4%	6%	8%	9%	10%	12%
6	76.52	81.12	86.41	91.79	95.01	97.98	104.71
7	90.21	96.61	104.07	111.78	116.43	120.77	130.67
8	104.18	112.73	122.83	133.40	139.86	145.92	159.93
9	118.44	129.50	142.74	156.81	165.48	173.70	192.89
10	132.99	146.94	163.88	182.13	193.51	204.38	230.04
11	147.84	165.09	186.32	209.54	224.17	238.25	271.90
12	163.00	183.96	210.15	239.19	257.71	275.66	319.06
13	187.64	203.60	235.44	271.29	294.39	316.97	372.21
14	194.26	224.03	262.30	306.01	334.52	362.58	432.10
15	210.37	245.29	290.82	343.59	378.41	412.95	499.58
16	226.82	267.40	321.09	384.56	426.41	468.57	575.62
17	243.60	290.40	353.23	428.27	478.92	530.00	661.31
18	260.73	314.33	387.35	475.90	536.35	597.83	757.86
19	278.21	339.23	423.58	527.43	599.17	672.73	866.66
20	296.05	365.13	462.04	583.20	667.89	755.44	989.26
21	314.26	392.08	502.87	643.55	743.05	846.78	1127.40
22	332.84	420.11	546.23	708.85	825.26	947.64	1283.07
23	351.81	449.27	592.25	779.52	915.18	1059.02	1458.47
24	371.81	479.61	641.12	856.00	1013.54	1182.01	1656.13
25	390.92	485.43	692.99	938.75	1121.21	1317.83	1879.85
30	495.98	689.12	1004.52	1466.38	1830.74	2241.29	3494.96
35	612.30	905.97	1424.71	2249.33	2941.78	3757.66	6430.96
40	741.10	1170.22	1991.49	3411.20	4681.32	6247.62	11764.77
45	883.72	1492.22	2755.99	5135.32	7404.88	10336.35	21454.69

2. What will a $10,000 car cost in three years if inflation is 5 percent?

You will use the Inflation Table (Table B) on pages 38–39 to answer this question and determine the effect of inflation. The Inflation Table can also be used to solve these typical inflation calculations:

1. To determine the equivalent income you might need during retirement.

2. To help establish realistic savings goals.
3. To determine future income expectations.
4. To determine the decreasing purchasing power of the dollar.
5. To determine the future value of a home due to inflation.
6. To determine the future cost of an item, such as a car, if a purchase is postponed.

TABLE B
INFLATION TABLE

To determine what $30,000 in today's dollars will be equivalent to in thirty years due to an inflation rate of 4 percent, follow these steps:

First, find 4 percent and 30 years on the table. The factor given is 3.24.

Second, multiply 3.24 × $30,000, which equals $97,200. Therefore, $30,000 in today's dollars with an inflation rate of 4 percent for thirty years is equivalent to $97,200.

Note: More inflation factors can be found in Table B in Appendix A.

PROJECTED INFLATION RATE

Years	3%	4%	5%	6%	7%	8%	9%	10%
1	1.03	1.04	1.05	1.06	1.07	1.08	1.09	1.10
2	1.06	1.08	1.10	1.12	1.14	1.17	1.19	1.21
3	1.09	1.12	1.16	1.19	1.23	1.26	1.30	1.33
4	1.13	1.17	1.22	1.26	1.31	1.36	1.41	1.46
5	1.16	1.22	1.28	1.34	1.40	1.47	1.54	1.61
6	1.19	1.27	1.34	1.42	1.50	1.59	1.68	1.77
7	1.23	1.32	1.41	1.50	1.61	1.71	1.83	1.95
8	1.27	1.37	1.48	1.59	1.72	1.85	1.99	2.14
9	1.30	1.42	1.55	1.69	1.84	2.00	2.17	2.36
10	1.34	1.48	1.63	1.79	1.97	2.16	2.37	2.59
11	1.38	1.54	1.71	1.90	2.10	2.33	2.58	2.85

PROJECTED INFLATION RATE—*Cont'd*

Years	3%	4%	5%	6%	7%	8%	9%	10%
12	1.43	1.60	1.80	2.01	2.25	2.52	2.81	3.14
13	1.47	1.67	1.89	2.13	2.41	2.72	3.07	3.45
14	1.51	1.73	1.98	2.26	2.58	2.94	3.34	3.80
15	1.56	1.80	2.08	2.40	2.76	3.17	3.64	4.18
16	1.60	1.87	2.18	2.54	2.95	3.43	3.97	4.59
17	1.65	1.95	2.29	2.69	3.16	3.70	4.33	5.05
18	1.70	2.03	2.41	2.85	3.38	4.00	4.72	5.56
19	1.75	2.11	2.53	3.03	3.62	4.32	5.14	6.12
20	1.81	2.19	2.65	3.21	3.87	4.66	5.60	6.73
21	1.86	2.28	2.79	3.40	4.14	5.03	6.11	7.40
22	1.92	2.37	2.93	3.60	4.43	5.44	6.66	8.14
23	1.97	2.46	3.07	3.82	4.74	5.87	7.26	8.95
24	2.03	2.56	3.23	4.05	5.07	6.34	7.91	9.85
25	2.09	2.67	3.39	4.29	5.43	6.85	8.62	10.83
30	2.43	3.24	4.32	5.74	7.61	10.06	13.27	17.45
35	2.81	3.95	5.52	7.69	10.68	14.79	20.41	28.10
40	3.26	4.80	7.04	10.29	14.97	21.72	31.41	45.26
45	3.78	5.84	8.99	13.76	21.00	31.92	48.33	72.86

Now look at some examples:

1. Jay and Debbie are considering buying a $10,000 car this year. If they postpone the purchase for three years, how much can they expect to pay for the same car if inflation is projected at 5 percent each year?

$10,000 × Factor *1.16* = *$11,600*

2. Craig and Pam are making plans for their child to attend one of the state universities. They have called several of the state schools

and found that education expenses presently cost $40,000 for a four-year university. If college expenses are increasing at a rate of 6 percent per year, how much should they be planning to pay for a four-year university seven years from now?

$40,000 × Factor *1.5* = $60,000

3. Gary purchased a $100,000 home in a well-established neighborhood. If homes have been increasing in value at a rate of 4 percent per year due to inflation, how much can he expect the value of his home to increase in ten years?

$_____ × Factor _____ = $_____

After you have consulted the Inflation Table and worked the problem, turn the book upside down to check your answer.

Answer:

$100,000 × Factor 1.48 = $148,000

3. **How much money do I need in a fund in order to have an annual outflow of _____ dollars for _____ years?**

You will use the Annual Outflow Table (Table C) on pages 42–43 to determine the "lump sum" needed to fund a specific cash flow over a predetermined number of years. The Annual Outflow Table can also help in:

1. Planning for retirement.
2. Planning for college expenses.
3. Determining how much you can withdraw each year from a specific fund for any purpose.

Here are some examples of how this table is used:

1. Jay, your only son, will be needing money each year to pay for college expenses. You need to withdraw $10,000 every year for four years. If your investment will earn 7 percent, how much will you need in an investment account one year prior to his freshman year in order to accomplish your goal?

$10,000 Annual Outflow × Factor *3.39* = *$33,900*

2. The Johnsons will be retiring and selling their business next year. The business will sell for $250,000. If this money can be invested and earn 7 percent each year, how much will they be able to withdraw from this fund each year for the next twenty-five years? (Note the new procedure used in this illustration.)

Investment Amount *$250,000* ÷ Factor *11.65* = *$21,459.23*

3. Sam and Kay are retiring, and they plan to withdraw $30,000 every year for thirty years. If their investments will earn 10 percent, how much will they need invested in a retirement account to accomplish their goal?

$_____ Annual Outflow × Factor _____ = $_____

After you have consulted the Annual Outflow Table and worked the problem, turn the book upside down to check your answer.

Answer:

$30,000 Annual Outflow × Factor *9.43* = *$282,900*

TABLE C
ANNUAL OUTFLOW TABLE

You are planning for retirement and decide you need an annual income of $30,000 each year for a total of twenty-five years. How much do you need to have in an investment account earning 8 percent when you retire at age sixty-five to fully fund your annual income needs?

First, find 8 percent and 25 years on the table. The factor given is 10.67.

Second, multiply 10.67 × $30,000, which equals $320,100. Therefore, $320,100 is needed in an investment account to fully fund an annual payout of $30,000 for twenty-five years.

Note: After the last payout is made in twenty-five years, you will have $0 in your investment account. During those twenty-five years you will be using principal and interest money. More annual-outflow factors may be found in Table C in Appendix A.

PROJECTED RATE

Years	2%	3%	4%	5%	6%	7%	8%	9%	10%
1	.980	.971	.962	.952	.943	.935	.926	.917	.909
2	1.94	1.91	1.89	1.86	1.83	1.81	1.78	1.76	1.74
3	2.88	2.83	2.78	2.72	2.67	2.62	2.58	2.53	2.49
4	3.81	3.72	3.63	3.55	3.47	3.39	3.31	3.24	3.17
5	4.71	4.58	4.54	4.33	4.21	4.10	3.99	3.89	3.79
6	5.60	5.42	5.24	5.08	4.92	4.77	4.62	4.49	4.36
7	6.47	6.23	6.00	5.79	5.58	5.39	5.21	5.03	4.87
8	7.33	7.02	6.73	6.46	6.21	5.97	5.75	5.53	5.33
9	8.16	7.79	7.44	7.11	6.80	6.52	6.25	5.99	5.76
10	8.98	8.53	8.11	7.72	7.36	7.02	6.71	6.42	6.14
11	9.79	9.25	8.76	8.31	7.89	7.50	7.14	6.81	6.50
12	10.58	9.95	9.39	8.86	8.38	7.94	7.54	7.16	6.81
13	11.35	10.63	9.98	9.39	8.85	8.36	7.90	7.49	7.10
14	12.11	11.30	10.56	9.90	9.29	8.75	8.24	7.79	7.37
15	12.85	11.94	11.12	10.38	9.71	9.11	8.56	8.06	7.61
16	13.58	12.56	11.65	10.84	10.11	9.45	8.85	8.31	7.82
17	14.29	13.17	12.17	11.27	10.48	9.76	9.12	8.54	8.02
18	14.99	13.75	12.66	11.69	10.83	10.06	9.37	8.76	8.20
19	15.68	14.33	13.13	12.09	11.16	10.34	9.60	8.95	8.36

Years	2%	3%	4%	5%	6%	7%	8%	9%	10%
20	16.35	14.88	13.59	12.46	11.47	10.59	9.82	9.13	8.51
21	17.01	15.42	14.03	12.82	11.76	10.84	10.02	9.29	8.65
22	17.66	15.94	14.45	13.16	12.04	11.06	10.20	9.44	8.77
23	18.29	16.44	14.86	13.49	12.30	11.27	10.37	9.58	8.88
24	18.91	16.94	15.25	13.80	12.55	11.45	10.53	9.71	8.98
25	19.52	17.41	15.62	14.09	12.78	11.65	10.67	9.82	9.08
30	22.40	19.60	17.29	15.37	13.76	12.41	11.26	10.27	9.43
35	25.00	21.49	18.66	16.37	14.50	12.95	11.65	10.57	9.64
40	27.36	23.11	19.79	17.16	15.05	13.33	11.92	10.56	9.78
45	29.49	24.52	20.72	17.77	15.46	13.61	12.11	10.88	9.86

4. How much will my investment be worth in thirty years?

You will use the Future Value Table (Table D) on pages 44–45 to determine the future value of a specific amount of money you presently have. The Future Value Table can also:

1. Show how much any single sum of money will be worth in the future.
2. Determine how much an *investment* will be worth without investing any additional money each year.
3. Determine how much a lump sum *pension distribution* will be worth in the future.
4. Determine if your current investments will reach a specific dollar goal in the future.

Here are some examples:

1. Yesterday Karen sold $10,000 worth of stock, and now she plans to reinvest the money. If her new investment will earn 6 percent for the next twenty-five years, what will it be worth?

$10,000 × Factor *4.29* = *$42,900*

2. Hank is forty years old and changed jobs two months ago. Today he received a lump sum distribution payout of $10,000 from his company pension plan. If his investment earns 8 percent for the next twenty-five years, what will it be worth when Hank is sixty-five?

$10,000 × Factor 6.85 = $68,500

3. Mike and Joan are newlyweds and have combined savings of $10,000. They project they will be earning 6 percent interest on their investment. In five years, they would like to buy a home and have $15,000 for the down payment. Will Mike and Joan have the $15,000?

After you have consulted the Future Value Table and worked the problem, turn the book upside down to check your answer.

$_____ × Factor _____ = $_____

Circle one: Yes   No

Answer:

$10,000 × Factor 1.34 = $13,400 No

TABLE D
FUTURE VALUE TABLE

You presently have $10,000 in an investment earning 8 percent compounded annually. You want to know how much your investment will be worth in thirty years (you do not plan to invest any additional money in the investment).

First, find 8 percent and 30 years on the table. The factor given is 10.06.

Second, multiply 10.06 × $10,000, which equals $100,600. Therefore, your investment of $10,000 will be worth $100,600 if it earns 8 percent compounded annually for thirty years.

Note: More future value factors may be found in Table D in Appendix A.

PROJECTED RATE

Years	3%	4%	5%	6%	7%	8%	9%	10%	12%
1	1.03	1.04	1.05	1.06	1.07	1.08	1.09	1.10	1.12
2	1.06	1.08	1.10	1.12	1.14	1.17	1.19	1.21	1.25
3	1.09	1.12	1.16	1.19	1.23	1.26	1.30	1.33	1.40
4	1.13	1.17	1.22	1.26	1.31	1.36	1.41	1.46	1.57
5	1.16	1.22	1.28	1.34	1.40	1.47	1.54	1.61	1.76
6	1.19	1.27	1.34	1.42	1.50	1.59	1.68	1.77	1.97
7	1.23	1.32	1.41	1.50	1.61	1.71	1.83	1.95	2.21
8	1.27	1.37	1.48	1.59	1.72	1.85	1.99	2.14	2.48
9	1.30	1.42	1.55	1.69	1.84	2.00	2.17	2.36	2.77
10	1.34	1.48	1.63	1.79	1.97	2.16	2.37	2.59	3.11
11	1.38	1.54	1.71	1.90	2.10	2.33	2.58	2.85	3.48
12	1.43	1.60	1.80	2.01	2.25	2.52	2.81	3.14	3.90
13	1.47	1.67	1.89	2.13	2.41	2.72	3.07	3.45	4.36
14	1.51	1.73	1.98	2.26	2.58	2.94	3.34	3.80	4.89
15	1.56	1.80	2.08	2.40	2.76	3.17	3.64	4.18	5.47
16	1.60	1.87	2.18	2.54	2.95	3.43	3.97	4.59	6.13
17	1.65	1.95	2.29	2.69	3.16	3.70	4.33	5.05	6.87
18	1.70	2.03	2.41	2.85	3.38	4.00	4.72	5.56	7.69
19	1.75	2.11	2.53	3.03	3.62	4.32	5.14	6.12	8.61
20	1.81	2.19	2.65	3.21	3.87	4.66	5.60	6.73	9.65
21	1.86	2.28	2.79	3.40	4.14	5.03	6.11	7.40	10.80
22	1.92	2.37	2.93	3.60	4.43	5.44	6.66	8.14	12.10
23	1.97	2.46	3.07	3.82	4.74	5.87	7.26	8.95	13.55
24	2.03	2.56	3.23	4.05	5.07	6.34	7.91	9.85	15.18
25	2.09	2.67	3.39	4.29	5.43	6.85	8.62	10.83	17.00
30	2.43	3.24	4.32	5.74	7.61	10.06	13.27	17.45	29.96
35	2.81	3.95	5.52	7.69	10.68	14.79	20.41	28.10	52.80
40	3.26	4.80	7.04	10.29	14.97	21.72	31.41	45.26	93.05
45	3.78	5.84	8.99	13.76	21.00	31.92	48.33	72.86	163.99

5. How much do I need in a fund today in order to accomplish a(n) _____ dollar goal in the future?

Use the Present Value Table (Table E) on pages 46–47 to determine how much you would need to invest *today* to accomplish a specific future financial goal. The Present Value Table can also be used in the following situations:

1. Exactly how much do I need to invest today in a lump sum in order to accomplish my financial goal several years in the future, without adding any additional money to the investment?
2. Saving the down payment for a home.
3. Buying a car.
4. Buying a business.
5. Saving for college expenses.

TABLE E
PRESENT VALUE TABLE

You estimate that you will need $75,000 in fifteen years. What lump sum dollar value do you need to invest today to accomplish your goal?

First, find 10 percent and 15 years on the table. The factor given is .23939.

Second, multiply $75,000 by .23939, which equals $17,954.25.

Therefore, you need to invest a lump sum of $17,954.25 earning 10 percent to accomplish your goal of $75,000 in fifteen years.

Note: More present value factors can be found in Table E in Appendix A.

PROJECTED RATE

Years	4%	6%	8%	9%	10%	12%	14%
1	.96154	.94339	.92592	.91743	.90909	.89285	.87719
2	.92455	.88999	.85734	.84168	.82644	.79719	.76964
3	.88899	.83962	.79383	.77183	.75131	.71178	.67497
4	.85480	.79093	.73503	.70842	.68301	.63552	.59208
5	.82192	.74726	.68058	.64993	.62092	.56742	.51937
6	.79031	.70496	.63017	.59626	.56447	.50663	.45558
7	.75991	.66505	.58349	.54703	.51316	.45235	.39963

Years	4%	6%	8%	9%	10%	12%	14%
8	.73069	.62741	.54027	.50186	.46650	.40388	.35056
9	.70258	.59190	.50025	.46042	.42409	.36061	.30750
10	.67556	.55839	.46319	.42241	.38554	.32197	.26974
11	.64958	.52678	.42888	.38753	.35049	.28747	.23661
12	.62459	.49697	.39711	.35553	.31863	.25667	.20756
13	.60057	.46884	.36769	.32618	.28966	.22917	.18207
14	.57747	.44230	.34046	.29924	.26333	.20462	.15971
15	.55526	.41726	.31524	.27454	.23939	.18269	.14009
16	.53391	.39364	.29189	.25187	.21763	.16312	.12289
17	.51337	.37136	.27027	.23107	.19784	.14564	.10780
18	.49363	.35034	.25025	.21199	.17986	.13004	.09456
19	.47464	.33051	.23171	.19449	.16350	.11610	.08295
20	.45638	.31180	.21455	.17843	.14864	.10366	.07276
21	.43883	.29415	.19865	.16370	.13513	.09256	.06382
22	.42195	.27750	.18394	.15018	.12284	.08264	.05598
23	.40572	.26179	.17031	.13778	.11678	.07378	.04911
24	.39012	.24698	.15770	.12640	.10152	.06588	.04308
25	.37511	.23300	.14601	.11596	.09229	.05882	.03779
30	.30832	.17411	.09937	.07537	.05731	.03337	.01962
35	.25341	.13010	.06763	.04898	.03558	.01894	.01019
40	.20829	.09722	.04603	.03183	.02209	.01074	.00529
45	.17120	.07265	.03132	.02069	.01372	.00610	.00275

Now let's look at some examples of how to use this table.

1. Wayne needs to have $5,000 five years from now. How much would he need to invest today at 8 percent?

$5,000 × Factor *.68058* = *$3,402.90*

2. Joe has an opportunity to sell his business, which he started five years ago. Joe is only thirty-five years old and would like to start another business. An important goal for Joe is to be able to accumulate

$1,000,000 in twenty-five years—specifically from the sale of this one business. If the proceeds from his business will earn 10 percent every year for the next twenty-five years, what would be the minimum amount Joe would need to receive from the sale of his business?

$1,000,000 × Factor .09229 = $92,290

3. Andrew is considering selling a piece of real estate. He wants to be sure he will be able to turn his proceeds into $50,000. His parents will be retiring in ten years and he would like to give them $50,000 to help with their needs. If his new investment earns 8 percent each year, how much does he need to sell his real estate for?

After you have consulted the Present Value Table and worked the problem, turn the book upside down to check your answer.

$_____ × Factor _____ = $_____

Answer:

$50,000 × Factor .46319 = $23,159.50

6. **I'm saving _____ dollars annually. What will this money be worth at _____ percent in _____ years?**
   Use the Annual Savings Table (Table F) on pages 50–51 to determine how much your savings will be worth if you are saving money on an annual basis. The Annual Savings Table can also be used in the following situations:

   1. To determine the future dollar value of any savings/investment program.
   2. To determine the future dollar value of your pension plan.
   3. To determine the future dollar value of your college savings plan.

4. To determine the future dollar value of your children's savings plan.

5. To determine the future dollar value of your mutual fund.

Here are some examples:

1. Ronald has established a savings goal of $5,000 every year for the next twenty-five years. If his investment can earn 6 percent interest, how much will it be worth?

$5,000 Annual Savings Amount × Factor *54.87* = *$274,350*

2. Todd's daughter had a baby this year. He would like to help relieve the burden of college expenses for his daughter and her husband. Todd's retirement income is very sufficient, and he really wants to help. He is considering these options listed below:

A. Save $1,000 each year, with projected earnings of 6 percent for fifteen years.

$1,000 Annual Savings Amount × Factor *23.28* = *$23,280*

B. Save $2,000 each year, with projected earnings of 6 percent for fifteen years.

$2,000 Annual Savings Amount × Factor *23.28* = *$46,560*

3. An investment Richard made nine years ago is beginning to produce new income for his family. He is expecting a steady stream of $4,000 per year. He does not plan to increase his spending but to save the additional income. Richard expects to receive 8 percent on his investment each year. How much will his investment be worth in fifteen years?

$_____ Annual Savings Amount × Factor _____ =
$_____

After you have consulted the Annual Savings Table and worked the problem, turn the book upside down to check your answer.

Answer:

$4,000 Annual Savings Amount × Factor *27.15* = *$108,600*

TABLE F
ANNUAL SAVINGS TABLE

You are saving $1,500 annually in a mutual fund account. You will do this for at least 10 years. You project you can earn 10 percent on your investment each year. How much will you have saved in ten years?

First, find 10 percent and 10 years on the table. The factor given is 15.94.

Second, multiply 15.94 × $1,500, which equals $23,910. Therefore, your annual deposit of $1,500 each year for ten years would be worth $23,910 if it earns 10 percent compounded annually.

Note: For more annual savings factors, see Table F in Appendix A.

PROJECTED RATE

Years	5%	6%	8%	9%	10%	12%	14%
1	1.00	1.00	1.00	1.00	1.00	1.00	1.00
2	2.05	2.06	2.08	2.09	2.10	2.12	2.14
3	3.15	3.18	3.25	3.28	3.31	3.37	3.44
4	4.31	4.38	4.51	4.57	4.64	4.78	4.92
5	5.53	5.64	5.87	5.99	6.11	6.35	6.61
6	6.80	6.98	7.34	7.52	7.72	8.12	8.54
7	8.14	8.39	8.92	9.20	9.49	10.09	10.73
8	9.55	9.90	10.64	11.03	11.44	12.30	13.23
9	11.03	11.49	12.49	13.02	13.58	14.75	16.09
10	12.58	13.18	14.49	15.19	15.94	17.55	19.34
11	14.21	14.97	16.65	17.56	18.53	20.66	23.05
12	15.92	16.87	18.98	20.14	21.38	24.13	27.27
13	17.71	18.88	21.50	22.95	24.52	28.03	32.09
14	19.60	21.02	24.22	26.02	27.98	32.39	37.58

Years	5%	6%	8%	9%	10%	12%	14%
15	21.58	23.28	27.15	29.36	31.77	37.28	43.84
16	23.66	25.67	30.32	33.00	35.95	42.75	50.98
17	25.84	28.21	33.75	36.97	40.55	48.88	59.12
18	28.13	30.91	37.45	41.30	45.60	55.75	68.39
19	30.54	33.76	41.45	46.02	51.16	63.44	78.97
20	33.07	36.79	45.76	51.16	57.28	72.05	91.03
21	35.72	39.99	50.42	56.77	64.00	81.70	104.77
22	38.51	43.59	55.46	62.87	71.40	92.50	120.44
23	41.43	46.99	60.89	69.53	79.54	104.60	138.30
24	44.50	50.82	66.77	76.79	88.50	118.16	188.66
25	47.73	54.87	63.11	84.70	98.35	133.33	181.87
30	66.44	79.06	113.28	136.31	164.49	241.33	356.79
35	90.32	111.44	172.32	215.71	271.02	431.66	693.57
40	120.80	154.76	259.06	337.88	442.59	767.09	1342.02
45	159.70	212.74	386.51	525.86	718.91	1358.23	2590.57

Now that you are familiar with these tables, let's look at some additional problems. However, this time, it will be up to you to read the problem and decide the appropriate table to use. (When you're finished, check your answer against the answer list at the end of the problems.)

PRACTICE PROBLEMS TO SOLVE

1. Jack and Donna graduated from college this month. Together they plan to begin an investment program with their first paychecks. If they can save at least $2,500 each year and earn 8 percent, how much will they have in thirty-five years?

Answer: $_____

2. Harry and Sandy are planning for retirement. When they begin their retirement, they would like to withdraw $30,000 from their

account each year (for twenty-five years). Their investment account will earn at least 8 percent each year. How much will they need in an investment account to accomplish their goal?

Answer: $_____

3. Randy expects inflation to continue at a rate of 5 percent each year. He is trying to determine the equivalent income he will need in five years to maintain his present standard of living. He is earning $30,000 in annual income this year. How much will he need to be earning in five years?

Answer: $_____

4. Robert purchased an investment valued at $18,000. He projects that the value will increase at 12 percent each year. What will his investment be worth in ten years?

Answer: $_____

5. Joe and Patty have a goal to buy a $75,000 house for cash before they are thirty-one years old. They finished college this month and are both twenty. They will be earning more than $60,000 in combined income. They believe even after paying for rent, they can still save enough each month to buy a house with cash in ten years. They expect to work hard managing their investment and earn at least 10 percent each year. How much will they have to save each month to accomplish this goal?

Answer: $_____

6. Mary wants to buy an expensive coin collection. She expects the coin collection to be worth $7,500 in three years. How much does she need to invest today at 9 percent to have $7,500 in three years?

Answer: $_____

Answers

1. Use the Annual Savings Table (Table F):
$2,500 Annual Savings × Factor 172.32 = $430,800

2. Use the Annual Outflow Table (Table C):
$30,000 Annual Outflow × Factor 10.67 = $320,100

3. Use the Inflation Table (Table B):
$30,000 × Factor 1.28 = $38,400

4. Use the Future Value Table (Table D):
$18,000 × Factor 3.11 = $55,980

5. Use the Monthly Savings Table (Table A):
$75,000 (Goal) ÷ Factor 204.38 = $366.96

6. Use the Present Value Table (Table E):
$7,500 × Factor .77183 = $5,788.73

Now apply these time-value tables to your own goals. List your goals here, check the appropriate time-value table to use, and then fill in the answer lines with the specific times and amounts of money you need to obtain those goals.

Goal 1. _____
Which table will you use?
_____ Monthly Savings Table
_____ Inflation Table
_____ Annual Outflow Table
_____ Future Value Table

_____ Present Value Table
_____ Annual Savings Table
Answer: _____

Goal 2. _____
Which table will you use?
_____ Monthly Savings Table
_____ Inflation Table
_____ Annual Outflow Table
_____ Future Value Table
_____ Present Value Table
_____ Annual Savings Table
Answer: _____

Goal 3. _____
Which table will you use?
_____ Monthly Savings Table
_____ Inflation Table
_____ Annual Outflow Table
_____ Future Value Table
_____ Present Value Table
_____ Annual Savings Table
Answer: _____

Goal 4. _____
Which table will you use?
_____ Monthly Savings Table
_____ Inflation Table
_____ Annual Outflow Table
_____ Future Value Table

_____ Present Value Table
_____ Annual Savings Table
Answer: _____

Goal 5. _____

Which table will you use?
_____ Monthly Savings Table
_____ Inflation Table
_____ Annual Outflow Table
_____ Future Value Table
_____ Present Value Table
_____ Annual Savings Table
Answer: _____

   Planning is critical to good money management! Without it you will struggle aimlessly through life. With it you will have a greater chance of succeeding. The decision will be yours.

The Dangerous Lure of Debt:

How Can Anyone Have $45,000 in Credit Card Debt?

One hot summer day in Dallas I got a call from a man I had met while speaking at a conference; he asked if I could have breakfast with him and his wife. My reply was "Great!" even though I had a hunch about the meeting since this was not the first time a couple had invited me to breakfast or lunch. (I wish more people would invite me out to dinner!) Sure enough, our meeting began with a little small talk about the weather, and then it quickly shifted to finances as this man unloaded his financial dump truck.

During a few years of marriage, he and his wife had accumulated more than $45,000 in credit card debt! To put it mildly, they were experiencing a financial cardiac arrest! They were paying over $8,000 in annual interest to carry this amount of debt ($45,000 × 18 percent = $8,100).

As I was driving back to my office after our meeting, I thought to myself, *How can someone accumulate $45,000 in credit card debt?* Let me show you how people do it (although I do not recommend it):

1. Fill out every credit card application that is sent to you in the mail. For example, in a two-month period I personally received "preapproved" credit card applications for a total credit line of $36,000. Just by mailing the applications back, I could have thousands of dollars in new credit. I decided to pass on these gracious invitations.

2. Run up each balance to its limit and beyond. When you reach your limit, many credit card companies will expand your limit to a higher level (just what you do *not* need to happen!).

3. Pay only the minimum payment each month.

Be careful! Most families don't wake up one morning and decide, *I think I will go out and put thousands of dollars on my credit cards today.* No, it happens gradually. Couples will charge twenty dollars at the department store, two hundred dollars for car repairs, ninety dollars for clothes, and on and on. Then one day, they realize they have accumulated thousands of dollars in credit card debt.

Easy access to debt can give you a false sense of success or security. Don't let it happen to you.

Unfortunately our federal government is setting a very poor example.

The Trillion-Dollar National Debt

America is *four trillion dollars in debt* and is once again at a strategic point in her history. During our two hundred years as a nation we have faced many trials: Our fight for independence from England.

The writing of our constitution. The Civil War. The Great Depression of the 1930s. World War I and World War II. The Vietnam War in the 1960s and 1970s. The elimination of prayer from our schools. And presently, abortion on demand.

However, I believe America will be facing her greatest challenge— an economic crisis—in the months to come. How we, as a nation and a people, deal with our national debt of four trillion dollars will ultimately determine the destiny of this great nation.

The Bible is not silent about the subject of debt. God gave us very careful instructions in the book of Deuteronomy:

> The LORD will open to you His good treasure, the heavens, to give the rain to your land in its season, and to bless all the work of your hand. You shall lend to many nations, but you shall not borrow. And the LORD will make you the head and not the tail; you shall be above only, and not be beneath, if you heed the commandments of the LORD your God, which I command you today, and are careful to observe them. So you shall not turn aside from any of the words which I command you this day, to the right or the left, to go after other gods to serve them (Deut. 28:12–14).

Then the Lord explains the consequences of disobedience in Deuteronomy 28:15:

> But it shall come to pass, if you do not obey the voice of the LORD your God, to observe carefully all His commandments and His statutes which I command you today, that all these curses will come upon you and overtake you.

And in Deuteronomy 28:43–44 He talks specifically about debt:

> The alien who is among you shall rise higher and higher above you, and you shall come down lower and lower. He shall lend to you, but

you shall not lend to him; he shall be the head, and you shall be the tail.

And also in Proverbs 22:7:

> *The rich rules over the poor,*
> *And the borrower is servant to the lender.*

The Bible is very clear about the consequences of debt for individuals and nations. So where is our nation headed? Only the Lord knows the future, but the national debt continues to escalate at a rapid rate. The chart on page 61 shows a brief history of our national debt.

The chart shows how our national debt has increased from $706 billion in 1977 to $4.4 trillion in 1993. We hear these numbers all the time, but have you ever stopped to think about what they mean? Every American's share (that's every man, woman, and child's share) of our nation's four-trillion-dollar debt is $16,000. That means if you have a family of four, your family's share of this debt is $64,000. If the government decided to send out bills to pay off the debt, how would you like to be responsible for $64,000?

Would it make it easier if they let you pay it out over the next thirty years? For some, it would add on another bill equivalent to a mortgage payment. Let's see, $64,000 financed at 10 percent over thirty years—that's a monthly payment of $561.65.

Next, let's consider the national deficit. To really understand this, let's consider what the word *deficit* really means. Deficit is the amount we are "overspending" in one given year. For example:

Expenses	$1,500,000,000,000
Income	*$1,200,000,000,000*
Deficit	$ 300,000,000,000

FEDERAL DEBT
1790 to 1993

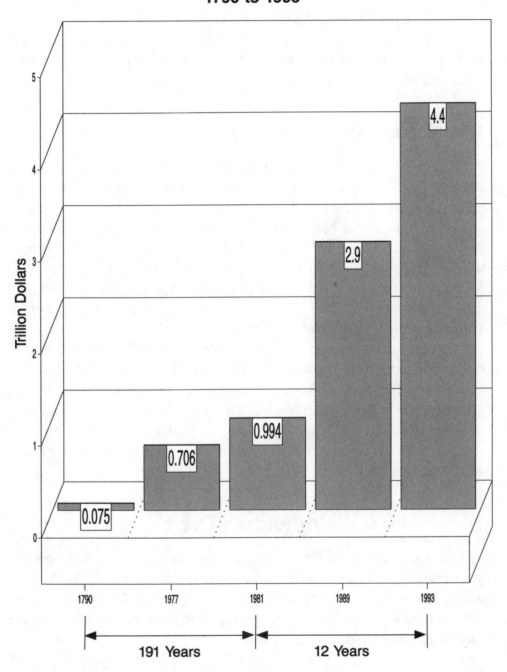

Fact Source: U.S. News & World Report, February 1, 1993, 13.

If the nation is running a deficit of $300 billion, that means we are *overspending* approximately *$1 billion every day!* At this rate, with no interest added on, we will overspend $1 trillion in just thirty-three months! Now let's apply that to the national debt.

What Does National Debt Mean?

Our *national debt* is the accumulated total of all our past annual deficits. The United States has presently accumulated more than four trillion dollars of debt.

Let's think about how much money four trillion dollars really is. If you could lay four trillion one-dollar bills end-to-end, you would have a line of dollar bills that would stretch 386,680,000 miles. To help put this into perspective, the circumference of the earth is 24,902 miles. Therefore, our line of dollar bills would wrap around the earth approximately sixteen thousand times!

The distance to the sun is only 92,957,000 miles, so our line of dollar bills could make more than two trips to the sun and back!

It seems like an impossible concept to grasp, but with God's help, all things are possible. Let's never forget where we should place our ultimate trust!

Yes, our federal government is drowning in debt, but so are many Americans.

Individual Debt

Too many Americans are living beyond their means. Some people who earn $30,000 a year live like they are earning $35,000 a year. And others who may be earning $70,000 a year spend $80,000 a year. Debt is the *only way* people can spend more than they earn, yet smart money managers control their debt.

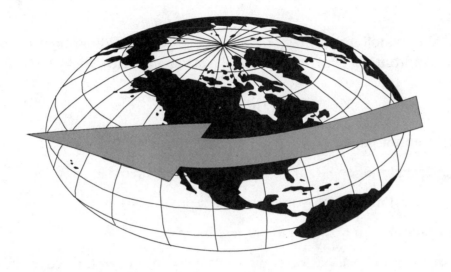

Our national debt: Four trillion one-dollar bills
would circle the earth sixteen thousand times.

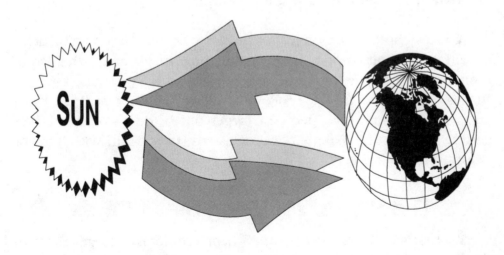

Our national debt: Four trillion one-dollar bills
would make two trips to the sun and back.

Take the following quick quiz to see if you are falling prey to the debt syndrome in America. Check the statements that apply to you:

QUICK QUIZ

_____ Cannot pay the bills in full at the end of the month.

_____ Spend money when you know you don't have it.

_____ Spend more than you earn on a regular basis.

_____ Spend money to make you feel happy.

_____ Write a check before you have money in the bank to cover it.

_____ Continually look for an easy way out.

_____ Have no savings in reserve.

_____ Feel as if you will never pay all your bills.

_____ Have contemplated filing for bankruptcy.

These symptoms are typical of people who are overcome by debt, usually as a result of poor decisions in three major areas: the use of their credit cards, the purchase of a home, and the purchase of a car. In this chapter and the two following it, we will look at these three areas to determine how people can get out of debt—or avoid ever getting into debt by making good decisions. Let's begin with a major culprit: credit card debt.

The Hazards of Using Credit Cards

My first step in solving people's debt problems is to get them to think about their use of credit cards. In fact I often give them a red sticker to apply to the front of their credit card that reads:

WARNING! THIS CREDIT CARD CAN BE HAZARDOUS
TO YOUR FINANCIAL FUTURE.

I advise people to take the following steps to keep themselves out of credit card debt:

1. Pay all your bills first.
The best way to get out of debt is to pay all your bills before you spend any of your money. When the paycheck arrives, pay your fixed expenses such as mortgage or rent, utilities, car payment, and all your credit card bills. Don't pay your credit card bill with what is left over; pay it first with all the other fixed bills. View your credit card bill as a fixed expense!

2. Avoid the minimum-balance mentality.
Some people are in the rut of only paying the minimum balance on their credit card debt. This is like trying to put out a house fire with a garden hose—a squirt here and a squirt there, here a squirt there a squirt, everywhere a squirt-squirt. With a strategy like this, old MacDonald would lose not only the farm, but the ranch too!

You will not get out of debt by paying only the minimum balance each month. In fact, you are barely paying the interest that is being added on each month. Have you ever been stuck in a mud puddle with your car? The wheels keep spinning, but you are getting nowhere fast! The same concept is true of always paying only the minimum balance. You are getting nowhere!

3. Use credit cards for convenience, not necessity.
There is nothing wrong with using credit cards as long as you don't abuse them, but most Americans walk around with several credit cards in their pockets. If ever there comes a point in your life when you are using these cards to meet basic living expenses, you are in serious trouble.

It is extremely expensive to pay for food and clothes when an 18 percent fee is added to the price. Learn to use credit cards properly!

The very first sign of credit card trouble is when you receive a bill in the mail, and you cannot pay it in full that month.

The very first sign of credit card trouble is when you receive a bill in the mail, and you cannot pay it in full that month. This means you are living beyond your income, and this is unacceptable. The problem has to be quickly resolved before disaster strikes. I believe that every credit card should be paid in full every month.

Unfortunately, credit card companies are now launching an advertising campaign on college campuses.

College Credit?

It used to be that graduating seniors were the only ones who received credit card applications. Not anymore. Now, credit cards are readily available to undergraduates as well. Billboards in college towns are advertising "college credit" for MasterCard and Visa. When will the credit cards become popular in high school and elementary school? Why not just send everyone a personal card at birth?

That's a summary of how to stay out of credit card debt. However, if you are already in debt to that plastic card, you must take more drastic steps.

A Sure Plan to Get Out of Credit Card Debt

All it takes to get deep into debt is a few credit cards and the stroke of a pen. To date, I have yet to see a credit card commercial that talks about the fact that you must actually pay for your purchases. The focus is always on how much fun you can have by using your credit card.

Well, someday you're going to have to pay for that fun. Eventually, it's time to pay the lender. I have seen more tears shed over the issue of debt than any other issue. If you are presently in debt, you know the emotional stress you are experiencing. Yet there is hope; you can get out of debt. However, it will involve a commitment on your part.

I advise people to follow these five steps to get out of credit card debt:

1. Buy everything with cash or a check.

Stop using credit cards for any purchase. If you have to use a credit card for a catalog purchase, write the check out to the credit card company the same day. Believe me, credit card companies will accept several checks each month. Operating on a pay-now system is critical to getting out of debt.

2. Carefully analyze every purchase.

Before you buy anything, ask yourself, "Do I really need to make this purchase?" Try to avoid all unnecessary purchases while paying off debt. Don't make a major purchase without waiting at least twenty-four hours to think about it.

3. List all your debt obligations.

Make a list of all your debt obligations. Each month update the list with payments and new amounts due. You should see the overall debt balance decreasing. Once you see the debt being reduced, this list becomes a motivational tool.

4. Determine what you will allocate each month to pay off debt.

Decide a set amount you will pay each month to reduce your debt, and either keep the debt-payment amount the same each month or try to increase it. *Never decrease* this amount until all your debts have been paid off.

For example, let's say you have five credit card bills and you are paying $50 per month on each card for a total of $250. When you finally get one of the five cards paid off, don't just keep sending the other four $50.00; instead, send each one of the other four companies $62.50. When you pay off the second credit card, send each of the remaining three credit card companies $83.33 each. The Monthly Payment Schedule below illustrates another way this could be done. Do not decrease your debt payments until all your credit cards have been paid in full!

MONTHLY PAYMENT SCHEDULE

Card	Jan.	Feb.	Mar.	Apr.	May	Jun.	Jul.
Gold Card	$ 50	$ 50	$ 10	*	*	*	*
MasterCard	50	50	60	$ 19	*	*	*
Visa	50	50	60	77	$ 70	*	*
Discover	50	50	60	77	90	$ 48	*
Universal	50	50	60	77	90	202	$84
Totals	$250	$250	$250	$250	$250	$250	$84

5. Begin to save.

Once you get your debt paid off, begin to save 50 to 100 percent of the money you had been sending to the credit card companies. Be very wise in how you use the money that was going to pay off debt. Build up an emergency fund for future needs and expenses.

In Chapter 5 we will look at the second area in which people make poor decisions and lead themselves into excessive debt: the purchase of a home.

PURCHASING A HOME:

Wise Investment or Murky Nightmare?

5

I remember advising a young couple from Dallas who were in the process of buying their first home. (We will use this couple throughout this section on mortgages to illustrate the various options available to—and the decisions to be made by—anyone of any age who decides to purchase a home.) This young couple had applied for their mortgage and had been meeting with the mortgage company right before they came to my office.

They brought in several papers and asked me to explain what they meant. I began by giving them a handout I use in my seminars that summarizes the common terms they needed to understand. I have listed those terms for you on the following page.

COMMON FINANCIAL TERMS
YOU NEED TO UNDERSTAND

Amortization Schedule

This is usually a computer printout that reflects how each monthly payment to the mortgage company is allocated between principal and interest. It also reveals the remaining principal due after each payment is made.

Point

In financial terms, a point represents 1 percent of a total amount. For example, on a $100,000 loan, one point equals $1,000, or 1 percent.

Prime Rate

The interest rate that banks will lend money to their "best" customers.

Prepaying a Mortgage

To prepay a mortgage means you pay more than your contract requires you to pay. If your monthly payment is $650 and you pay $750, you are prepaying your mortgage. One hundred percent of the payment that exceeds the required amount should go toward principal reduction.

After the couple had looked at this paper, we went through the information the bank had given them. One of the papers had the disclosure information for the loan: a summary of the loan amount, the interest rate, the monthly payment, the number of payments, and the total cost for the mortgage. One of the boxes had a figure of

$236,944.32. I explained to them that this indicated they would be paying $236,944.32 for their house.

I will never forget the look on their faces. Their first question was, "How can that be? Our mortgage is only for $75,000!"

To explain, I showed them that their monthly payment was $658.18. Together we multiplied $658.18 × 12 months × 30 years, which equals $236,944!

The Shocking Expense of Buying a Home

For most people, their home will be their largest, single purchase during their lifetime. For most, buying a home is a wise investment, but for some who have made mistakes it becomes their greatest nightmare!

Do you have a mortgage on your home? If your answer is yes, how much do you think you will be paying for your home? Would you like to know? It is actually very simple. Take your monthly payment for principal and interest and multiply it by 12. Then multiply the annual amount times the number of years for your loan. For example, let's assume your mortgage payment is $750 per month.

$750	×	12	=	$9,000	×	30	=	$270,000
Monthly Payment				Annual Payment		No. of Years		Total Cost for Loan

Now let's use this formula to figure the total cost of your own home.

_____	×	12	=	_____	×	_____	=	_____
Monthly Payment				Annual Payment		No. of Years		Total Cost for Loan

THIRTY-YEAR AMORTIZATION SCHEDULE

An amortization schedule shows how each monthly payment is allocated toward principal and interest. Below, you will find a partial schedule for a thirty-year $75,000 mortgage at 10 percent interest. Due to a lack of space, we can only include the twelve payments for the first year, the last payment of the fifteenth year, and the final six payments for the last year.

Payment Number	Payment	Amt. Allocated to Principal	Amt. Allocated for Interest	Balance Due After Payment
1	$658.18	$ 33.18	$ 625.00	$74,966.82
2	658.18	33.46	624.72	74,933.37
3	658.18	33.73	624.44	74,899.63
4	658.18	34.02	624.16	74,865.62
5	658.18	34.30	623.88	74,831.32
6	658.18	34.58	623.59	74,796.73
7	658.18	34.87	623.31	74,761.86
8	658.18	35.16	623.02	74,726.70
9	658.18	35.46	622.72	74,691.24
10	658.18	35.75	622.43	74,655.49
11	658.18	36.05	622.13	74,619.44
12	658.18	36.35	621.83	74,583.09
Totals for Year 1		$416.91	$7,481.24	
180	$658.18	$146.55	$ 511.62	$61,248.42
355	$658.18	$626.21	$ 31.97	$ 3,210.19
356	658.18	631.43	26.75	2,578.77
357	658.18	636.69	21.49	1,942.08
358	658.18	641.99	16.18	1,300.08
359	658.18	647.34	10.83	652.74
360	658.18	652.74	5.44	$ 0.00

Did you realize how much you would be paying for your home during the next thirty years? Most of us are quite surprised the first time we face this reality.

Some people might respond by saying, "I don't plan to live in my home for thirty years." Well, that only makes it worse! If you live in a home for five years and then move to another home and obtain a new thirty-year loan, you are now paying your mortgage for thirty-five years. And the most expensive years of a mortgage are the first few years! Every time you buy a new home and obtain a new mortgage, you are reentering the high-interest payment years.

On pages 74–80 are two partial amortization schedules for a $75,000 mortgage. One illustrates a thirty-year mortgage and the other is for a fifteen-year mortgage. You can quickly see that the young couple with the thirty-year mortgage would really be paying $236,944.

Look again at the thirty-year amortization schedule on page 74 and notice the following important factors:

1. The amount of the first payment that is actually applied toward principal is $33.18.

2. The first payment applied toward interest is $625!

3. At the end of fifteen years of paying 180 monthly mortgage payments, you still owe the bank $61,248.42 on a $75,000 loan! You have paid $118,472.40 (180 payments × $658.18) to the bank, and your mortgage has been reduced just $13,751.58! The remaining $104,720.82 went to pay interest for the first fifteen years.

4. The total principal repaid after 360 payments is $75,000. The young couple will finally have paid off their mortgage. However, they have paid more than *double* this amount in interest.

5. The total interest they will have paid after 360 payments will be $161,944.32.

6. Total cost: $236,944.32

Now let's look at each year of this couple's thirty-year mortgage by glancing at the annual totals for a thirty-year amortization schedule.

THIRTY-YEAR AMORTIZATION SCHEDULE / ANNUAL TOTALS

This is a partial schedule for a $75,000 mortgage at 10 percent for thirty years. Annual payment each year: Monthly payment ($658.18) × 12 = $7,898.16. Thus, for each year, if you add the principal paid and interest paid, the total will be $7,898.16.

Year	Principal Paid	Interest Paid	Balance Due at End of Year	Percentage of Mortgage Still Due at Year End
1	$ 416.91	$7,481.24	$74,583.09	99.44
2	460.56	7,437.58	74,122.53	98.82
3	508.79	7,389.35	73,613.73	98.15
4	562.07	7,336.08	73,051.67	97.40
5	620.93	7,277.22	72,430.74	96.57
6	685.94	7,212.20	71,744.80	95.65
7	757.77	7,140.37	70,987.03	94.65
8	837.12	7,061.02	70,149.91	93.35
9	924.78	6,973.37	69,225.13	92.30
10	1,021.61	6,876.53	68,203.51	90.93
11	1,128.59	6,769.55	67,074.92	89.43
12	1,246.77	6,651.38	65,828.16	87.77
13	1,377.32	6,520.82	64,450.84	85.93
14	1,521.54	6,376.60	62,929.29	83.90
15	1,680.87	6,217.28	61,248.42	81.66
16	1,856.88	6,041.27	59,391.54	79.19
17	2,051.32	5,846.83	57,340.22	76.45
18	2,266.12	5,632.03	55,074.11	73.43
19	2,503.41	5,394.73	52,570.70	70.09
20	2,765.55	5,132.59	49,805.15	66.40
21	3,055.14	4,843.00	46,750.01	62.33
22	3,375.05	4,523.09	43,374.95	57.83
23	3,728.46	4,169.68	39,646.49	52.86
24	4,118.88	3,779.26	35,527.61	47.36
25	4,550.18	3,347.96	30,977.42	41.30

Year	Principal Paid	Interest Paid	Balance Due at End of Year	Percentage of Mortgage Still Due at Year End
26	$5,026.65	$2,871.50	$25,950.77	34.60
27	5,553.00	2,345.14	20,397.77	27.20
28	6,134.48	1,763.67	14,263.29	19.02
29	6,776.84	1,121.31	7,486.46	09.98
30	7,486.46	411.69	00.00	00.00

Totals:

Principal	$ 75,000.00
Interest	$161,944.32
Principal and Interest	$236,944.32

Again, let's take a second look at this schedule to see what is happening. In the first year of their mortgage, after the couple pays the mortgage company $7,898.16 ($7,481.24 in interest and $416.91 toward the principal), they have only obtained approximately one half of 1 percent additional equity (ownership) in their home. During this same one-year period they paid the mortgage company more than 10 percent ($7,898.16) of their original loan amount of $75,000, yet they still owe 99.44 percent of their loan!

All in all, they do not pay more on their principal than on their interest until the twenty-third year of their thirty-year mortgage (see the graph on page 79).

Now let's suppose this young couple had decided to obtain a $75,000 mortgage for fifteen years, rather than thirty, at the same 10 percent interest rate (see the chart on page 78).

FIFTEEN-YEAR AMORTIZATION SCHEDULE

This is a partial schedule for a $75,000 mortgage at 10 percent for fifteen years.

Payment Number	Payment	Amt. Allocated to Principal	Amt. Allocated for Interest	Balance Due After Payment
1	$805.95	$ 180.95	$ 625.00	$74,819.05
2	805.95	182.46	623.49	74,636.58
3	805.95	183.98	621.97	74,452.60
4	805.95	185.52	620.44	74,267.09
5	805.95	187.06	618.89	74,080.03
6	805.95	188.62	617.33	73,891.40
7	805.95	190.19	615.76	73,701.21
8	805.95	191.78	614.18	73,509.44
9	805.95	193.38	612.58	73,316.06
10	805.95	194.99	610.97	73,121.07
11	805.95	196.61	609.34	72,924.46
12	805.95	198.25	607.70	72,726.21
Totals for Year 1		$2,273.79	$7,397.66	
84	$805.95	$ 360.34	$ 445.62	$53,113.56
175	$805.95	$ 766.81	$ 39.15	$ 3,930.95
176	805.95	773.20	32.76	3,157.76
177	805.95	779.64	26.31	2,378.12
178	805.95	786.14	19.82	1,591.98
179	805.95	792.69	13.27	799.29
180	805.95	799.29	6.66	0.00

What a difference the fifteen-year mortgage makes. Notice:

1. The amount of the first payment applied toward the principal is $180.95 (rather than only $33.18 with the thirty-year mortgage).

2. The amount of the first payment applied toward the interest is $625.00 (the same as the thirty-year mortgage).

3. The amount of principal due after paying eighty-four payments for seven years is $53,113.56. This couple has already paid off $21,886.44 of their $75,000 mortgage.

4. The amount of principal due after paying 180 payments for fifteen years is $0 (rather than the $61,248.42 they still owed after fifteen years of the thirty-year mortgage).

5. The total principal repaid after 180 payments is $75,000. Their house is truly their own!

6. The total interest paid after 180 payments is $70,071.69 (rather than $161,944.32 at the end of the thirty-year mortgage).

7. The total cost of their home is $145,071.69 (rather than the $236,944 that so surprised them when they came to see me).

MORE PRINCIPAL THAN INTEREST

Begins in 23rd Year

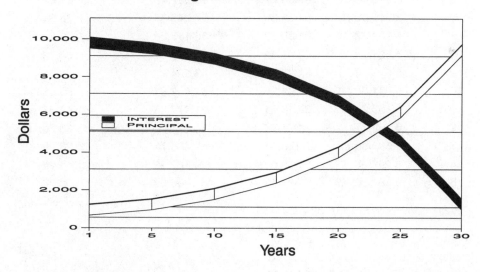

$75,000 at 10 percent for thirty years

Now let's look at each year of the fifteen-year mortgage by looking at the chart of the annual totals for a fifteen-year amortization schedule below.

FIFTEEN-YEAR AMORTIZATION SCHEDULE / ANNUAL TOTALS

Annual Payment Each Year: Monthly Payment $805.95 × 12 = $9,671.40. For each year, if you add the principal paid and interest paid the total will be $9,671,40.

Year	Principal Paid	Interest Paid	Balance Due at End of Year	Percent of Mortgage Still Due at Year End
1	$2,273.79	$7,397.66	$72,726.21	96.97
2	2,511.88	7,159.56	70,214.33	93.62
3	2,774.91	6,896.54	67,439.42	89.92
4	3,065.48	6,605.97	64,373.94	85.83
5	3,386.48	6,284.97	60,987.46	81.32
6	3,741.08	5,930.36	57,246.38	76.33
7	4,132.82	5,538.62	53,113.56	70.81
8	4,565.58	5,105.86	48,547.97	64.73
9	5,043.66	4,627.79	43,504.31	58.01
10	5,571.80	4,099.65	37,932.51	50.58
11	6,155.24	3,516.21	31,777.28	42.37
12	6,799.77	2,871.67	24,977.51	33.30
13	7,511.80	2,159.65	17,465.71	23.29
14	8,298.38	1,373.07	9,167.33	12.22
15	9,167.33	504.12	00.00	00.00

Totals:

Principal	$ 75,000.00
Interest	$ 70,071.69
Principal and Interest	$145,071.69

My first observation about the fifteen-year mortgage is that you own the home in fifteen years! When you compare the fifteen-year schedule to the thirty-year schedule, it is obvious you are paying less interest and are obtaining ownership faster.

Another observation is that you pay more on your principal than on your interest in the ninth year of your fifteen-year mortgage (rather than the twenty-third year of the thirty-year mortgage). See how the graph below illustrates this.

MORE PRINCIPAL THAN INTEREST

Begins in 9th Year

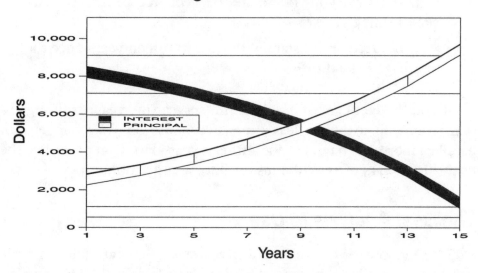

$75,000 at 10 percent for fifteen years

Analysis of the Fifteen-Year Plan

The monthly payment for a $75,000 mortgage at 10 percent for fifteen years is $805.95. The total cost for the young couple is

$145,071 ($805.95 × 180 payments = $145,071.00). What I am showing you here is that by choosing a fifteen-year loan over a thirty-year one, your savings will be $91,873.80 ($236,944.80 − $145,071.00 = $91,873.80). And in fifteen years you will own your home outright.

Some people have said, "I can't afford a fifteen-year loan." But I ask you, "Can you afford the additional $90,000 it will cost you for a thirty-year loan?" I guess you can see why I recommend that people opt for a fifteen-year mortgage!

- Why not pay thousands of dollars less in interest?
- Why not own your home and be debt free in fifteen years versus thirty years?
- Why not free up substantial income in fifteen years once the mortgage is paid off?

If your budget cannot handle a fifteen-year mortgage, my suggestion would be to buy a less expensive house so your budget *can* handle a mortgage payment for a fifteen-year loan. Don't sacrifice the next thirty years of your life just to have a larger home.

The Best Analysis to Use

I believe one of the most effective ways to analyze any financial decision, particularly a home mortgage, is to look at the big picture.

Using this question, here is an interesting analysis for you. Think back to the monthly payment for that thirty-year, $75,000 mortgage at 10 percent interest, which was $658.18. The total cost out of the couple's checkbook would be $236,944.80 ($658.18 × 360 payments = $236,944.80). After thirty years the young couple would have their house paid for—and no additional money in savings.

Now here is the bonus! If the young couple paid their mortgage off in fifteen years and started saving $510.41 each month for the next fifteen years, earning 8 percent on their investment, they would accumulate an additional $176,621.37 in savings.

Ask yourself, "How much money will I have to spend out of my personal checkbook?"

The total cost out of their checkbook during this thirty-year period would be $236,944.80—*exactly the cost of the thirty-year mortgage!*

Calculations

For the first fifteen years (180 months), they will pay a monthly mortgage payment of $805.95. For the second fifteen years (180 months) they write themselves a check and invest $510.41 each month.

$$\begin{aligned}
\$805.95 \times 180 \text{ months} &= \$145,071.00 \text{ MORTGAGE} \\
+ \$510.41 \times 180 \text{ months} &= \underline{\$\ 91,873.80} \text{ SAVINGS} \\
&\ \$236,944.80
\end{aligned}$$

Which would be the wiser use of your resources?

☐ Thirty-year mortgage
   Money out of your checkbook: $236,944
   House is paid in full after thirty years
   After thirty years you have $0.00 in savings.

☐ Fifteen-year mortgage (with fifteen-year savings plan)
   Money out of your checkbook: $236,944
   House paid for after fifteen years
   After thirty years you have $176,621 in savings.

Who is making the money here? You or the bank? The comparison of mortgages below shows the difference graphically.

15-YEAR VS. 30-YEAR
You Decide

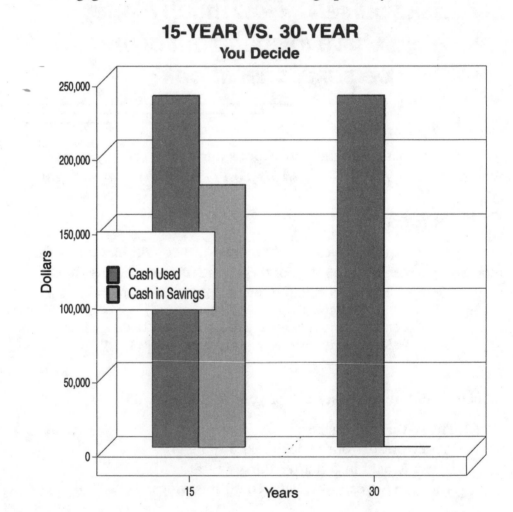

Since this young couple had already obtained a thirty-year mortgage, I suggested they consider prepaying their mortgage whenever possible.

Prepaying Your Mortgage

For most mortgages, any additional money you send to the mortgage company is applied 100 percent to reduce the principal owed. Our young couple originally obtained a $75,000 loan at 10 percent interest for thirty years. Let's assume they make twelve monthly payments of $658.18 before they feel able to prepay their mortgage. Then they decide to add an additional $200 each month in "prepayment money." Now they will be sending $858.18 each month ($658.18 + $200.00 = $858.18).

The chart below shows how prepaying affects the amount of money being used to reduce the principal. Notice that during the first year this couple is not prepaying and the principal reduction is very low. Next, notice that beginning with the thirteenth payment the prepayment money significantly increases the amount being applied to principal reduction!

HOW PREPAYMENT DIRECTLY AFFECTS INTEREST

Payment Number	Payment	Amt. Allocated to Principal	Amt. Allocated for Interest	Balance Due After Payment
1	$658.18	$33.18	$625.00	$74,966.82
2	658.18	33.46	624.72	74,933.37
3	658.18	33.73	624.44	74,899.63
4	658.18	34.02	624.16	74,865.62
5	658.18	34.30	623.88	74,831.32
6	658.18	34.58	623.59	74,796.73
7	658.18	34.87	623.31	74,761.86

HOW PREPAYMENT DIRECTLY
AFFECTS INTEREST—*Cont'd*

Payment Number	Payment	Amt. Allocated to Principal	Amt. Allocated for Interest	Balance Due After Payment
8	$658.18	$35.16	$623.02	$74,726.70
9	658.18	35.46	622.72	74,691.24
10	658.18	35.75	622.43	74,655.49
11	658.18	36.05	622.13	74,619.44
12	658.18	36.35	621.83	74,583.09

Now compare that to what happens when they add $200.00 more each month to their payment!

Payment Number	Payment	Amt. Allocated to Principal	Amt. Allocated for Interest	Balance Due After Payment
13	$858.18	$236.65	$621.53	$74,346.44
14	858.18	238.63	619.55	74,107.81
15	858.18	240.61	617.57	73,867.20
16	858.18	242.62	615.56	73,624.58
17	858.18	244.64	613.54	73,379.94
18	858.18	246.68	611.50	73,133.26
166	858.18	842.45	15.73	1,045.29
167	858.18	849.47	8.71	195.82
168	197.45	195.82	1.63	0.00

Now compare this second schedule to the regular schedule for their thirty-year mortgage. Notice the following important facts:

1. The total principal repaid after 168 payments is $75,000.
2. The total interest paid after 168 payments, which has now paid off the loan, is $66,113.29, rather than a total interest of $161,944.32 at the end of the thirty-year mortgage.

3. The total cost of the $75,000 mortgage is $141,113.29, rather than their original $236,944.32!

4. It only took fourteen years to pay off the mortgage, rather than the original term of thirty years.

Obviously, prepaying the mortgage would save this young couple a great deal of money. However, if they could not afford to pay $200 more each month, they could also consider a one-time prepayment on their mortgage.

One-Time Prepayment on a Mortgage

What would happen if this young couple made a one-time pre-payment of $1,000 when they paid their thirteenth payment? On the Prepayment Schedule for Thirty-Year Mortgage on pages 87–88, notice that all the payments are "normal" with the exception of payment thirteen, when the couple added $1,000 to their payment.

PREPAYMENT SCHEDULE FOR THIRTY-YEAR MORTGAGE

Payment Number	Payment	Amt. Allocated to Principal	Amt. Allocated for Interest	Balance Due After Payment
1	$658.18	$33.18	$625.00	$74,966.82
2	658.18	33.46	624.72	74,933.37
3	658.18	33.73	624.44	74,899.63
4	658.18	34.02	624.16	74,865.62
5	658.18	34.30	623.88	74,831.32
6	658.18	34.58	623.59	74,796.73
7	658.18	34.87	623.31	74,761.86
8	658.18	35.16	623.02	74,726.70
9	658.18	35.46	622.72	74,691.24
10	658.18	35.75	622.43	74,655.49
11	658.18	36.05	622.13	74,619.44
12	658.18	36.35	621.83	74,583.09

The chart below clearly shows what happens when they add a one-time payment of $1,000 to the thirteenth monthly payment. The $1,000 was applied directly to principal reduction!

EFFECT OF ONE-TIME PAYMENT
ON THIRTY-YEAR MORTGAGE

Payment Number	Payment	Amt. Allocated to Principal	Amt. Allocated for Interest	Balance Due After Payment
13	$1,658.18	$1,036.65	$621.53	$73,546.44
325	658.18	598.28	59.90	6,590.11
326	658.18	603.26	54.92	5,986.85
327	658.18	608.29	49.89	5,378.56
328	658.18	613.36	44.82	4,765.20
329	658.18	618.47	39.71	4,176.73
330	658.18	623.62	34.56	3,523.11
331	658.18	628.82	29.36	2,894.29
332	658.18	634.06	24.12	2,260.23
333	658.18	639.34	18.84	1,620.89
334	658.18	644.67	13.51	976.22
335	658.18	650.04	8.14	326.17
336	328.89	326.17	2.72	000.00

Let's compare this schedule to their original thirty-year mortgage schedule. Notice these important facts:

1. Their total interest paid is $146,818.75, rather than $161,944.32.

2. The total cost of their loan is $221,818.75, rather than $236,944.32.

3. Their thirty-year mortgage originally took 360 payments, but now they only have 336 payments; therefore their $1,000 investment saved them twenty-four payments ($15,796.32).

360 Payments − 336 Payments = 24 payments!
24 × $658.18 = *$15,796.32* in savings

Looks like a pretty good "return" on their $1,000 investment!

Most mortgage companies do allow you to prepay on your mort-gage. *Be sure to check with your lender for approval and details.*

Our young couple had two other options:

1. Pay a thirty-year mortgage like a fifteen-year mortgage!

Most people are like this young couple. They already have obtained a thirty-year mortgage on their home. What can they do now? Even if you have a thirty-year mortgage, if you make the same monthly payment as a fifteen-year payment would be, you will be debt free in fifteen years. Even prepaying $25 a month would save our young couple money.

2. Prepay the loan by a small amount per month.

By increasing their payment by $25 each month starting with the first payment on a $75,000 mortgage at 10 percent interest for thirty years, the young couple's loan would be paid off after 297 payments (the ninth payment in the twenty-fifth year of the loan) with a savings to them of $34,163.89.

Just because you cannot make large monthly prepayments does not mean you should not prepay your mortgage.

Unfortunately, this young couple had bought into a common prob-lem: obtaining a mortgage that was too big for their budget.

Both spouses were working, and they felt they could afford a $75,000 loan. This shows why it is wise to qualify for your mortgage using only one income, even if you both are working. Having a mort-gage dependent on two incomes becomes very stressful if one of you must stop working due to children or personal illness.

Several years later that same young couple called my office. "Now that interest rates are so low, should we refinance our home?" they asked. This is a common question since interest rates fluctuate with economic conditions.

What About Refinancing Your Home?

The rule of thumb for refinancing your home is as follows:

1. You must be able to reduce your interest rate by at least two percentage points. For example, the young couple's present interest rate was 10 percent. I told them, "You must be able to finance a new loan at 8 percent or less."

2. You must believe you will be living in your home long enough to recover your closing costs to refinance. For example, this young couple paid monthly payments of $658.18 on their $75,000, thirty-year mortgage at 10 percent. Their mortgage was fifteen years old, and they presently owed $61,248 since they had never prepaid their mortgage as they had hoped. If they refinanced their home at 7 percent for fifteen years, their monthly payment would become $550.51. However, the closing costs to refinance would be $1,500. Should they refinance?

First, did their interest percentage drop more than two points? Yes.

Second, how long would it take them to recover their closing costs of $1,500 through their monthly savings?

$658.18 (old monthly payment)
− $550.51 (new monthly payment)
$107.67 (monthly savings due to refinancing)

$1,500 ÷ $107.67 = 13.93 or 14 months

Did they plan to live in their home for at least fourteen months? Their answer was yes, so I told them to proceed with refinancing. It would take them fourteen months to recover their refinancing costs, but beginning with the fifteenth month, they would be saving $107.67 every month for almost fourteen years ($107.67 × 166 months = $17,873.22).

An Even Better Plan

Actually, a better plan in this example would be to *keep* their monthly payment at $658.18 (old payment) and refinance at 7 percent. Their home would be paid in full in eleven years and three months. They were already accustomed to paying $658.18, so why not keep doing the same? They would get out of debt faster!

Now that you have watched this young couple struggle through the many facets of a mortgage decision, take a moment to carefully examine your own situation.

How Much Mortgage Can I Afford?

Have you ever wondered how much of a mortgage you can afford? If your answer is yes, I have just the worksheet for you! Of course, the mortgage amount will depend on what term mortgage you are obtaining—a fifteen-year or a thirty-year contract (and I trust that I have influenced you to seriously consider the fifteen-year option!).

But before you can calculate how much mortgage you can afford, you must first understand how to calculate your potential mortgage payment for any loan amount.

The Mortgage Monthly Payment worksheet on pages 93–94 will allow you to calculate the approximate monthly payment for a mortgage of any amount. It does not matter if it is for $1,000 or $10,000,000! The process is so simple, anyone can do it!

I remember the first time I purchased a home. I probably asked my real estate agent twenty-five times how much my monthly payment would be if I bought a home for _____. My agent was always punching a long series of numbers into the calculator before I would receive my answer.

I felt helpless, not knowing how to figure it out for myself! I thought you surely had to be a financial wizard to use one of those fancy financial calculators that had about forty different keys.

Well, I have figured out a way for *anyone* to do exactly the same thing *without* having to be a wizard at using a financial calculator. The result of my effort is the Mortgage Monthly Payment Worksheet.

You will be able to calculate your approximate monthly mortgage payment with any interest rate from 4 percent all the way up to 17 percent!

How to Use the Worksheet

Let's look at a sample problem first. A family wants to buy a house with an $81,500 loan at a 9 percent interest rate for fifteen years:

1. Amount of loan: *$81,500* ÷ 1,000 = *81.50* (a)
2. On the Mortgage Monthly Payment Factor chart on pages 93– 94, find the factor corresponding to your interest rate and term. In this case, the factor corresponding to your interest rate *(9 percent)* and the years for the loan *(15)* is *10.14* (b).
3. Multiply (a) *81.50* × (b) factor *10.14* = *$826.41* monthly payment.

Now estimate your own monthly payment using the following worksheet:

MORTGAGE MONTHLY PAYMENT WORKSHEET

1. Amount of loan: $_____ ÷ 1,000 =   _____(a)

2. On the chart, find the factor corresponding to your interest rate and
   term. Your interest rate is _____% and the term (years for the
   loan) is _____, so your factor is   _____(b)

3. Multiply (a) _____ × (b) _____ = $_____ monthly payment.

MORTGAGE MONTHLY PAYMENT CHART

Interest Rate	Years of Loan 15 Factor	Years of Loan 30 Factor	Interest Rate	Years of Loan 15 Factor	Years of Loan 30 Factor
4.00	7.40	4.77	8.00	9.56	7.34
4.25	7.52	4.92	8.25	9.70	7.51
4.50	7.65	5.07	8.50	9.85	7.69
4.75	7.78	5.22	8.75	9.99	7.87
5.00	7.91	5.37	9.00	10.14	8.05
5.25	8.04	5.52	9.25	10.29	8.23
5.50	8.17	5.68	9.50	10.44	8.41
5.75	8.30	5.84	9.75	10.59	8.59
6.00	8.44	6.00	10.00	10.75	8.78
6.25	8.57	6.16	10.25	10.90	8.96
6.50	8.71	6.32	10.50	11.05	9.15
6.75	8.85	6.49	10.75	11.21	9.33
7.00	8.99	6.65	11.00	11.37	9.52
7.25	9.13	6.82	11.25	11.52	9.71
7.50	9.27	6.99	11.50	11.68	9.90
7.75	9.41	7.16	11.75	11.84	10.09

MORTGAGE MONTHLY
PAYMENT CHART—*Cont'd*

Interest Rate	Years of Loan 15 Factor	Years of Loan 30 Factor	Interest Rate	Years of Loan 15 Factor	Years of Loan 30 Factor
12.00	12.00	10.29	15.00	14.00	12.64
12.25	12.16	10.48	15.25	14.17	12.85
12.50	12.33	10.67	15.50	14.34	13.05
12.75	12.49	10.87	15.75	14.51	13.25
13.00	12.65	11.06	16.00	14.69	13.45
13.25	12.82	11.26	16.25	14.86	13.65
13.50	12.98	11.45	16.50	15.04	13.85
13.75	13.15	11.65	16.75	15.21	14.05
14.00	13.32	11.85	17.00	15.39	14.26
14.25	13.49	12.05	17.25	15.57	14.46
14.50	13.66	12.25	17.50	15.75	14.66
14.75	13.83	12.45	17.75	15.92	14.87

Now that you know what your monthly payment will be, you are ready to determine the proper mortgage. I hope the following "How Much Mortgage Can I Afford?" worksheet will be of help. The worksheet is based upon some common guidelines that most lending institutions use. For example, most lenders will allow you to have a mortgage payment that does not exceed the larger of:

28 percent of your gross income or
36 percent of your gross income minus all other current monthly obligations (such as payments on cars, credit cards, and school loans).

First, let's work a sample problem. The answers are at the end of the worksheet.

HOW MUCH MORTGAGE CAN I AFFORD?

1. What is your total monthly gross (before taxes) income? $ __3,500__ (1)

2. Total monthly payment of all present loans (car, school, credit cards) $ ___150__ (2)

3. Maximum monthly payments for your mortgage, taxes, and insurance is the larger of the two calculations below:

   A. Gross income $_____ × .28 = $_____(3a)

   B. Gross Income $_____ × .36 = $_____

       Minus line 2 $_____

       Equals $_____(3b)

4. Price of the home you plan to purchase: $ _81,500_ (4a)

   Add: Estimated closing expenses (2 percent to 4 percent of line 4) $ _3,260_ (4b)

   Total (4a) + (4b) $_____(4c)

5. Assets or cash available for down payment $ _12,000_ (5a)

   Minus 2.5 percent of (4a) to be used for house repairs $_____(5b)

   Subtract 5b from 5a $_____(5c)

6. Amount of loan you need to obtain (4c) − (5c) = $_____(6a)

7. Calculate your monthly mortgage payment: (Use Mortgage Calculation Table: 15 years @ 9 percent) $_____(7a)

   Add: Projected monthly insurance premium $ _25.00_ (7b)

   Add: Projected monthly real estate taxes $ _90.00_ (7c)

   Equals total payment for mortgage, taxes, and insurance $_____(7d)

8. Is (7d) less than the amount calculated in either steps (3a) or (3b)?

   If yes, you are within your limits. If no, the amount of the price of home (4a) needs to be lowered. Reduce (4a) and recalculate.

Answers:

3a. $980 ($3,500 × .28 = $980)

3b. $1,110 ($3,500 × .36 = $1,260; $1,260 − $150 = $1,110)

4c. $84,760 ($81,500 + $3,260 = $84,760)

5b. $2,038 ($81,500 × 2.5% = $2,038)

5c. $9,962 ($12,000 − $2,038 = $9,962)

6a. $74,798 ($84,760 − $9,962 = $74,798)

7a. $758 ($74,798 ÷ 1,000 = 74.80 × Factor 10.14 = $758.45)

7d. $873 ($758 + 25 + $90 = $873)

8.   YES

On page 97 is a blank worksheet for your personal use.

Now that we have worked through buying a home, in the next chapter we will look at the purchase of a car. Most people use debt to buy a car. However, I believe there is a better plan.

HOW MUCH MORTGAGE CAN I AFFORD?

1. What is your total monthly gross (before taxes) income? $_____(1)

2. Total monthly payment of all present loans (car, school, credit cards) $_____(2)

3. Maximum monthly payments for your mortgage, taxes, and insurance is the larger of the two calculations below:

   A. Gross income $_____ × .28 = $_____(3a)

   B. Gross Income $_____ × .36 = $_____

      Minus line 2 $_____

      Equals $_____(3b)

4. Price of the home you plan to purchase: $_____(4a)

   Add: Estimated closing expenses (2 percent to 4 percent of line 4) $_____(4b)

   Total (4a) + (4b) $_____(4c)

5. Assets or cash available for down payment $_____(5a)
   Minus 2.5 percent of (4a) to be used for house repairs $_____(5b)

   Subtract 5b from 5a $_____(5c)

6. Amount of loan you need to obtain (4c) − (5c) = $_____(6a)

7. Calculate your monthly mortgage payment:
   (Use Mortgage Monthly Payment Chart on pages 93–94: _____ years @ _____ percent) $_____(7a)

   Add: Projected monthly insurance premium $_____(7b)

   Add: Projected monthly real estate taxes $_____(7c)

   Equals total payment for mortgage, taxes, and insurance $_____(7d)

8. Is (7d) less than the amount calculated in either steps (3a) or (3b)?
   If yes, you are within your limits. If no, the amount of the price of home (4a) needs to be lowered. Reduce (4a) and recalculate.

PURCHASING A CAR:

Buy Four, Get the Fifth One Free!

Congratulations," said a friendly voice on the telephone. "You have been selected as one of our winners. You can receive five magazines of your choice for only two dollars and fifty cents per week." The person paused a moment and then said, "I know this is an offer you just will not be able to refuse."

"How long will the subscriptions last?" I asked.

"Five years."

I began to do some rough calculations aloud on the phone. "Now, two dollars and fifty cents a week, that's ten dollars a month ($2.50 × 4 weeks) and one hundred and twenty dollars a year ($10 × 12 months). And for five years, that would be *six hundred dollars* ($120 × 5 years)!"

I said, "I am very sorry but I cannot commit six hundred dollars for five magazines."

Well, I think the poor woman was personally embarrassed. She had never taken the time to calculate the commitment she was asking people to make. You see, only $2.50 a week sounded reasonable, yet the total cost was outrageous.

Many people have been raised by their parents to make financial decisions based upon the monthly payment. I personally want to know the total cost for the purchase. And better yet, I want to know if I can afford to buy it with cash.

An essential perspective in debt: What is the total cost?

This is especially applicable when it comes to buying a new car.

Purchasing a New Car

So you want to buy a new car. Before you sign on the dotted line, carefully consider the proposal presented below. It just might change the way you buy cars for the rest of your life.

Let's assume you are in the process of buying a new car that is selling for $10,000. The loan company says you can get a forty-eight-month (four-year) loan at 10 percent interest. Your monthly payments will be $253.63, which amounts to $3,043.56 per year ($253.63 × 12 = $3,043.56).

It is always beneficial to look at financial decisions from a perspective of *several years* as opposed to basing your financial decision on how much the monthly payment is.

In the Buying a Car Using Debt chart below, we will use a sixteen-year time frame in which an individual will be using debt to purchase four cars.

BUYING A CAR USING DEBT

Year	Cash Paid Out of Checkbook	Price of Car	Amount in Savings
1	$ 3,043.56	$10,000	$0
2	3,043.56		0
3	3,043.56		0
4	3,043.56		0
5	3,043.56	10,000	0
6	3,043.56		0
7	3,043.56		0
8	3,043.56		0
9	3,043.56	10,000	0
10	3,043.56		0
11	3,043.56		0
12	3,043.56		0
13	3,043.56	10,000	0
14	3,043.56		0
15	3,043.56		0
16	3,043.56		0
Total	$48,696.96		$0

Note the following important observations about the cars related to the Buying a Car Using Debt chart:

1. You are purchasing four cars during a sixteen-year period.
2. You are paying $10,000 for each car. Don't get too caught up in the fact that I have not increased the price of the car every

four years due to inflation. I will deal with this fact later in the illustration.

3. Your monthly payments are $253.63.
4. Your cost is $3,043.56 per year ($253.63 × 12 months).
5. Your total cost per car is $12,174.24 ($253.63 × 48 months).
6. You are paying $2,174.24 in interest for each car. For four cars you are paying $8,696.96 in interest.
7. Your total cost to purchase four cars with debt is $48,697 out of your checkbook.
8. At the end of the sixteenth year you have a car that is four years old.
9. *At the end of the sixteenth year you have nothing in savings.*

There must be a better way! And indeed there is: *It's called paying cash.*

If you position yourself on the "earning" side of interest and not always on the "paying" side, you will be able to drive around in a new car you bought with cash!

The Cash Payment Plan

If you were asking my advice about buying a car, I would suggest the following plan:

1. Pay off your present car as quickly as possible.
2. Once you have your car paid off, begin writing *yourself* a car-payment check every month. Naturally, the amount will depend upon the price of the car you plan to purchase. If you are purchasing a $10,000 car, as we are using in our illustration, your check would be for $253.63 every month. The dollar

amount in this illustration does not matter. This plan will work for any price car! You would simply have to raise or lower your monthly savings amount.

3. Invest *your car payment* in a money market (or mutual fund) account, ideally one that earns at least 6 percent interest. If interest is higher, our plan will take less time; if interest is lower, our plan will be delayed two to eight months, a small price to pay for such wonderful results.

4. Keep driving your old car for at least four more years.

5. Use your savings account to pay for all the needed repairs to your old car during these years until you can purchase your new car for cash.

The chart below is an example of buying a car for cash.

BUYING A CAR USING CASH

Year	Cash Paid Out of Checkbook	Price of Car	Amount in Savings
1	$ 3,043.56		$ 3,128.67
2	3,043.56		6,450.31
3	3,043.56		9,976.82
4	3,043.56		13,720.83
5	3,043.56	$10,000.00	3,128.67
6	3,043.56		6,450.31
7	3,043.56		9,976.82
8	3,043.56		13,720.83
9	3,043.56	10,000.00	7,078.99
10	3,043.56		10,644.28
11	3,043.56		14,429.46
12	3,043.56		18,448.11
13	3,043.56	10,000.00	12,097.84

BUYING A CAR USING CASH—*Cont'd*

Year	Cash Paid Out of Checkbook	Price of Car	Amount in Savings
14	$ 3,043.56		$15,972.68
15	3,043.56		20,086.51
16	3,043.56		24,454.07
17 (January 1)		$10,000.00	14,454.07
Total	$48,696.96		

Let's walk through this time period together and take a closer look at the figures in this illustration:

Year One: You are still driving your old car. Committed to buying your next car for cash, you are faithfully paying yourself $253.63 every month. By the end of the first year, $3,043.56 has come out of your checkbook, but your savings are now worth $3,128.67, thanks to interest earned.

Year Two: On the first of each month, you continue to save $253.63. By the end of year two, you have $6,450.31 in your savings!

Year Three: Can you believe it, at the end of year three you actually have $9,976.82 in savings?

Year Four: Yes, you are still driving your old car. Who knows? By now it might be four, eight, or fifteen years old. But since you have faithfully saved every month for four years, you have put yourself in a financial position that will be paying rewards for the rest of your life! Was it worth the wait? Absolutely yes!

If you have paid for all your car repairs with money other than car savings, you now have $13,720.83 to purchase your new car for cash! Even if you had to use your car savings to pay for car repairs of up to $3,000 during the last four years, you should still have at least $10,000 in savings at the end of year four!

Year Five: It's January 2. You are ready to buy your car for cash.

You have more than $10,000, and you even have your "old" car to sell or trade, which will cover any increase in price due to inflation. At the beginning of year five you purchase your new car for cash.

But during year five, you continue to pay *yourself* a monthly car payment of $253.63 every month. Having a new car that is paid for is a strong motivator to write the check out to yourself each month!

At the beginning of year five, we will assume you used every dollar in your car savings to purchase your new car. But after twelve more months of saving, you have $3,128.67 (and a car that's paid for).

After you purchase your new car, we are assuming you will have very limited repairs and that you will pay for all repairs out of a budgeted car-repair category, not from your new-car savings account.

Year Six: You are still enjoying a fairly new car, and you keep paying yourself every month. At the end of year six your new-car savings account is worth $6,450.31.

Year Seven: Every month you are writing yourself a check. You now have $9,976.82 in your car savings.

Year Eight: Can you believe it? It's been another four years. You now have $13,720.83 in your car savings, and a car that is only four years old.

Year Nine: You have driven your first new car for four years and are ready to make another purchase. You have $13,720.83 at the beginning of year nine. In January you purchase another car for $10,000. In fact, you will be able to purchase a car for *more than* $10,000 because you again have a four-year-old car to sell or trade in!

The $7,078.99 you have in savings at the *end* of year nine represents the following actions: (1) You began the year with $13,720.83. (2) In January you spent $10,000 for a new car, leaving $3,720.83 in your account. (3) You continued saving $253.56 each month, and you now have $7,078.99 in your savings account.

Year Ten: It sure is nice driving around in that new car you paid for with cash. Just think, at the *beginning* of year ten, you already have $7,078.99 in savings and a car that is only one year old. Much better than the debt plan, wouldn't you say?

Year Eleven: Yes, you are still paying yourself $253.63 every month, and at the end of year eleven, you will have $14,429.46 in your car savings.

Year Twelve: Wow! Since you have been so faithful to pay yourself, your car savings account is worth $18,448.11!

Year Thirteen: It's January and time to go shopping again for that new car! You think, "This is great!" You have now driven your second new car for four years and are ready to make another purchase. You have $18,448.11 at the beginning of year thirteen. In January you purchase another car for $10,000. In fact, you will be able to purchase a car for *more than* $10,000 because, once again, you have a four-year-old car to sell or trade in!

The $12,097.84 you will have in savings at the end of year 13 represents the following: (1) You began the year with $18,448.11. (2) In January you spent $10,000 for a new car, leaving $8,448.11 in your account. (3) You continued your savings of $253.56 each month, and you now have $12,097.84 in your savings account at the end of year thirteen.

Year Fourteen: You started the year with $12,097.84 and saved $253.63 every month. With interest, your car savings are worth $15,972.68 at the end of the year.

Year Fifteen: *Incredible!* you think. How can this be? You have more than $20,000 in savings.

Year Sixteen: Keep on faithfully saving every month. You are now a believer. It *does* pay to be on the earning side of interest and *avoid debt!* At the end of year sixteen your car account has accumulated the grand sum of $24,454.07!

Year Seventeen: It's January again and time to go shopping for that fourth new car in just over sixteen years!

You have $24,454.07 at the beginning of year seventeen. In January you purchase another car for $10,000. In fact, you will be able to purchase a car for *more* than $10,000 because, as usual, you have a four-year-old car to sell or trade in!

Our illustration stops here at the beginning of year seventeen, but it could go on and on. And just look what you have accomplished. You are debt free, have a brand new car, and $14,454.07 in savings!

By positioning yourself on the earning side of interest, you have literally saved enough to buy your next car out of the savings you earned by not having to pay interest on money you borrowed from a bank. It's like getting a new car for free!

It's like getting a new car for free!

This concept can be wrapped up in a simple summary chart:

Number of cars purchased:
Debt Plan: 4
Cash Plan: 4

Total amount of cash out of your checkbook:
Debt Plan: $48,696.96
Cash Plan: $48,696.96

Total amount in savings at beginning of the seventeenth year:
Debt Plan: $0.00
Cash Plan: $14,454.51   (This is the money for your "free" car. At the end of the sixteen-year period, either you or the banker will have control of this $14,454.51.)

Age of car beginning year seventeen:
Debt Plan: Four years old
Cash Plan: One month old

Since both plans cost exactly the same amount out of your checkbook, which plan makes the most sense to you?

You are probably wondering how to calculate the monthly savings amount that will allow you to buy your cars for cash and accumulate savings at the same time. The following worksheet is designed to answer that question.

Calculating the Monthly Savings Amount for Purchasing a Car with Cash

Many factors could enter into this decision, such as present loan rates and what your savings will be able to earn each year, but by using the calculations below, you will be headed in the right direction.

First, determine how often you would like to buy your new cars. Will it be once every three, four, five, or six years? Second, determine the general price of the cars you plan to purchase each time. Once you know these two factors, you can determine the amount you need to *pay yourself* each month.

CAR SAVINGS CALCULATION CHART

Years	Factor
Three-year plan	32.27
Four-year plan	25.37
Five-year plan	21.25
Six-year plan	18.53

Let's work a sample problem to show how to use this chart. Suppose you want to buy a $14,000 car on the four-year plan.

1. Price of Car: *$14,000* ÷ 1,000 = *$14.00* (a)

2. Multiply (a) (which, in this case, is *$14.00*) × the appropriate factor from the Car Savings Calculation Chart (in this case, *25.37*) = *$355.18,* the amount you need to save each month.

Now work this calculation for your own car:

1. Price of Car: $_____ ÷ 1,000 = _____ (a)

2. Multiply (a) _____ × the appropriate factor from the Car Savings Calculation Chart _____ = $_____, the amount you need to save each month.

But what if you don't want a savings program built into your car-purchasing savings plan? If not, here is another car-for-cash plan that allows you to save enough money on a monthly basis to buy your next car for cash. The following worksheet *does not allow for any buildup of savings.* You will simply have enough money to purchase your next car for cash.

CAR-FOR-CASH WITHOUT ACCUMULATING SAVINGS

Step One:	Selling price of a new or used car	$ 8,000 (1)
Step Two:	Trade-in or selling price of your present car	$ 2,500 (2)
Step Three:	Dollars needed to buy car (line 1 minus line 2)	$ 5,500 (3)
Step Four:	Number of years until purchase	4 (4)
Step Five:	Interest rate you can earn on money	8% (5)
Step Six:	Use the Monthly Savings Table (page 110) to find the appropriate division factor by using information in lines 4 and 5. Factor =	56.26 (6)

Step Seven: Divide the dollars needed to buy the car (line 3) by the factor from the Monthly Savings Table (line 6) to see how much you need to save each month to buy a car for cash: $ __97.76__ (7)

$5,500 ÷ 56.26 = $97.76 (7), the amount you need to save each month.

TABLE A
MONTHLY SAVINGS TABLE

(This is a condensed chart of interest rates and years; see Table A in Appendix A for more interest rates and years.)

Years Until Purchase	Projected Interest Rate				
	6%	8%	9%	10%	12%
1	12.34	12.45	12.51	12.56	12.68
2	25.43	25.91	26.19	26.44	26.97
3	39.34	40.49	41.15	41.76	43.08
4	54.10	56.26	57.52	58.67	61.22
5	68.77	73.32	75.42	77.36	81.67
6	86.41	91.79	95.01	97.98	104.71
7	104.07	111.78	116.43	120.77	130.67
8	122.83	133.40	139.86	145.92	159.93
9	142.74	156.81	165.48	173.70	192.89
10	163.88	182.13	193.51	204.38	230.04

Now fill in your own car worksheet.

CAR-FOR-CASH WITHOUT
ACCUMULATING SAVINGS

Step One: Selling price of a new or used car $_____ (1)

Step Two: Trade-in or selling price of your current car $_____ (2)

Step Three: Dollars needed to buy car (line 1 minus line 2) $_____ (3)

Step Four: Number of years until purchase   _____ (4)

Step Five: Interest rate you can earn on money   _____ % (5)

Step Six: Division factor from Monthly Savings Table (use information in lines 4 and 5) Factor: _____ (6)

Step Seven: Divide the dollars needed to buy the car (line 3) by the factor from the Monthly Savings Table (line 6) to see how much you must save each month to buy a car for cash.

Savings needed each month: $_____ (7)

I told you I had a better plan for buying cars. Do you agree? I view it this way: Year after year, most people make monthly payments for a car. Postpone the purchase of your next car for four years, and begin paying yourself. If you can just stop the cycle of always paying a bank and begin paying yourself, it will be to your advantage. Guaranteed!

Finally, has anyone ever challenged you to *have a goal to be debt free?* If not, I want to be the first! If someone already has, I desire to do it again. In the next chapter we will look at how being debt free is really being a smart money manager.

THE DEBT-FREE OPTION:

Why Pay Later If You Can Pay Now?

7

Life can seem overwhelming if you begin to think about your financial future. The car payment, the house payment, upcoming college expenses for your kids, retirement needs. How is a person to pay for all these things and still have money to live on?

I'd like to suggest a plan that lets you live debt free, pay for all these things, and still have money for your expenses. Yes, have a goal to live debt free! You *can do it!*

I can hear you saying, "Did you say to have a goal to be debt free? But, don't you understand? This is *America!*"

You're right, this is America, where the overwhelming philosophy is, Why pay now, when you can pay later? And along with this philosophy come the following corollaries:

I will have debt till I die!
Why would anyone want to pay cash?
You only go around once in life!

Despite these attitudes, being debt free is gradually becoming popular in America. It's becoming one of the "in" status symbols. No, it is not widespread, but more and more people are talking about it. Debt is the anchor for most financial ships that try to set sail—without success. If you can get rid of debt, you're a smart money manager who's headed for a fantastic future. Get ready to set sail like never before!

Here is a three-step plan for becoming debt free:

The Debt-Free Plan

1. Get out of credit card debt.

Pay off all your credit cards and begin paying the balance due in full each month. This is where you begin the process. Be faithful in paying the bill in full each month, and be careful not to charge more than you can pay in one month.

2. Get out of car debt.

Once you are out of credit card debt, begin allocating this money toward saving for your next car. If you are presently making car payments, work toward getting the loan paid off as soon as possible. The very next month after you make your last payment, write a check to yourself and deposit it in a savings or money market account designated for purchasing your next car with cash. Don't miss even one month. Review the plan presented in Chapter 6, and make a commitment to buy all future cars with cash!

3. Begin a mortgage prepayment program.

Your next goal is to work on getting your mortgage paid in full. Begin a prepayment schedule—the sooner the better. Talk with your mortgage company about prepaying.

And once you've accomplished all this, relax and enjoy the advantages of living debt free!

Advantages of Being Debt Free

Just think, no credit card payments, no car payment, no mortgage payment! When you live debt free you have freed up several thousand dollars each year for other expenses. It does take a plan and work, but it is not impossible by any means. I can cite seven quick advantages to being debt free:

Advantage 1: You can pay for educational expenses.

If at all possible, time your mortgage to be paid off one or two years before your first child enters college, just to give you a jump start on saving your money. If your mortgage is paid in full, this money can now be used to cover educational expenses for your children. If your monthly mortgage payment has been $600, you will free up $7,200 each year to pay for college. If your mortgage was $800, you will free up $9,600 each year for college expenses. And best of all, when your children finish college, they do not have a college loan of $30,000 tagged to their diploma.

Advantage 2: You can meet your retirement income needs.

Once you get the kids through school, you can begin an aggressive savings program to plan for your retirement income. Every person should have a goal to have their home fully paid for before their retirement years. Expenses are high enough without having to pay a mortgage.

Advantage 3: You are prepared for a potential financial collapse.

We never want to see a financial collapse in our economy, but if the economy does collapse those who are debt free will suffer the least. Why? They will have fewer financial obligations, and their house will be paid for. No bank can repossess what is yours. You and your family will have a place to live without fear of losing your home.

Advantage 4: You will have less financial stress.

Becoming debt free will relieve some of the ongoing stress most families face. Many times we buy things we believe will bring us happiness only to find that having to pay for them every month takes away most of the joy.

Advantage 5: You will be able to seize investment opportunities.

With additional funds available, you will have the opportunity to make good investments that were never available before.

Advantage 6: You can increase your charitable giving.

You will have greater flexibility to support your local church and other ministries and charities. Once your fixed financial obligations are removed, your flexible income increases.

Advantage 7: You will be financially independent.

You will see your savings accumulate rapidly when you begin saving the money you have been spending on mortgage payments. One glance at the tables on page 117 will assure you of this if you have any doubts. We'll look at both 7 percent and 10 percent return on your money and see how fast your savings could build with monthly savings amounts of $500, $750, or $1,000.

7 PERCENT RETURN

Monthly Savings	5 Years	10 Years	20 Years	30 Years
$ 500	$35,796	$ 86,542	$260,463	$ 609,986
750	53,695	129,814	390,695	914,978
1,000	71,593	173,085	520,927	1,219,971

10 PERCENT RETURN

Monthly Savings	5 Years	10 Years	20 Years	30 Years
$ 500	$38,719	$102,422	$379,684	$1,130,244
750	58,078	153,634	569,527	1,695,366
1,000	77,437	204,845	759,369	2,260,488

Analyzing Your Current Debt Load

It sounds great, doesn't it? But you may be looking at a stack of bills and thinking, *I could never live debt free.* Perhaps you're overwhelmed with too much debt for your current income. Maybe it seems like there's never enough money. Let's take a look at how you're doing with your current debt.

The Debt Guideline Chart on page 118 should be helpful in analyzing your present financial circumstances. The goal is to determine what percentage of your income is allocated to pay off debt. I'll show you how the Debt Guideline Chart works by taking the hypothetical Jackson family through a debt analysis.

JACKSON FAMILY DEBT ANALYSIS

Monthly net income: $3,750

Consumer debt payments:

Car	$180.00
TV	0.00
Visa	0.00
Total	$180.00

Mortgage debt payment:

Home $755.00

Total consumer and mortgage debt: $935.00

How are the Jacksons doing in their consumer debt?

$180 ÷ $3,750 = .048 or 4.8 percent

(Check the Debt Guideline Chart for the answer.)

Answer: *Good*

How are the Jacksons doing in their mortgage debt?

$755.00 ÷ $3,750.00 = .20 or 20 percent

(Check the Debt Guideline Chart for the answer.)

Answer: *OK*

How are the Jacksons doing in their combined debt?

$935.00 ÷ $3,750.00 = .24 or 24 percent

(Check the Debt Guideline Chart for the answer.)

Answer: *OK*

DEBT GUIDELINE CHART

	Best	Good	OK	Danger
Consumer	0%	1–6%	7–14%	15 + %
Mortgage	0%	1–19%	20–28%	29 + %
Combined	0%	1–21%	22–35%	37 + %

DEBT ANALYSIS WORKSHEET

Monthly net income: $_____(a)

Consumer debt payments:

_____ $_____

_____ $_____

_____ $_____

_____ $_____

_____ $_____

      Total $_____(b)

Mortgage debt payment:

_____ $_____

_____ $_____

      Total mortgage debt $_____(c)

Total consumer and mortgage debt: $_____(d)

How are you doing with consumer debt?

(Total consumer debt ÷ net income)

$_____(b) ÷ $_____(a) = _____ OR _____%

(Check Debt Guideline Chart for answer.)

Answer: _____

How are you doing in mortgage debt?

(Total mortgage ÷ net income)

$_____(c) ÷ $_____(a) = _____ OR _____%

(Check Debt Guideline Chart for answer.)

Answer: _____

How are you doing in your combined debt?

(Consumer and mortgage debt ÷ net income)

$_____(d) ÷ $_____(a) = _____ OR _____%

(Check Debt Guideline Chart for answer.)

Answer: _____

The following notes should be helpful as you use the Debt Guideline Chart.

1. Percentages should be based on your net income (take-home pay).
2. Consumer debt includes things such as cars, appliances, and furniture purchased on credit.
3. Mortgage debt is what you owe for the home you are living in. How much is your mortgage payment each month?
4. Use this chart as a general guideline, not as an absolute rule.
5. If you receive a high "OK" or "Danger" signal, changes are in order.

Now think about your own situation. How are you doing?

Avoid Debt

At this point, you have had an overview of the problems and pitfalls of debt. Debt is dangerous. It is wasteful. It destroys marriages, and it can destroy a business. Debt can lead a church into financial bondage. Debt is destroying our federal government.

Please don't let debt do to you what it did to Nancy, a single woman who let excessive debt cause her to become depressed and eventually lose job after job.

And don't follow in the footsteps of Jimmy, who, from all outward appearances, seemed to be a big success. However, due to lack of self-control, he owes the bank thousands of dollars and owes thousands more to credit card companies. He continues to drain every penny of equity out of his home. Jimmy is always waiting to close the big deal that will clear up his financial problems. Well, it's been more than ten years, and Jimmy's debt is growing, but he's still waiting for the big deal.

And the list goes on.

Then there's Don, who carefully executed a plan to become debt free. He now owns his home debt free, pays his credit card bills in full each month, and buys his cars for cash. He has cash in the bank and is looking for good places to invest it!

Whether or not you become debt free will depend on *you*. And part of that decision will involve your determination to live within your means, a topic we will discuss in Chapter 8. You are the only person who can write your story. Will your story be one of freedom or frustration?

QUICK QUIZ

Now that we've covered several areas related to debt, let's take a moment for a quick quiz to review what you've learned. Complete the following statements by choosing an answer from the following list. Write the corresponding letter in the blank at the beginning of each statement.

A. Eighth year
B. Deficit
C. Two
D. $236,944
E. $145,071
F. Twenty-third year
G. National debt

1. _____ When your expenses are more than your income, you have a _____.

2. _____ The sum total of all the nation's past deficits is called the _____.

3. ____ The total cost of a $75,000 mortgage at 10 percent interest for thirty years is _____.

4. ____ The total cost of a $75,000 mortgage at 10 percent interest for fifteen years is _____.

5. ____ How many interest points does your mortgage need to drop before you should consider refinancing your home?

6. ____ In what year does more of your money go toward principal reduction than interest reduction in a thirty-year mortgage?

7. ____ In what year does more of your money go toward principal reduction than interest reduction in a fifteen-year mortgage?

Answers:

7. A
6. F
5. C
4. E
3. D
2. G
1. B

8

LIVING WITHIN YOUR MEANS:

Will More Money Really Solve Your Financial Problems?

We had just finished eating dinner, and I was anticipating an enjoyable evening with my family when the telephone rang. A casual friend of Janet's and mine, Susan, asked, "Ethan, can I come by and see you for about ten minutes?" Her voice sounded strained so I told her to come right over. When Susan arrived, the look on her face further confirmed my hunch that she was in trouble. She began to explain, "I have not made my rent payment for several months, and I have been served notice: I must move tonight!"

I immediately called one of my best friends, explained the situation to him, and solicited his help. We obtained a truck and moved all of Susan's things to a secure location. When we had finished, the furniture, books, and beds were stacked to the ceiling. Several weeks later, we were able to help move Susan into another apartment. As Susan found out, learning to live within your God-given means is no small task!

It is said that a reporter asked one of the wealthiest men in the world, "Sir, how much is enough?" The man paused, thought for a moment, and responded, "Just a little bit more!" That seems true for many of us; we are always thinking we need "just a little bit more" to be happy in life.

One day I came across an article in a newspaper with a headline that said, "We Want More!" The article went something like this: Those who are presently earning $15,000 think they need $18,000 to live a "comfortable" life. Those who are earning $18,000 think they need $22,000. Those who are earning $22,000 think they need $30,000. Those who are earning $50,000 think they need $60,000 or $70,000 in annual income to live a comfortable life.

Can you identify with this article? If you are like most people, your answer is *yes!*

I believe our basic desire to succeed in life is given to us by God. It is honorable to have a goal for excellence in your work. If work and drive were not good, God would not castigate the sluggard as a fool. Our goal is to keep our aspirations in perspective.

Now, please understand me: I am not saying that more income is a bad thing. I am saying that more money is not your most important goal. From your personal perspective, you will never have enough, and someone else will always have more than you do.

I will be the first to agree that having more money will solve some short-term financial problems. However, if your problems are the result of living beyond your means, more money is not the ultimate solution!

I made this very clear to Mike, a person I have never forgotten. We were having breakfast one day when Mike, who was then earning $76,000, mentioned his long list of financial "concerns," as he called them. He had a large house payment, various credit card debts, additional personal debt, and no savings. He, did, indeed need to be "concerned"!

I asked Mike, "How much were you earning five years ago?"

"About $24,000," he said.

"Mike, if we were sitting here five years ago and I told you, 'You will be earning $76,000 a year,' would you have thought you were going to have any financial problems?"

I think he got the point. (In fact, we both got the point.) Mike had bought into the prevalent misconception that "More money will solve my financial problems."

It would not matter if Mike were earning $26,000, $76,000, or $176,000; he would still find himself in financial difficulty. The more you earn, the bigger your problems become. If you are having financial problems at any income level, you must attack them. Do not think that more money is the "ultimate" answer to your problems.

The Games Adults Play

Grown Americans are great at playing a game we learned as children: the game of pretend. The word *pretend* means to make believe or to deceive, to be someone you are not. It is living a lie. When people live beyond their means, they are living a lie. What our world needs is more authentic people.

In all my years of speaking and counseling I have learned that there are two types of people: the savers and the spenders. And because opposites attract, they frequently marry each other.

The philosophy of the saver is usually:

> *Get all you can,*
> *Can all you get,*
> *Sit on your can.*

The philosophy of the spender is usually:

Buy things you don't need
with money you don't have
to impress people you don't even like.

This is, indeed, a strange world we live in!

A smart money manager learns to live within his or her God-given means. If God has entrusted $40,000 to your family in income this year, you must learn to live within this amount. The diagram on page 127 illustrates this.

If you have the money to support your lifestyle, you are not living beyond your means. If not, you are living a lie and are conformed to the world's economy.

When a person chooses to live beyond his or her God-given means, that person is saying to God, "I reject Your will and plan for my life. I have a better plan. Even though You have given me $40,000 this year, I plan to live as if I am earning $45,000." In my opinion, this attitude is sinful. That's correct; let's call it exactly what it is: sin.

What a miserable life to go through every day, every week, every month, every year, never content with what God has given you! Living beyond your means is obviously financially destructive as well as

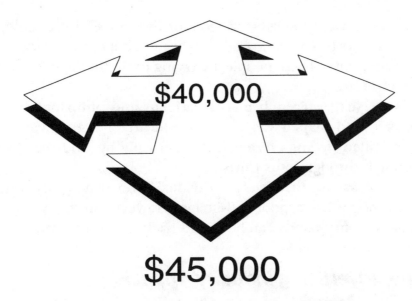

$45,000

You are earning $40,000, but you expand
your lifestyle and spend $45,000!

spiritually destructive. You cannot spend yourself rich. Spending 110 percent of your income only leads to financial ruin. Why would anyone put his or her family in a position of financial ruin? Let me list a few reasons for you.

Why People Live Beyond Their Means

People live beyond their means for three primary reasons.

1. *Poor Self-Esteem*

A person who lacks self-confidence will tend to spend more money trying to prove to everyone that he or she is worthwhile and significant. Poor self-esteem *can* be reflected by the person who has to drive the newest car, wear the latest fashion, or live in the nicest home. Yet there will always be someone else who has a better car, fancier clothes, and a bigger house. These people are trying to fill the vacuum in their lives with _things_.

Blaise Pascal, a French mathematician and philosopher, said, "There is a God-shaped vacuum in the heart of every man which cannot be filled by any created thing, but only by God the Creator, made known through Jesus Christ."

I am not saying that every individual who drives nice cars or has a nice home has a poor self-image. However, in many cases an individual's money habits can be traced back to this problem.

2. The Advertising Industry Appeals to Our Greed

Advertisers spend billions of dollars reminding us that we are not perfect. However, they tell us, if we buy their product we will be prettier, sexier, happier, and really have more fun! And do you know what? We believe them. We have taken their bait—hook, line, and sinker!

3. No Self-Discipline

Living within your means takes discipline. When you literally cannot afford to purchase that new couch, don't buy it! If you cannot afford to eat out three times a week, don't do it. Self-control is one of the fruits of the Spirit (see Gal. 5:22–23). It means saying "No!" to yourself. If you are weak in this area, commit it to God and ask for His help.

Take this quick quiz to determine if you have any of the common danger signals of living beyond your means.

ARE YOU LIVING BEYOND YOUR MEANS?

Check the statements below that apply to you. During the last six months, have you:

_____ Used one credit card to pay off another credit card?

_____ Mailed a check before the actual money was deposited in the bank? (Played the timing game?)

_____ Not paid all your credit card bills in full?

_____ Bounced a check due to lack of funds?

_____ Taken funds out of a company pension plan or IRA account for anything other than retirement?

_____ Not saved any money?

_____ Stopped or cut back in your giving?

_____ Applied for a personal loan just to pay your bills?

_____ Taken a loan from the IRS for past-due taxes?

_____ Knowingly charged something you knew you could not afford?

If you checked even one of the above questions, it is possible you are living beyond your means. If you checked three or more, you are definitely living beyond your means. Be warned! You are walking on dangerous ground. Make changes before it's too late.

Now that we have looked at some of the reasons why people live beyond their means, let's look at the solution to this problem.

Seven Solutions to Living Beyond Your Means

1. Understand that God is sovereign.

Begin by acknowledging that God, in His sovereign power, has given you exactly what you need to live on today. No more and no less. (See Phil. 4:11–13; Heb. 13:5.)

2. Don't focus on others and what they have.

Stop focusing on what others have; instead, be thankful for what you have. There are many people who would love to have your car, your home, or your job. In fact, most people in the world don't even own a car!

Get away from "if only" thinking:

If only I had a bigger house, I would be happy.
If only I had a nicer car, I would be happy.
If only I made more money, then I would be happy.
If only I could buy nicer clothes, then I would get a promotion.
If only I could move to another city.
If only I could change jobs.

"If only" thinking focuses on what others have and on what you don't have. We are saying, "*If only* I could be like (or have something like) someone else, I would be happy or content, or life will be easier."

3. Don't always expand your lifestyle after receiving a raise.

When you receive a raise, don't immediately increase your expenses. Try to be faithful to live well within your means. You will find far more freedom and happiness if you don't spend every penny you earn each month.

4. Don't succumb to "when-then" thinking.

Have you ever said, "*When* _____, *then* I will _____"?

When I get a raise, then I will begin to save more.
When I get my bonus, then I will give more to the church.
When I finish college, then I will start balancing the checkbook.
When I change jobs, then I will manage my money better.
When I get the kids through college, then I will have it made.
WHEN I retire, THEN I will . . .

When-then thinking never acknowledges the joy in the present. The truth is: When the *when* happens, there is usually another *when*, not a *then*.

5. Learn to be content.

Thomas Aquinas said, "There is within every soul a restless search for happiness and meaning." When I was growing up there was a song titled, "Looking for Love in All the Wrong Places." Well, people are continually looking for happiness and meaning in all the wrong places too.

Contentment is like a mirage in the desert. It always eludes you. Psalm 73:25 says, "Whom have I in heaven but Thee? / And besides Thee, I desire nothing on earth" (NAS). Psalm 23:1 says, "The LORD is my shepherd; / I shall not want."

6. Understand materialism.

Materialism. Everybody talks about it, but very few can clearly explain the concept or define it. Some say materialism is "having too many worldly possessions." Others define it "as loving things more than God." Still others say, "It's a matter of the heart." What is the correct perspective? Are all wealthy people materialistic? Can a person living in poverty also be materialistic?

Nowhere in the Bible does God condemn wealth. In fact, many godly men and women in the Bible were wealthy: Abraham, Job, Solomon, David, and Lydia, to name a few. If these men and women of God loved and served God, and God loved and continued to bless them, we must conclude that having wealth is not sinful or wrong in His eyes. But we must acknowledge that the Bible is full of warnings and cautions for those who are already wealthy and those who are pursuing wealth (see Deut. 8:11–19; Prov. 23:4–5; Matt 6:19–24; and 1 Tim. 6:6–11).

After many hours of studying the Bible, I decided to define materialism in the following manner:

Materialism is a philosophy (that is chosen in preference over any other philosophy, religion, or value in life), which has, as its ultimate goal, the unrestrained pursuit (and accumulation) of worldly goods and pleasures in this life.

The word _philosophy_ is used in my definition because materialism is a value system of beliefs that help you make decisions. Materialism is more an "attitude" or "value" issue than anything else. The _results_ of materialism might be an _accumulation of "things,"_ but the real determining factor of whether people are materialistic is not how much they own but what their values are and what they are pursuing!

The most convincing illustration of this point can be found by comparing two very wealthy men in the Bible: Job and the rich man in Luke 12.

Study the chart on page 133, which compares these two men. _Notice that each man was wealthy, but the similarities end there._ One was materialistic; the other was not. Notice also that the difference begins with their "philosophies," which overflow into all other aspects of their lives!

You might want to read the parable of the rich man in Luke 12:15–21 and then read Job 1:1—2:10 before you study this chart.

A STUDY OF THE "RICH MAN" AND JOB

Area	Luke 12:15–21	Job 1:1–22
Wealthy men?	Yes	Yes
Philosophy in life:	Eat, drink, and be merry.	The Lord gives, the Lord takes away . . .
View of possessions:	100 percent mine	100 percent God's
Acknowledge God?	No	Yes
Acknowledge eternity?	No	Yes
Wise man or fool	Fool	Wise
Reasoned with:	Self	God
Rich toward whom?	Self	God
Spend eternity:	In hell	In heaven
Materialistic?	Yes	No

© *Ethan Pope, 1987*

7. Be willing to make the necessary changes in your life.

I recall a couple who came to me because of their financial problems. As we began to look at their income and expenses, I immediately recognized some areas where they could save money. The husband ate lunch out every day, which was costing him about $140 a month (28 days × $5), or $1,680 a year. I suggested that he cut back on this expense by taking a brown-bag lunch.

Then I said, "I know it is amazing, but a family can live without cable TV. This would save you thirty-four dollars a month and four hundred eight dollars a year." Within ten minutes, I had made four recommendations that would have saved them two thousand dollars a year. Since this family was earning less than thirty thousand dollars a year, saving two thousand dollars during one year was significant. And I was just getting started!

Well, there was immediate tension in the office! The attitude I sensed was, *How dare you suggest that I stop eating out for lunch!*... and *Cable TV is only thirty-four dollars a month!* They seemed to resent me for my suggestions, yet, I personally had adopted these suggestions during some phase of my married life.

This couple never returned to my office. I believe that unless they changed their attitude toward money, this marriage would eventually end in divorce because of their financial stress. Everyone must be willing to make necessary changes in their financial lives if needed. Let me share our personal story.

When we were living in Dallas, Janet and I purchased a red-brick, two-story house with tall, beautiful trees. Its spacious yard was perfect for our children. We could envision raising our family in this beautiful home in this lovely neighborhood.

Yet this home had been on the market for almost two years. After we took our first tour, we knew why! It had old wallpaper, poor plumbing, holes in the carpet, loose tiles in the bathroom, and a leaky roof. Still we fell in love with the old house and bought it. After hundreds of hours of labor in the evenings and on the weekends, we transformed the house into a real home.

Three years later we were making plans to launch our ministry, so we decided to scale back our expenses—and the major expense at that time was our home. Our plan was to sell our home so we could pursue God's calling in our lives. Well, we put our home on the market, and sure enough, it sold.

It was a happy/sad day for us. We were happy because we had the freedom to follow God's calling for our lives—and sad because of all the memories we'd lived in that house: Bringing our second child home from the hospital. Seeing our four-year-old daughter's excitement when we had new carpet installed. (When she saw the new carpet for the first time, she fell to her knees and yelled, "Look how beautiful and blue the carpet is, Daddy!") Building a playroom for the kids under the stairs. Watching the kids roll down the hill in the front yard. Working on the house together . . .

When the time came to pack up and leave our home, we went through the empty house room by room and wept. As we made our way downstairs, I crawled into the play space under the stairs and asked myself, *What am I doing to my family? Why are we moving?* Finally, Janet reached in and said, "Honey, we have to go now; the other family will be moving in very soon." To this day I have not driven by that house!

Within several weeks we found another "destitute" home and bought it—this time for cash! No, it wasn't anything like our other home, but it was perfect for us. We paid 40 percent of the sale price of our other home—and we started to build more memories. In the scorching Texas heat on the Fourth of July weekend, we painted the outside with three coats of paint! We also painted the inside and had the hardwood floors revarnished. By the time God once again called us to move, we had once again fallen in love with our home.

I believe with all my heart that we must *be willing* to make the hard decisions that will allow us to live within our means and follow God's calling. If you asked me, "Would you do it again?" my answer would be, *Absolutely, positively yes!*

If you want to overcome discontentment, I suggest that you get a goal bigger than life. Earlier, I suggested that you set realistic financial goals, but now I'm talking about something else. My wife explains it this way: "You must have a purpose for your *life,* a goal that is so big it makes everything else that you want seem small. You must have a goal that is worth any sacrifice, any hardship, or any suffering. You must have a goal that consumes your thoughts and motivates your soul. You must have a purpose so that when you look back at the end of your life, you will have no regrets. That goal will help you focus on the important things in life!" I agree 100 percent!

Here's something else I've learned during my journey: Overspending a little can equal a lot.

Overspending a Little Can Equal a Lot

We usually don't realize the significant cost of wasting a few dollars every day or week. If I were to tell you that overspending just $10 a week during your *working life* could cost you anywhere from $62,000 to over $700,000, what would you think? But it's true. The chart below shows how it happens—and also shows the damage of wasting $25 or $50 or $100 a week.

RESULTS OF OVERSPENDING VERSUS SAVING

Amount Saved or Overspent	25-Year/ 45-Year Total If Saved at 4 Percent	25-Year/ 45-Year Total If Saved at 6 Percent	25-Year/ 45-Year Total If Saved at 8 Percent	25-Year/ 45-Year Total If Saved at 10 Percent	25-Year/ 45-Year Total If Saved at 12 Percent
$1.43 daily ($10/week, $520/year)	$ 21,656/ 62,935	$ 28,530/ 110,627	$ 38,015/ 200,983	$ 51,140/ 373,831	$ 69,334/ 706,280
$3.57 daily ($25/week, $1,300/year)	54,140/ 157,338	71,324/ 276,567	95,038/ 502,457	127,851/ 934,576	173,334/ 1,765,699
$7.14 daily ($50/week, $2,600/year)	108,279/ 314,676	142,648/ 553,133	190,075/ 1,004,914	255,702/ 1,869,153	346,668/ 3,531,398
$14.29 daily ($100/week, $5,200/year)	216,559/ 629,352	285,295/ 1,106,266	380,151/ 2,009,829	511,405/ 3,738,305	693,336/ 7,062,796

It should be our goal to make the very best use of our God-given resources. This doesn't mean I am advocating that families account for every penny they spend or every soft drink they buy during the day. I have met far too many people who do this, and personally, I think it is foolish. It can drive a spouse (and children) crazy!

In my opinion, if the money is available and you are living within your means, it is fine to buy new clothes, go to the movies, and eat out. But if you need to cut your expenses, I have a few suggestions for you. Spending less and saving more can lead to tremendous advantages for a family. We must recognize that there are no independent financial decisions. If you spend money on one thing, it cannot be used for another purpose. This is why it is so important for you to make the best use of your resources and be a smart money manager.

How to Cut Your Expenses

If you are living with a tight cash flow, the following suggestions might help you cut your expenses. If you have ample resources, you probably don't need to implement these suggestions, but you just might pick up an idea that will help you save money!

When looking for ways to trim your monthly expenses, *always* start with the categories that have the largest expenditures. It is less stressful to cut $100 out of one category than to take $10 out of ten categories. Start by looking at housing and transportation expenses. Then consider the following areas:

Food

1. The best time to go grocery shopping is when you (and the kids) have full stomachs. Don't go when you are hungry; you are likely to buy more food, eat more snacks, and therefore spend more money.

2. Be sure you take the time to write out your grocery list for the things you need before you go to the store. Buy only what you need for your family. Don't buy everything you see that looks good.

3. Most well-known brand-name foods cost more. You know about them because of all the advertising money they have spent on the product. Give the other, less expensive ones a try. They might just taste the same but cost far less.

4. Realize that you and the kids can go to the grocery store and buy a half-gallon of ice cream and twenty-five ice-cream cones for about the same price as four people going out to buy four ice-cream cones at an ice-cream shop. Try buying your own ice-cream cones and ice cream at the store, then dip your own ice-cream cones. For the same amount of money, the family fun can literally last for days.

5. Take the time to clip a few coupons and you will be amazed at how much you will be able to cut your food bill each month and year. It is easy to save $4.00 each week by clipping just a few coupons, and that $4.00 saved weekly becomes $208.00 saved each year!

6. Use restaurant coupons when you eat out. Let the coupons help you determine your choices. For example, if ABC Pizza is offering a half-off coupon, why not go there instead of XYZ pizza place? Depending on your family size, your savings could be $5 to $10 each time you eat out. The chart below shows how much you could save over a year's time by using coupons.

YEARLY SAVINGS BY USING RESTAURANT COUPONS

Average Times Family Eats Out Each Month	Savings Each Time	Savings Each Year
1	$7.50	$ 90.00
2	7.50	180.00
3	7.50	270.00
4	7.50	360.00
10	7.50	900.00

7. As you are driving, read the restaurant and fast-food billboards for specials. You can find some great deals!

8. When traveling for a full day, pack a breakfast and lunch in a cooler and save from $30 to $50 for a family of four in just one day!

9. Save fast-food coupons for eating out while you're taking car trips. Combined with bring-along breakfast and lunch, this means even more savings.

10. If you love to have friends over for meals but it's getting too expensive, have a potluck (each family bring something). Everyone has lots of fun, the food is great, and your expenses are cut by about 90 percent.

11. When eating out with friends, agree beforehand that each individual or family will pay for their own meal. Don't feel compelled to pick up the entire check.

12. Before going to the park or on a family outing, slip a candy bar or a snack in your purse or pocket.

13. As a general rule, try to eat at home more than eating out.

14. When barbecuing, cook several days' worth of food. You will not be spending any more money for charcoal or gas, so this will save you money as well as *time*.

Entertainment

1. After dinner, invite friends over to your home just to play some board games. The fellowship is great and the expense is negligible. Don't feel like you have to go out and buy a new game; ask each friend or couple to bring their favorite game with them, then the group can choose which game to play!

2. Rent movies during the week and not during the weekend. Weekday video rentals are usually less expensive than weekend rentals.

3. Go to the park or city zoo for free entertainment. (Yes, some zoos *are* free.)

4. Go to a state park. There is often a fee, but it's usually small. This can be an inexpensive way to spend a very enjoyable afternoon— or the whole day.

5. Check newspaper listings for free entertainment in your area.

6. Young children love fire trucks. Check with your local fire station to see if they will give your family a tour. You will be a hero to your kids for weeks after this one. By the way, it should be free!

7. On a Saturday or Sunday afternoon, take the family on a picnic. Pack a lunch and some snacks and spend an inexpensive day with the family.

8. Keep your eyes open for discount tickets for major attractions. One day I took my family to an attraction that usually costs $7 per person but on this special day, the park was offering admission for 77¢ per person!

9. When going to a college or professional ball game, you can usually pick up some discounted tickets immediately after the game begins. There are no guarantees, but you just might save a bundle!

10. If you are really a sports fan, you might consider buying season tickets. Watch for discounts and special offers. The university in our town recently offered a season ticket family plan for four people at about one-third the normal ticket cost.

Home

1. Stick with the basic telephone plan, and don't get add-on features. Most families really don't need more than basic local service.

2. Turn down the thermostat by two degrees in the winter and turn up the thermostat two degrees in the summer.

3. Whenever you leave the home, be sure to adjust the thermostat.

4. If home ownership is just too expensive for your budget, sell your home and move into an apartment.

5. When you're going on vacation, turn off the hot water heater. Why should you be heating hot water every day when it will not be used for several days or weeks? (Be sure to turn it back on the minute you get home, or you'll have cold showers the next morning!)

6. If your budget needs help, consider discontinuing your cable TV service. Not only will it save you twenty dollars or more each month, but you can work on productive projects during the time you used to spend in front of the TV. You might even have time to begin a money-producing hobby involving all the family members, or perhaps you could read more and spend more time with your spouse and kids.

7. Start a baby-sitting co-op.

Financial

1. Pay all bills on time. Avoid late charges.

2. Pay your credit card bill in full each month.

3. Be careful to keep your checkbook register up to date! One of the most expensive mistakes I see people making is bouncing checks. Most banks charge $10 to $25 for processing bad checks.

4. Find a bank that doesn't charge a monthly fee on a checking account.

Clothing

1. Buy clothes at the end of a season or at outlet stores.

2. If you have an adult brother or sister with a child a little older than yours, ask for their children's clothes when they outgrow them. Children very seldom wear out clothes when they are babies.

Transportation

1. Begin a car pool for school or work.
2. Buy used cars versus new ones.
3. When possible, walk instead of ride; it's great exercise too!
4. Try to run all your errands in one day.
5. Keep your car well maintained; change your oil, rotate your tires, etc., when needed. It will cost less in the long run.

Insurance

1. Consider increasing the deductible of your health insurance from $250 to $500 or $1,000.
2. As your car becomes older, increase the deductible.

Once you have learned to live within your means, you're ready to develop a consistent savings program, which is the topic of the next chapter.

A Consistent
Savings Program:

It's Easier Than You Think to Be a Millionaire

9

Want to be a millionaire? If you are just finishing college, all it will take is $3,500 a year and at least 7 percent return on your money! That's right! Save $3,500 every year during your working life (forty-five years) and earn at least 7 percent on your savings each year, and you will end up with $1,000,122.59. And for most couples, this can all be done tax deferred.

As an example, let's look at Harry and Joseph, two young men who graduated from the same college the same year with the same degree. Both obtained similar-paying jobs. Shortly after graduation, when they were both twenty-five years old, they each married and began a family.

One evening the topic of financial planning came up. They each decided they would need about $750,000 in a retirement account to meet their needs.

The very next day Harry went to a local investment adviser and told him he would like to have $750,000 in forty years. The investment adviser told Harry, "If you invest $2,895.12 each year in a tax-deferred investment and earn 8 percent interest, you will accomplish your goal." Harry began his investment program that day.

In contrast, by the next day, Joseph had forgotten about his and Harry's conversation about retirement savings. In fact, he forgot about the conversation for almost five years. He was now thirty years old, but he still desired to have $750,000 for retirement. But now he had only thirty-five years to accumulate it, instead of forty. Joseph finally decided to begin an investment plan. An investment adviser said, "If you invest $4,352.45 each year in a tax-deferred investment and earn 8 percent, you will accomplish your goal of having $750,000." Joseph said, "I'll think about that and call you back."

Ten years later, Joseph finally called him back. Joseph was now forty, but he still needed $750,000 when he retired, which was now only twenty-five years away. This time the investment adviser told Joseph, "If you invest $10,259.08 each year in a tax-deferred investment and earn 8 percent, you will accomplish your goal." Again Joseph said, "I'll think about that and call you back."

Well, Joseph is now fifty. He is only fifteen years away from retirement and has finally realized, *I must do something!* This time an investment adviser said, "You will need to save $27,622.16 each year for the next fifteen years and earn 8 percent on your investment in order to accomplish your goal." "That's impossible!" Joseph answered, and his investment adviser said, "You're probably right!"

By this time, Harry (also age fifty) had been faithfully saving $2,895.12 every year in a tax-deferred investment for the past twenty-five years at 8 percent. His investment account was worth $211,650.47!

In the coming year Harry's investment account would increase by $16,932.04 *in interest alone!*

The graph below shows the savings needed annually to accumulate $750,000 by age sixty-five if you start saving at age twenty-five, thirty, or forty. It only takes a quick look at the graph to understand the moral of this story: The earlier you start a systematic saving program, the better.

ANNUAL SAVINGS NEEDED
Goal: $750,000 at Age 65

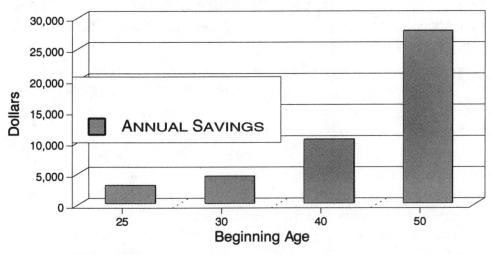

(Projected 8 percent return)

A good money manager has a consistent savings program. However, it has been my observation that one of the most difficult things for human beings to do is to save money. It's just not our nature.

Ninety-nine percent of all families push their lifestyle to the absolute limit, with no margin left for saving or giving. We only have so much money to be spent, saved, and given. The more we spend, the less we have to save or give.

The solution is to give and save first, not last. Over the years I have found some effective ways to systematically save money. The key is to have a plan and to implement that plan in a systematic way.

Ten Important Saving and Investing Concepts

On the pages that follow you will find ten concepts to help you better understand saving and investing. As you read through these concepts, it may be that you will be able to understand for the first time some of the "why's" and "how's" of financial planning.

Concept One: Steady plodding leads to prosperity.

Let's suppose Johnny made a commitment to save $2,000 every year for the first ten working years of his life and then let it compound at 9 percent for the next thirty-five years.

And let's suppose that Dan made a commitment to do just the opposite. "I will save nothing for the first ten working years of my life," he decided, "and then make up for it by saving $2,000 at 9 percent for the remaining thirty-five years."

Who would have the most money at the end of the thirty-five years?

Well, Johnny will have invested $20,000 and Dan will have invested $70,000. Yet after forty-five years Johnny will have $620,285, and Dan will have $431,421. And Johnny only saved for ten years while Dan saved for thirty-five years!

Even if Dan saved $2,000 every year for the next 1,000 years (and Johnny added nothing to his savings), Dan would never catch up with Johnny! It's called the magic of compounding interest. The earlier you start saving, the better.

This illustration may seem incredible or even unbelievable, but it's true. Look at it again and find the financial principle:

<small>Simple Simon</small> saved a small sum and soon he saw a SIZABLE SAVINGS!

We'll explore this further in concept two.

Concept Two: Compounding interest can perform magic.

The most fundamental principle in financial planning has to be the concept of compound interest. It is the common thread that is woven throughout just about every (but not all) concept in financial planning.

This is how it works. I will use 10 percent interest to make the illustration easier to understand. If you invest $1,000 and it earns 10 percent every year, during the first year you earn *$100 in interest* ($1,000 × 10 percent = $100). So at the end of the first year, your initial investment of $1,000 is worth $1,100 ($1,000 + $100 interest earned = $1,100).

Year	10 Percent Interest Earned on Investment in One Year	Total Amount in Investment
1	$100	$1,100

During the second year you earn $110 more in interest ($1,100 × 10 percent = $110). So at the end of the second year, your initial investment of $1,000 is worth $1,210 ($1,100 + $110 interest earned = $1,210).

Year	10 Percent Interest Earned on Investment in One Year	Total Amount in Investment
2	$110	$1,210

The third year, your investment, now worth $1,210 (at the beginning of the year), earns *$121 in interest* during the year ($1,210 × 10 percent = $121). At the end of the third year, your initial investment of $1,000 is worth $1,331 ($1,210 + $121 interest earned = $1,331).

The key principle to learn is that your money is earning "interest on interest." Therefore, we use the name "compounding interest."

Follow this same $1,000 investment through the tenth year in the chart below.

Year	10 Percent Interest Earned on Investment in One Year	Total Amount in Investment
3	$121	$1,331
4	133	1,464
5	146	1,610
6	161	1,771
7	177	1,948
8	194	2,142
9	214	2,356
10	235	2,591

By year ten, your $1,000 investment is earning $235 in interest, and the total value of your investment is $2,591. After ten years your money has earned $1,591 dollars in interest ($2,591 − $1,000 = $1,591).

This growth can be seen in the graph below. Above the $1,000 original investment (the solid area on the graph), all the earnings (the shaded area) are interest. Each year you are earning interest on the interest you have earned in previous years as well as the interest on your one-time investment of $1,000.

COMPOUND INTEREST

Earning Interest on Interest

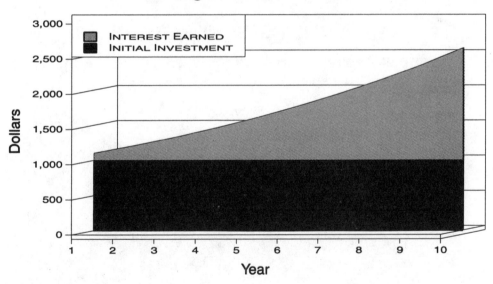

Concept Three: Always seek the highest interest.

It is amazing what one or two percentage points will do to a savings plan. For example, look at the table on page 150 and notice how, if you save $1,000 each year, different interest rates affect the return on your total investment over the years.

INTEREST EARNED

Years	4%	6%	8%	10%	12%
5	$ 5,416	$ 5,637	$ 5,866	$ 6,105	$ 6,353
10	12,006	13,180	14,487	15,937	17,549
25	41,646	54,864	73,106	98,347	133,334
45	121,029	212,744	386,506	718,905	1,358,230

Just look at how much four interest points affect a plan of saving $1,000 a year for twenty-five years. At 4 percent, you earn $41,646. At 8 percent, you earn $73,106! The graph below illustrates the difference in interest earned after twenty-five years of saving.

SEEK THE HIGHEST RETURN

$1,000 Annual Investment for Twenty-Five Years

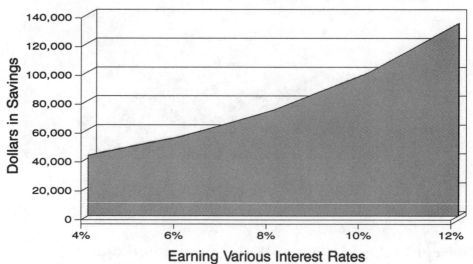

Concept Four: Extra months will pay off.

It always pays to invest at your earliest opportunity. It even makes a big difference when you invest on January 1 versus investing at the end of the year on December 31. For example, in the chart below, assume we will be investing $1,000 every year for forty-five years.

	Earn 8%	Earn 10%	Earn 12%
Invest on Jan. 1	$417,426	$790,795	$1,521,217
Invest on Dec. 31	386,505	718,904	1,358,230
Difference	30,921	71,891	162,987

Concept Five: Use the "rule of 72" to determine how fast your money will double.

To quickly determine how fast your money will double, use the rule of 72: Divide 72 by the interest rate you are earning to determine how many years it will take for your money to double. For example: If I invest $5,000 at 10 percent interest, how many years will it take for my investment to double (be worth $10,000)?

Divide 72 by 10 = 7.2 years
What if I will earn 5 percent?
Divide 72 by 5 = 15 years.

Now try two sample problems for yourself. The answers are at the end of the problems.

1. How many years will it take for my money to double if I earn 4 percent interest? _____ years
2. How many years will it take for my money to double if I earn 12 percent interest? _____ years

(Answers: 1. 18 years 2. 6 years)

Concept Six: Consider the difference in tax-free versus taxable investments.

Is it better for a person in a 28 percent tax bracket to invest in a 7.5 percent tax-free investment or in a 9.5 percent taxable investment?

Here is how to figure the taxable equivalent yield of a tax-free investment:

Step 1:
Subtract your tax bracket from 1.
If you are in a 28 percent tax bracket, the answer is 0.72.
(1.00 − .28 = .72)

Step 2:
Divide the tax-free yield by the answer in step 1.
The number you obtain is the yield you would need on a taxable investment to match the tax-free yield. For example: If a tax-free investment is yielding 7.5 percent, the equivalent taxable yield is 10.42 percent (.075 ÷ .72 = 0.1042 or 10.42 percent).

Try another problem for yourself:
Assume you are in a 28 percent tax bracket.
What is the taxable equivalent yield of a 6.5 percent tax-free investment? _____

(Answer: 9.03 percent)

Concept Seven: Be sure to diversify.
    Be sure to spread your investments into a variety of areas (see pie charts on page 153). An example of not being diversified:

$20,000	Money Market

An example of being diversified:

$ 5,000	Money Market
$ 5,000	Certificate of Deposit
$ 5,000	Mutual Fund
$ 5,000	Bonds

NON-DIVERSIVIED

Investing in a Single Source

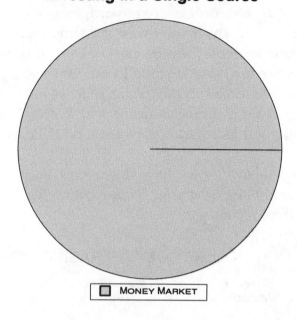

| MONEY MARKET |

DIVERSIFIED

Spreading Out Your Investments

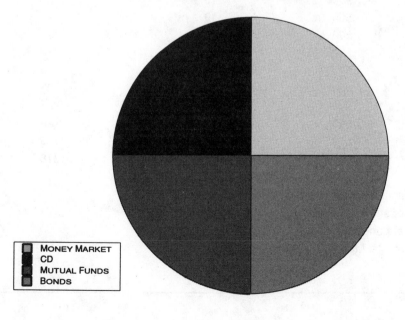

| MONEY MARKET
| CD
| MUTUAL FUNDS
| BONDS

Concept Eight: Use dollar cost averaging.

This is a plan in which you invest the same specific dollar amount on a systematic schedule. You do not try to read or time the market. When prices are low, you are able to buy more shares. When prices are high, you are forced to buy fewer shares—but you keep doing it methodically. This planning concept will keep you from following the crowd (a good idea, since they are usually headed in the wrong direction!).

The chart below shows how dollar cost averaging works—and how consistently investing your money over a long period of time is a valid investment strategy.

HOW DOLLAR COST AVERAGING WORKS

Date	Amount Invested	Market Price Paid	Number of Shares Purchased
Jan	$ 500	$20	25
Feb	500	15	33
Mar	500	14	36
Apr	500	16	31
May	500	19	26
Jun	500	21	24
Jul	500	23	22
Aug	500	26	19
Sep	500	22	23
Oct	500	19	26
Nov	500	18	28
Dec	500	20	25
	$6,000	$19.42	318

Total amount invested: $6,000

Total number of shares purchased: 318

Average market price: $19.42

Average Cost: $18.87 ($6,000 ÷ 318 = $18.87)

Concept Nine: Use shorter times of compounding interest.

How much difference does it make if my money compounds monthly, quarterly, semiannually, or annually?

To answer that question, in the chart below we will use a $10,000 investment and let it earn 8 percent interest.

COMPARING MONTHLY, QUARTERLY, SEMIANNUALLY AND ANNUALLY COMPOUNDING

Years	Monthly	Quarterly	Semiannually	Annually
1	$10,830.00	$10,824.30	$10,816.00	$10,800.00
5	14,898.50	14,859.50	14,802.40	14,693.30
10	22,196.40	22,080.40	21,911.20	21,589.20
25	73,401.80	72,446.50	71,066.80	68,484.80

There is a definite advantage to obtaining a shorter compounding period! However, the difference is always somewhat surprising once people see the actual numbers. For instance, my $10,000 investment will earn $73,401.80 if the interest is compounded monthly versus $68,484.80 if it is compounded annually over a period of twenty-five years. Naturally, *the larger the investment amount and the longer the time period, the more significant the difference.*

Concept Ten: The greater the risk, the greater the potential for gain or loss on your investment.

The Investment Chart on page 156 will be helpful as you read this section of material. As I frequently mention in my seminars, there are thousands of ways to illustrate investment concepts and investment risk. I trust this chart will help you to simplify the concepts of risk and return. Let's go through the categories on the chart together:

INVESTMENT CHART

LEVEL 1	LEVEL 2	LEVEL 3	LEVEL 4
NO RISK*	LOW RISK	MEDIUM RISK	HIGH RISK
Money Market	Balanced Mutual Funds	Growth Mutual Funds	Oil & Gas
Treasury Securities	Real Estate	Stock	Precious Metals
U.S. Savings Bonds	High Grade Bonds	Real Estate	Speculative Stocks
CDs	Life Insurance	Business Venture	Futures
Saving Accounts			

Amount of Risk Involved
LOW   HIGH

Potential for Return or Loss on Investment
LOW   HIGH

Loan	Own

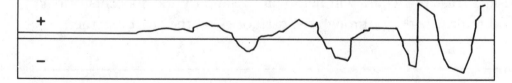

Four Levels of Risk

I have divided all investments into four basic levels. Level 1 is the "no-risk" category while level 4 is "high-risk." On the chart, an asterisk is placed next to the words *No Risk* for the following reason: I do not believe there are any no-risk investments. Sure, it might say, "Guaranteed by the federal government," but what does that really mean?

Common Investments for Each Level

The next line on the chart records the various investment vehicles that are typical for each level of risk. Certificates of deposit (CDs) most definitely fall into a level-one, no-risk category while investments in speculative stocks fit best in a level-four, high-risk category. (At the end of this chapter I will briefly describe each type of investment.)

Risk versus Return

The next line analyzes the return on your investment. Notice that the amount of risk you are willing to take is proportionate to the "potential" for gain or loss on your investment. If you are not willing to take any risk, the return on your investment is very low. If you are willing to take more risk, the potential for gain or loss increases. *The greater the risk, the greater the potential for gain or loss!*

Loan versus Own

The next-to-last line records ownership. Even though you "own" your investments, a level-one investment is typically viewed as a "loan." You are "loaning" the bank your $1,000 in return for its promise to pay you 5 percent return on your money. The level-two or higher investments are viewed from an ownership perspective: A higher degree of risk comes with any ownership.

The final line is the "heartbeat" line, which represents your potential to gain or lose money. You will make a small return for a level-one investment 99 percent of the time. You will typically have a gain with level two, but on occasion you will lose some money. You will find your gains and losses more frequent with level three. With level four, you can make large sums of money or literally lose every penny you invested.

Now that we have looked at ten concepts for investing, I would like to help you avoid the six most common investing mistakes I see people make.

The Six Most Common Investing Mistakes

1. Following the crowd.

When everyone buys, you buy. When everyone sells, you sell. Many times buying and selling is motivated by fear or greed! Fearful people think, *Since everyone appears to be selling, I don't want to be the last fool, therefore I should sell too!*

Greedy people think, *Since everyone appears to be making money, I don't want to be left behind; therefore I should buy too!*

I will never forget the man who told me how he had taken out a second mortgage on his home to make a "sure" get-rich investment. Well, the investment went into bankruptcy, he lost all his money, and the family is suffering the consequences. It was a true confession when he looked me square in the eyes and said, "It was only because I was greedy and wanted to get rich quick." Few people ever admit their greed as this man did. Now God has worked greatly in his life, and he will make it through his trial.

When a person becomes greedy, it's as if someone flips a switch that turns off all rational thinking. Why are so many financial scams successful? They appeal to people's greed, which entices them with the prospect of making enormous amounts of money, usually in a short time.

Financial-advice newsletters also appeal to greed. It is hard to resist ordering a publication when you see how "You too can turn thousands into millions over the next few years!"

Many families have been sacrificed on the altar of greed because a man or woman has walked away from a precious family to seek greater financial security, not a greater marriage.

The epitome of a selfish, greedy individual has to be Henrietta Green, who lived from 1835 to 1916. Her son injured his leg and eventually had to have it amputated because of her delays in attempting to find a "free" medical clinic to attend to his leg. Henrietta went so far as to eat cold oatmeal because she didn't want to pay to heat it on the stove. When she died, her estate proved to be worth $95 million (*1986 Guinness Book of World Records,* 333)!

Don't let fear or greed determine your financial future.

2. Avoiding risk.

If you are never willing to take any risk, you will be paralyzed in your investments. For most investors some calculated risk is fine. Note that I said "calculated risk," not "foolish risk." Your goal is to make the best decision with the information you have. If you succeed or fail, you have done the best you could!

3. Acting on a "hot tip."

Many a dollar has been lost on a hot tip. I've learned to view a hot tip as seeing money burn up in smoke. Good investments are made by hard work and research. Good investments are made when _you_ know _why_ an investment will or will not work!

4. Failing to carry through on your determination to save.

Remember Harry and Joseph? Your greatest enemy may be yourself. You must make the decision to save and invest your money today. _Intentions mean nothing_ in the investment world! _Action means everything!_

5. Failing to monitor your investment's performance.

You need to be sure your money is working hard for you! Most people don't need to monitor their investments every day, but they should keep up-to-date on how they are doing at least once every month.

6. Buying into a financial scam.

In 1989 the North American Securities Administrators Association (NASAA) and the Council of Better Business Bureaus produced a report entitled, "Preying on the Faithful: False Prophets of the Investment World." According to their report, more than fifteen thousand investors have been conned since 1985.

Frequently con artists target key leaders in a community or church and win them over, and then these influential leaders spread the word to others in the community. People who initially get involved receive investment reports and spread the "good news" about their success to multitudes of other people.

In one scheme reported, 193 investors, mostly from one city and one particular church, were taken for an estimated $18 million. They were "earning" 8 to 30 percent profit each month. The good news spread like wildfire. Money was pouring in from everywhere. Each investor received monthly statements, and just to make the investors feel good, a Bible verse was printed on the statement each month! According to one victim, "It was comforting to see the Bible verse. . . ."

However, it was all a scam! Don't let it happen to you.

How to Detect a Scam

Here are some things that might clue you in to a potential scam:

- *Vague answers to your questions.*

- *The group will not offer or provide extra written information if you ask for it.* Get everything in writing.

- *The promoter calls you several times, asking you to consider investing more money since you are making so much already.* This strategy feeds on our greedy human nature. He might say, "You have already earned 10 percent just this one month. I really hate to see you lose out by not investing more in the program today. What do you have to lose? I assure you, you can get your money out whenever you want to. But who would want to take money out of an investment earning 10 percent a month?"

- *Promises that seem too good to be true.* If the promoter is offering you unbelievable promises, ask yourself the question, "Why did he choose to operate out of my town or my church?" If he can earn 10 percent a month on our money, why does he spend all this time soliciting new investors? Why doesn't he just take his money and become a self-made billionaire in the next few years and not have to hassle with people?

- *Pressure to make a decision today.* If this is the case, don't do it. Any legitimate investment adviser will not pressure you into making your decision today. If you sense any pressure, don't invest with him or her!

• *If you hear the words, "This is a proven success," or "This is a sure thing," run!* These words are only in the vocabulary of a con artist trying to get your money! They will actually never guarantee anything, but you get the impression, "It's guaranteed."

Let me review. If any one of the following signs are present, be careful!

• *Vague* answers
• No *written* information
• *Numerous* phone calls
• *Promises* too good to be true
• *Pressure* to make a decision
• "It's a *sure* thing."

As you consider investing in low- or high-risk vehicles, review the brief descriptions of the various investments below and select the ones that fit your needs. This material is not intended to give you detailed or exhaustive information, but to provide a general overview of each investment vehicle.

Twenty Investment Vehicles

1. Passbook savings.

This is your simplest kind of investment. Most banks pay a set amount of interest—usually very low. Passbook savings are not the best place to invest your money. As we will learn, there are other investments that are equally as safe and just as liquid but will pay more interest.

2. Interest-bearing checking.

Everyone should have an interest-bearing checking account; most banks today will offer it. This means the bank will pay you interest on the money sitting in your checking account. Why should you let a bank use your money without paying for the use of it? Some banks pay a fixed rate; others will pay more interest on larger amounts.

3. Money market accounts.

These accounts usually pay more interest than passbook savings or interest checking, but there are certain limitations. For example, usually (but not always), you need at least $1,000 to open the account and you must keep a minimum balance level at all times. Most will allow you to write a maximum of three checks during the month. Money market accounts are generally offered by banks.

4. Money market mutual funds.

These instruments are very similar to money market accounts, but there are two main differences. Money market "accounts" are generally insured by the Federal Deposit Insurance Corporation (FDIC), but money market funds with mutual fund companies are *not* insured. However, they usually pay just a little higher return than money market accounts.

5. U.S. savings bonds.

Savings bonds are an excellent investment for the conservative investor. Presently, they pay a flexible interest rate based upon 85 percent of yields on five-year government treasury securities. The rates change each May 1 and November 1.

If you hold the bond for five years, you will receive the average of all the rates in effect while you owned the bonds, but they pay a fixed rate if cashed before five years. You can buy a $50 bond for $25 or a $10,000 bond for $5,000. The maximum amount of bonds a person can purchase during one year is $15,000 ($30,000 face value).

The most common U.S. savings bond is the Series EE, which the United States treasury began issuing on January 2, 1980, to replace the Series E bond. Series EE bonds also have a guaranteed minimum yield if the bonds are held for five years. (Call your local bank and ask for present minimum yield.) Presently, U.S. savings bonds are exempt from state and local taxes, and federal tax is deferred until the year cashed. As of January 2, 1990, Series EE bonds that are used for higher education are exempt from federal tax. Note: They must be bought in the parent's name, not the child's.

U.S. savings bonds Series HH are sold at face value, with $500 being the minimum investment. The bonds mature in ten years. The interest is paid every year; therefore, when the bond matures you have already received your interest. Interest is taxed each year.

6. Treasury bills.

Treasury bills are short-term federal debt. They are sold in denominations of $10,000 to $1,000,000 and mature in three to twelve months. They are sold at a discount and pay no set amount of interest. The one-year bills are auctioned off once a month, and the shorter ones are auctioned off weekly. They can be purchased through brokers, commercial banks, or directly from the Federal Reserve.

Treasury notes mature in one to ten years and are sold in denominations of $1,000 to $100,000.

Treasury bonds mature in five years or more and sell in denominations of $1,000 to $1,000,000.

7. Certificates of deposit (CDs).

CDs pay a fixed interest for a set period; maturities generally range from one month to five years. You can buy them at commercial banks, savings and loans, and credit unions. There is no risk if the institution is federally insured and you do not exceed insurance limits.

8. Life insurance.

Whole life insurance policies create a cash value. Many times the interest paid is flexible, and you can borrow against the cash value. Insurance should be seen as "protection" first and as an alternative for "saving" second.

9. Preferred stock.

This is another type of fixed-income security. It is an instrument that pays fixed dividends—if the company has the ability to pay them. If they cannot pay, the dividends are said to be *in arrears,* meaning they must be paid *before* any dividends can ever be paid to common stock holders.

10. Bonds.

When working with debt instruments (bonds), you should be aware of three terms. *Principal* is what you originally invest. The *maturity date* is the date on which the loan must be paid in full; it can range from one day to twenty or thirty years. If it is less than one year, it is called short-term debt and if longer than one year, it is called long-term debt. *Interest* is the money you receive in return for loaning your money.

There are three types of risk involved in bonds: (1) The interest will not be paid. (2) The principal will not be returned. (3) The market value of the instrument might decline due to rising interest rates, making your investment worth less.

Unless the government defaults, there is "no risk" when you loan money to the federal government. So government securities are the safest of all debt instruments available. But government securities can lose market value if interest rates rise.

Corporate bonds can be purchased the same way as stocks—through a brokerage firm. Government securities can be purchased through commercial banks or a federal reserve branch bank.

11. Mutual funds.

Mutual funds can be divided into five main categories: (1) Income, (2) Growth, (3) Balanced, (4) Specialty, and (5) Money market.

Income funds usually buy bonds and short-term securities that pay interest. These types of funds can provide cash flow if you need it.

Growth funds are more interested in buying stock in new and developing companies. Your profits (or losses) will come from the success (or failure) of these growing companies.

Balanced funds are exactly what they sound like: They invest in both stocks and bonds; therefore, they're considered "balanced."

Specialty funds invest in only one area. For example, you can buy a mutual fund that invests only in gold or silver or in transportation, health care, banks, or real estate.

Money market funds invest only in short-term securities and pay consistent interest.

12. Common stocks.

Now our discussion enters the more specialized area of investment vehicles. Up to this point, the investment vehicles have been very simple and easy to understand. But selecting a stock takes additional experience and knowledge. When you buy stock, you are buying part of a company; you literally own part of it. Stocks are bought and sold through stockbrokers.

13. Real estate (residential).

Real estate is one of the best investments you can make, but you must know what you are doing. Just because a home is a good investment does not mean it's a "sure thing." When you buy a home, you are probably making one of the largest investments you will ever make, so you need to totally understand the basics of making such a purchase. If a home is bought in the right *location* and at the right *price,* it can be very worthwhile. But, if you make a mistake in either of these areas you can be in big trouble.

14. Collectibles.

Collectibles are such things as jewelry, antiques, stamps, coins, or artwork. This type of investing is very specialized. For most people, buying things like antiques is a good investment because you can use the item, and then later you can usually sell it for more than you paid for it. But, once again, you must know what you are doing.

15. Precious metals.

Gold and silver and other precious metals have always been considered a good investment. You can buy gold or silver coins and store them in a safe-deposit box, or you can buy shares in mutual funds that buy gold or silver. You can also buy stock in gold or silver companies. Gold and silver are good investments to "hedge" against inflation. In other words, when inflation goes up, the price of gold and silver rises also.

16. Stock options.

These instruments give the purchaser the right to buy or sell a particular stock for a guaranteed price within a fixed amount of time. This type of investing is very risky.

When you buy a *call,* you are buying options for rights to buy stock shares at a certain price within a set time. When you buy a *put,* you are buying the right to sell shares for a fixed price within a certain time period. A person could buy a put or call for $3 a share when the stock is selling for $50.

Example: You buy 100 *call options* to buy 100 shares of XYZ stock for $55 at any time during the next three months. You paid

$300 for your 100 options. If the stock is selling for $65.00, you could *exercise* your options to buy the stock at $55 to make an instant profit of $700 (100 × $10 = $1,000 − $300 = $700). But if the stock falls to $45 you would not want to exercise your options; therefore, you would lose your $300.

17. Speculative common stock.

This is a very risky type of investment. You are buying stock on a new, unproven company, hoping it will survive and grow. Shares will sell for pennies or several dollars per share.

18. Speculative bonds.

Speculative bonds are rated by several companies. Standard and Poor's Bond Rating denotes AAA for the highest quality; other ratings, in descending order, are AA, A, BBB, BB, B, CCC, C, or D. D means the bond is in default. Bonds with a B or lower rating are classified as speculative.

19. Your own business.

Don't overlook this one. Most of the time an investment in your own business is your best investment because you are investing in yourself! And you are in control of how your money will be used. I would assume if you own your own business, this would be your greatest strength.

20. Yourself.

Investing in yourself will often yield the greatest return on investment. Money spent on education, training, and self-improvement can pay dividends for the rest of your life. When you spend money this way consider it an investment in yourself, but, as with any investment, you must make wise decisions as to where and how much to invest.

Before making any investment, be sure you understand the risk involved, and if necessary seek professional advice! If you are going to be involved in the investment arena, you should have a working knowledge of some of the most widely used terms. These terms are defined below:

COMMON INVESTMENT TERMS YOU SHOULD KNOW

Bear market: A term used to describe a long-term downward trend in the overall price of stocks.

Bull market: A term used to describe a long-term upward trend in the overall price of stocks.

Liquidity: Can your investment be converted into cash quickly without losing any of the principal? A money market account is more "liquid" than an investment in real estate.

Load: This term is common for mutual funds. You must pay a commission, or "load," to buy into the fund. For example: If the load is 3 percent and you invest $1,000, you will pay an up-front commission of $30 ($1,000 × 3 percent = $30). Your initial investment is now worth $970.

Risk: This relates to the potential to gain or lose money on an investment. For example, there is greater risk to gain or lose money on stocks than there is on a money market account.

ROI: Return on investment.

Principal: The amount you originally invest. If you invest $1,000 in a certificate of deposit (CD), your principal is $1,000.

Yield: A ratio where the numerator (top number) is the annual amount of money received and the denominator (bottom number) is the total amount of your investment. Example: If you invested $1,000 in a CD this year and at the end of the year it is worth $1,100, your "yield" is 10 percent ($100 ÷ $1,000 = .10).

Is It Biblical to Save?

A common question I am asked is, "Ethan, is it biblical to save?" I always reply by reminding the person that balance is as important in finances as it is in other areas. Some people save too little while others save far too much!

A reasonable savings plan is not only good common sense, but I believe it is also biblical. The Bible says, "The wise man saves for the future, but the foolish man spends whatever he gets" (Prov. 21:20 TLB).

Who is wiser? Those who spend every penny they earn or the ones who decide to save a small portion of their income? Our savings can help us overcome financial hardships; without savings, we frequently are left to the mercy of a lender or credit card company. Scripture says, "A prudent man foresees the difficulties ahead and prepares for them; the simpleton goes blindly on and suffers the consequences" (Prov. 22:3 TLB).

In the next chapter we will talk about how to prepare for possible difficulties by planning for crises.

Review

We've gone through a lot of important information in this chapter. Take a moment now for a quick review of the major points we've covered, then try the quick quiz that follows.

- Steady plodding leads to prosperity. Be faithful to save on a regular basis.

- Use the magic of compounding interest. It is great for your money to be earning interest on interest.

- Seek the highest interest. Only two percentage points can make a huge difference over time.

- Invest at your earliest opportunity. Don't wait to invest in December if you can do it in January.

- The rule of 72 will help you quickly determine how fast your money will double. (Divide 72 by the rate of your return.)

- Keep your investments diversified. Don't put all your eggs into one basket.

- Dollar cost averaging is a good investment plan.

QUICK QUIZ

Complete the following statements by choosing an answer from the following list. Write the corresponding letter in the blank at the beginning of each statement.

A. Bull market
B. Diversification
C. Bear market
D. Rule of 72
E. Compound interest

1. _____ Term used when stock prices are moving in an upward trend.

2. _____ Term used when stock prices are moving in a downward trend.

3. ____ Term used to explain earning interest on interest.

4. ____ Method to quickly help you determine how many years it will take your money to double.

5. ____ Spreading your investment over several different areas.

Answers:

5. B

4. D

3. E

2. C

1. A

PROTECTING YOURSELF AGAINST RISK:
Should You Become Self-Insured?

I would like for you to meet two families. Jay and Susan lived in North Carolina and had three young children: Adam was in the first grade, Audrey was three, and Allison was six months old. They were a picture-perfect family. Jay was an architect and becoming very successful. Their marriage was happy and fulfilling.

Mike and Ann lived in Texas, and they also had three young children: Jimmy was in the first grade, James was three, and Janice was six months old. They were also a picture-perfect family. Mike was an architect and becoming very successful. Their marriage was happy and fulfilling.

On one rainy morning, both of the men were killed in car accidents as they drove to work. Naturally, both families had suffered an irreplaceable loss.

Several days later, an insurance agent came to Susan's house. He expressed his sympathy and then presented Susan with a life insurance check for $500,000.

Amazingly, on the exact same morning, a different life insurance agent came to Ann's house. He also expressed his sympathy and then presented Ann with a life insurance check for $25,000.

The similarities between these two families end at this point. One family had prepared for this potential crisis; the other family had failed to plan. One family would have provision for many years; the other family would be at the mercy of the world!

Even though Mike loved his family very much, he had not provided for their needs in the event of his death. Not only would the people he loved so much have to daily deal with the loss of their loved one, they would have to move from their home. Ann, his precious wife, would have to carry financial pressures that would be hard to bear. The $25,000 check would last maybe a year if she was very careful. Then what?

Though dramatic, this illustration is played out every day with real people, real kids, real wives, and real money.

First Timothy 5:8 says, "But if anyone does not provide for his own, and especially for those of his household, he has denied the faith and is worse than an unbeliever."

A smart money manager plans for a crisis. There are four ways to protect against risk. Consider the following descriptions and decide which one would be appropriate for you.

Four Ways to Protect Against Risk

1. Avoid risk altogether.

If you want to protect yourself from risk, you might simply avoid the cause of risk—yet this is not always practical in financial matters.

For example, if you want to avoid the risk of being involved in a car accident, you never ride in a car. That's obviously not very practical. There must be a better way.

2. Reduce the risk.

You can also reduce the likelihood of a risk; this involves prevention and safety measures. For example, if you want to drive a car, you can take a driver's education class to help prevent any common driving mistakes. You could wear a seat belt or buy a car with air bags. You could install smoke alarms in your home to alert you to fire before it's too late. Risk reduction is more practical than risk avoidance, but it does not remove the risk.

3. You can retain the risk.

Another option is to retain the risk; this is generally the best plan when the item at risk is inexpensive. For example, a person can absorb the cost of losing a $19.95 calculator, but he or she probably cannot risk losing a $19,000 car or a $190,000 home.

4. You can transfer the risk.

A final way to deal with risk is to transfer it to someone else. This is the most common method to deal with risk. We transfer the risk to an insurance company in exchange for regular "premiums."

Insurance: Protection Against Risk

Suppose you own a home valued at $100,000. One day a man invites you to lunch and begins talking to you about home insurance. "Our research reveals that there is one chance in a thousand that your home will burn down this year," he says. Then he explains the following two options:

Option 1: Take all the risk personally upon yourself.

By not having insurance, you are at 100 percent risk for any loss suffered. In reality, every day you are personally taking the risk of losing $100,000.

Option 2: Transfer the risk to his insurance company.

The insurance agent explains how his company operates. "We are asking one thousand people to pay a premium of $240 each to protect their homes during the coming year. If one of the thousand homes burns, our company will replace it with the money collected in the premiums." He asks you, "Which option makes more sense? Taking personal responsibility for a $100,000 risk every day or paying $240 and transferring the entire risk to my company?"

Let's take a closer look at this simplistic illustration.

Total income to the insurance company:
1000 homes × $240 premiums = $240,000 in income for the insurance company

If one house burns down:
$100,000 to rebuild home
$140,000 profit to insurance company (less administrative costs)

If two houses burn down:
$200,000 to rebuild homes
$ 40,000 profit to insurance company (less administrative costs)

If three houses burn down:
$300,000 to rebuild homes
$ 60,000 loss to insurance company (less administrative costs)

If no homes burn down:
$240,000 profit (less administrative costs)!

The theory behind insurance depends upon four primary factors:

1. A statistical analysis and probability of risk
2. A pooling of large numbers of people
3. A spreading out of the risk
4. The administration of the plan

Another vital aspect of insurance lies with the financial strength and integrity of the insurance company. In our illustration above, does the insurance company have the financial resources to come up with $60,000 to cover its loss for the year if three homes burn?

Please understand that insurance is *far more complicated* than I have made it out to be. But for the sake of a simple illustration, I hope you now better understand the insurance concept. The same concepts are true in dealing with property insurance, life insurance, health insurance, or disability insurance.

We all need adequate insurance. In today's world, it has become a necessity. Very few people have the financial resources to suffer major financial loss without the help of an insurance company.

Most families need to consider the following insurance coverage:

1. Life insurance
2. Health insurance
3. Disability insurance
4. Property insurance

Let's take a more detailed look at each of these areas.

Life Insurance

One of the first questions people ask me is, "Why do I need life insurance?"

I always mention four important reasons:

1. To provide a financial base in which consistent income will be provided to meet basic living expenses. A family can end up in financial bondage if the husband or wife dies and leaves the family with no income.
2. Life insurance can help pay off any debt still outstanding.
3. It can be used to pay any medical and burial expenses.
4. If a mother dies and leaves small children, insurance can provide in-house child care and other household assistance normally provided by a homemaker.

The next common question is, "How much insurance do I need?" Generally, the younger you are, the more insurance you need. When you are young you usually have little or no savings, small children, and a mortgage on your home. The older you become, the less you will need because, ideally, you will have investments, your children will have finished college and moved out of your home, and your home mortgage will be paid off.

You need enough insurance so your family can live the same lifestyle if the major wage earner dies. For example, if a family is living on $25,000 a year in salary, they would need to buy an insurance policy that would give them 80 percent to 100 percent of $25,000 a year in income—ideally, without having to use the principal. That means if you can earn 10 percent on your money, you would need approximately $250,000 in insurance coverage.

If $250,000 is invested at 10 percent, you would have $25,000 a year to deposit in your checking account. Your family's lifestyle would not have to change. You could pay the mortgage, school expenses, buy clothes, and repair the car.

A good rule of thumb is:

Annual income \$_____ × (7 or 10) = \$_____ insurance needs.

This may seem like a lot of coverage, but in reality, you cannot afford to be without adequate protection!

When you purchase life insurance your number one concern is to obtain adequate coverage for your family. The most important thing is not the type of insurance you buy but that you buy enough coverage!

Your Objective in Buying Life Insurance

During one of my appointments I met with a couple who were paying \$90 a month for \$30,000 in life insurance coverage. They were grossly underinsured for a family of four (with two young children). Their whole-life policy (death insurance and savings) was not meeting their family's need for protection even though it was allowing for tax-free savings. They definitely needed more protection than they were receiving, and therefore they needed to add to (or replace) their protection. Term insurance (death insurance for a specified time without savings) will cost less initially, and in this case they could obtain 10 times the coverage (\$300,000) for less than half the cost.

There is absolutely nothing wrong with comparing prices and companies. I recommend you obtain at least three quotes from different companies.

COMMON TERMS YOU SHOULD UNDERSTAND

Face value: The face value of a life insurance policy is the amount of payment you will receive in the event of the death of the person insured.

Beneficiary: The beneficiary is the person to whom the proceeds of the life insurance policy will be paid. The most common beneficiaries would be a spouse or children.

Grace period: Most insurance policies will not lapse if not paid by the due date. It is possible you will have thirty days to make your premium payment before the policy is canceled. It is best to pay your premium before the due date. Be sure to check your personal policy to see if your policy has a grace period.

Premium: The premium is the amount you pay to receive your insurance. Depending on the policy, premiums can be paid monthly, quarterly, semiannually, or, in some cases, annually.

I have developed a Life Insurance Worksheet to help people determine the amount of insurance they need. First work through the following sample exercise; then do the blank worksheet to determine your particular needs.

LIFE INSURANCE WORKSHEET

Be sure to recalculate each year due to changing income, investments, debt, and needs.

1. Current annual income needs for
   entire family $ _25,000_ × 80 percent = $_____(1)

2. Continued or new income to be received after death:

      Income of living spouse $_____0_____

      Social Security $____7,500____

      Other income $_____

      Total $_____(2)

3. Net annual income needs after death of spouse (line 1 minus line 2) $_____(3)

4. Lump sum needed to fund annual cash needs determined in line 3 $_____(4)

   Multiply line 3 times the factor below. (This assumes 8 percent interest and 5 percent inflation.)

Number of years income needed (Use 25 years to work this problem.)	Factor
5	4.58
10	8.53
15	11.94
20	14.88
25	17.41
35	21.49

5. College funding needs $___30,000___(5)

6. Outstanding debt to be paid $___60,000___(6)

7. Medical and burial expenses (estimate $5,000 to $10,000) $___7,500___(7)

8. Emergency fund (line 1 divided by 12 multiplied by 3) $_____(8)

9. Total needs (add lines 4 + 5 + 6 + 7 + 8) $_____(9)

10. Liquid assets/investments available to offset total needs $___15,000___(10)

11. Face value of all life insurance coverage you presently have on yourself $_200,000__(11)

12. Total funds available at death (add lines 10 + 11) $_____(12)

13. Additional life insurance needs (if any) (subtract line 9 minus 12) $_____(13)

NOTES:

Line 2:   Call 1-800-234-5772 for Social Security information and projections.

Line 4:   Will you need additional income until (1) You can go to work, (2) The children finish college, (3) Retirement income begins? Use Table C in Appendix A if you want to change the assumptions of 8 percent interest and 5 percent inflation. These factors come from the 3 percent column of Table C (8 percent – 5 percent = 3 percent).

Line 5:   The college funds will need to be invested and earn at least 6 percent to keep up with college inflation costs.

Line 6:   Do you want to pay off credit card debt, mortgage, personal loans?

Line 10: Investments, CDs, stocks, mutual funds.

Answers:

1. $25,000 × 80% = $20,000
2. 7,500
3. 12,500
4. 17.41 × 12,500 = 217,625
5. 30,000
6. 60,000
7. 7,500
8. 20,000 ÷ 12 = 1,667 × 3 = 5,000
9. 217,625 + 30,000 + 60,000 + 7,500 + 5,000 = 320,125
10. 15,000
11. 200,000
12. 215,000
13. 320,125 – 215,000 = 105,125

Now go through the blank worksheet to determine your own insurance needs.

LIFE INSURANCE WORKSHEET

Be sure to recalculate each year due to changing income, investments, debt, and needs.

1. Current annual income needs for entire family $_____ × 80 percent = $_____(1)

2. Continued or new income to be received after death:

   Income of living spouse $_____
   Social Security $_____
   Other income $_____
   Total $_____(2)

3. Net annual income needs after death of spouse (line 1 minus line 2) $_____(3)

4. Lump sum needed to fund annual cash needs determined in line 3 $_____(4)

   Multiply line 3 times the factor below. (This assumes 8 percent interest and 5 percent inflation.)

Number of years income needed	Factor
5	4.58
10	8.53
15	11.94
20	14.88
25	17.41
35	21.49

5. College funding needs $_____(5)

6. Outstanding debt to be paid $_____(6)

7. Medical and burial expenses (estimate $5,000 to $10,000) $_____(7)

8. Emergency fund (line 1 divided by 12 multiplied by 3) $_____(8)

9. Total needs (add lines 4 + 5 + 6 + 7 + 8) $_____(9)

10. Liquid assets/investments available to offset total needs $_____(10)

11. Face value of all life insurance coverage you presently have on yourself $_____(11)

12. Total funds available at death (add lines 10 + 11) $_____(12)

13. Additional life insurance needs (if any) (subtract line 9 minus 12) $_____(13)

NOTES:

Line 2:   Call 1-800-234-5772 for Social Security information and projections.

Line 4:   Will you need additional income until (1) You can go to work, (2) The children finish college, (3) Retirement income begins? Use Table C in Appendix A if you want to change the assumptions of 8 percent interest and 5 percent inflation.

Line 5:   The college funds will need to be invested and earn at least 6 percent to keep up with college inflation costs.

Line 6:   Do you want to pay off credit card debt, mortgage, personal loans?

Line 10: Investments, CDs, stocks, mutual funds.

The second type of insurance all families need is health insurance.

Health Insurance

Before we can discuss health insurance you will need to understand the following basic definitions:

Deductible: Most health and property insurance policies have a deductible for each person, which is paid 100 percent by the policy holder. Once you have paid your deductible for the year, you do not pay any more deductible until the next year. For example, the most common deductibles for health insurance are $100, $250, $500, $1,000, or $2,500.

Coinsurance: It is common for health insurance to have a coinsurance clause. For example, an 80/20 coinsurance arrangement is very common. Once you have paid your deductible, the coinsurance comes into effect; the insurance company will pay 80 percent, and you pay 20 percent. It is common for this kind of coinsurance arrangement to be limited to the first $5,000 of a claim; this is the breakpoint (see below).

Breakpoint (stop-loss): Once you have paid your deductible and have reached your coinsurance limit, the insurance company will begin to pay 100 percent of the related costs—up to a predetermined limit. This is very common for health insurance policies. Your policy might read: "For the first $5,000 of covered expenses in excess of the deductible amount—80 percent."

Waiting period: Some health policies have a waiting period before you can file your first claim. For example, you might have to wait thirty days before your coverage becomes effective. Be sure to ask about this aspect of your policy.

Grace period: Some policies have a grace period of thirty days before they will cancel your policy due to a late premium payment.

Lifetime maximum benefit or maximum benefit: Most health insurance policies have a maximum benefit. Examples are $250,000, $500,000, $1,000,000 or $2,000,000. If the covered person's total expenses exceed this limit, you will be responsible for 100 percent of those expenses above the limit.

Now let's look at a typical health insurance situation. Let's assume you have the following health insurance policy:

Deductible:	$ 250
Coinsurance:	80 percent
Stop-Loss:	$ 5,000
Maximum benefit:	$1,000,000

If you incurred medical expenses that totaled $2,000, who would pay how much?

	You	Insurance Company
Deductible	$250	$ 0
Coinsurance	350	1,400
	$600	$1,400

Notes: $2,000 − $250 = $1,750
$1,750 × 20 percent = $350
$1,750 × 80 percent = $1,400

If you incurred additional expenses of $1,000 during the same year, who would pay how much?

	You	Insurance Company
Deductible	$ 0	$ 0
Coinsurance	200	800
	$200	$800

With escalating insurance rates, some people are choosing to become self-insured for noncatastrophic expenses. What does it mean to be self-insured?

Becoming Self-Insured

What you are saying is, "I will personally pay for all the expenses incurred up to a specific deductible amount. The deductible could be $500, $1000, $2,500, or even $5,000 or more. You are retaining the small risks and transferring the catastrophic expenses to the insurance company.

The money you save in premiums each month can be used to pay any additional expenses you face because you have increased your deductible.

Should you increase your deductible? Let's answer that question with a hypothetical situation. Suppose an insurance company presents you with three options:

Option 1: Keep your present insurance coverage.

Let's assume you presently have a monthly premium of $365 for your family of three with a deductible of $250 per person for the calendar year.

Option 2: Raise your deductible to $500 per person.

Your health insurance company offers you a policy with a monthly premium of $300 with a $500-per-person deductible for the calendar year.

Option 3: Raise your deductible to $1,000 per person.

Your health insurance company offers you a policy with a monthly premium of $215 with a $1,000-per-person deductible for the calendar year.

Here is a summary of those options:

Monthly Premium	Deductible per Person
$365	$ 250
$300	$ 500
$215	$1,000

Let's evaluate each option using three different levels of medical bills for the year. We will first evaluate option 1 using the following worksheets with three different levels of medical expenses.

MEDICAL BILLS PROJECTED
AT $250 PER PERSON

Amount of monthly premium:	$ 365
Amount of deductible:	$ 250
Coinsurance	80 / 20
Stop-Loss	$ 5,000
Maximum	$ 1,000,000

1	2	3	4	5
Name	Amount of Medical Bills	Amount You Pay for Deductible	Amount You Pay for Coinsurance	Total Amount You Will Be Paying
John	$250	$250	$0	$ 250
Jan	250	250	0	250
Jimmy	250	250	0	250

Monthly insurance premium *$365* × 12 months = $4,380

Total Out-of-Pocket
Cost to You: $5,130

Calculations: Column 2
This column is a projection of medical bills for the coming year, or you can use the actual numbers for last year.

Column 3
The amount in this column will not exceed your deductible. If medical bills are less than or equal to your deductible, put the amount of the bills in this column.

Column 4
Column 2 − your deductible × your coinsurance portion:
$250 − $250 = $0 × 20 percent = $0
If column 2 is less than your deductible put 0 in column 4.

Should You Become Self-Insured? _____

Calculations: Column 5
              Column 3 + Column 4 = Column 5
              $250 + $0 = $250

Now let's look at what happens when the medical bills for your family of three rise to $500 per person.

MEDICAL BILLS PROJECTED
AT $500 PER PERSON

Amount of monthly premium:	$ 365
Amount of deductible:	$ 250
Coinsurance	80 / 20
Stop-Loss	$ 5,000
Maximum	$ 1,000,000

	1	2	3	4	5
	Name	**Amount of Medical Bills**	**Amount You Pay for Deductible**	**Amount You Pay for Coinsurance**	**Total Amount You Will Be Paying**
John		$500	$250	$50	$ 300
Jan		500	250	50	300
Jimmy		500	250	50	300

Monthly insurance premium *$365* × 12 months = $4,380

                    Total Out-of-Pocket
                    Cost to You: $5,280

Calculations: Column 2
              This column is a projection of medical bills for the coming year, or you can use the actual numbers for last year.

Calculations: Column 3
The amount in this column will not exceed your deductible. If medical bills are less than or equal to your deductible, put the amount of the bills in this column.

Column 4
Column 2 – your deductible × your coinsurance portion:
$500 – $250 = $250 × 20 percent = $50
If column 2 is less than your deductible put 0 in column 4.

Column 5
Column 3 + Column 4 = Column 5
$250 + $50 = $300

Finally, let's assume your medical bills for the year are $1,000 per person.

MEDICAL BILLS PROJECTED
AT $1,000 PER PERSON

Amount of monthly premium:	$ 365
Amount of deductible:	$ 250
Coinsurance	80 / 20
Stop-Loss	$ 5,000
Maximum	$ 1,000,000

1	2	3	4	5
Name	Amount of Medical Bills	Amount You Pay for Deductible	Amount You Pay for Coinsurance	Total Amount You Will Be Paying
John	$1,000	$250	$150	$ 400
Jan	1,000	250	150	400
Jimmy	1,000	250	150	400

Should You Become Self-Insured?

Monthly insurance premium *$365* × 12 months = $4,380

                            Total Out-of-Pocket
                            Cost to You: $5,580

Calculations: Column 2
This column is a projection of medical bills for the coming year, or you can use the actual numbers for last year.

Column 3
The amount in this column will not exceed your deductible. If medical bills are less than or equal to your deductible, put the amount of the bills in this column.

Column 4
Column 2 − your deductible × your coinsurance portion:
$1,000 − $250 = $750 × 20 percent = $150
If column 2 is less than your deductible put 0 in column 4.

Column 5
Column 3 + Column 4 = Column 5
$250 + $150 = $400

These options are summarized on the comparison table below.

COMPARISON OF TOTAL OUT-OF-POCKET COST FOR HEALTH INSURANCE OPTIONS

	Medical Bills per Person in One Year		
	$250	$500	$1,000
Option 1 $365 premium $250 deductible	$5,130	$5,280	$5,580
Option 2 $300 premium $500 deductible	$4,350	$5,100	$5,400
Option 3 $215 premium $1,000 deductible	$3,330	$4,080	$5,580

Which One Is Best for Your Family?

From this basic analysis, it appears that option 3 is the best choice for this family. They will pay a considerable amount *less* in total medical expenses with medical bills of $250 and $500 per person. For medical bills totaling $1,000 per person, option 3 is right in line with the other two options.

Discuss this issue with your insurance agent. Every family is different, and every analysis is based upon specific circumstances. Just because option 3 was best in this illustration does not mean it would be best for your family. *You* must analyze the specific details using your personal information. Use the worksheets below to assess three possible options for your own family.

WORKSHEET FOR ASSESSING HEALTH INSURANCE OPTIONS

Option 1

Amount of monthly premium:	$_____
Amount of deductible:	$_____
Coinsurance	_____ / _____
Stop-Loss	$_____
Maximum	$_____

1	2	3	4	5
Name	Amount of Medical Bills	Amount You Pay for Deductible	Amount You Pay for Coinsurance	Total Amount You Will Be Paying
_____	$_____	$_____	$_____	$_____
_____	_____	_____	_____	_____
_____	_____	_____	_____	_____
_____	_____	_____	_____	_____

Should You Become Self-Insured? _____

1 Name	2 Amount of Medical Bills	3 Amount You Pay for Deductible	4 Amount You Pay for Coinsurance	5 Total Amount You Will Be Paying
_____	$_____	$_____	$_____	$_____
_____	_____	_____	_____	_____
_____	_____	_____	_____	_____

Monthly insurance premium _____ × 12 months = $_____

Total Out-of-Pocket
Cost to You: $_____

WORKSHEET FOR ASSESSING HEALTH INSURANCE OPTIONS

Option 2

Amount of monthly premium: $_____
Amount of deductible: $_____
Coinsurance   _____ / _____
Stop-Loss $_____
Maximum $_____

1 Name	2 Amount of Medical Bills	3 Amount You Pay for Deductible	4 Amount You Pay for Coinsurance	5 Total Amount You Will Be Paying
_____	$_____	$_____	$_____	$_____
_____	_____	_____	_____	_____
_____	_____	_____	_____	_____
_____	_____	_____	_____	_____
_____	_____	_____	_____	_____
_____	_____	_____	_____	_____

Monthly insurance premium _____ × 12 months = $_____

                                                Total Out-of-Pocket
                                                Cost to You: $_____

WORKSHEET FOR ASSESSING HEALTH INSURANCE OPTIONS

Option 3

Amount of monthly premium: $_____
Amount of deductible: $_____
Coinsurance   _____ / _____
Stop-Loss $_____
Maximum $_____

1	2	3	4	5
Name	Amount of Medical Bills	Amount You Pay for Deductible	Amount You Pay for Coinsurance	Total Amount You Will Be Paying
_____	$_____	$_____	$_____	$_____
_____	_____	_____	_____	_____
_____	_____	_____	_____	_____
_____	_____	_____	_____	_____
_____	_____	_____	_____	_____
_____	_____	_____	_____	_____
_____	_____	_____	_____	_____

Monthly insurance premium _____ × 12 months = $_____

                                                Total Out-of-Pocket
                                                Cost to You: $_____

Now let's look at the third type of insurance every family needs: disability insurance.

Disability Insurance

Many people overlook disability insurance because they either assume it is covered by their health insurance or they have never thought about the consequences of becoming disabled.

Stop a moment and run through the scenario quickly. If you were to become disabled and not able to work, the bills would still become due. Your family would still need food, transportation, and living money. Without income, what would you do?

It's obvious that disability insurance is necessary. So the question becomes, How much disability coverage is enough? In general, your disability insurance should equal 60 to 70 percent of your before-tax earnings, with benefits starting ninety days after you become disabled. (Your emergency fund—savings—can be used to cover expenses during this ninety-day period.)

Most insurers only cover you to the point at which your disability income from all sources, including Social Security and company benefits, would equal 70 percent of your current before-tax earnings.

Equally important in deciding the amount of coverage you need is the way your policy defines *disability.* The most generous disability insurance is described as "own occ," in which the insurers agree to pay full benefits if you can't work in your "own occupation" as long as you are under a physician's care. A less generous disability insurance is described as "any occ." It pays only if you are unable to work in "any occupation" (your occupation or any other type work you could do).

Every family also needs to consider the final type of insurance: property insurance.

Property Insurance

Everyone needs proper insurance on the home, car, and any other valuable personal property. The goal of property insurance is to be able to replace your asset in the event of a loss.

For example, if your home burns to the ground, you need insurance to replace the home and personal items in it. If your car is wrecked, you need insurance to repair it or replace it. If you damage someone else's car, you need insurance to repair or replace it. If you have equipment in an office, you need protection from fire and theft.

The most common types of property insurance are automobile, homeowners, jewelry/valuables, office, and renters.

Next, let's discuss ways to decrease your insurance premiums. However, let me say once again, discuss your insurance needs with your agent before making changes. This book is addressing general principles, not specific personal applications.

Ways to Decrease Your Premiums

The two primary ways to decrease your premiums are to increase your deductible or to decrease your benefits. You will find a substantial difference in the cost of a deductible of $250 versus a deductible for $1,000 or $2,500. When you raise your deductible, you are telling the insurance company that you will be paying 100 percent of all the smaller expenses. This costs the insurance company less in administrative fees and payments for smaller claims.

I also recommend that every family have the equivalent of one to three months of take-home pay in a very liquid investment to use for emergencies.

Reasons to Establish an Emergency Fund

Why do we need to establish a short-term savings plan like this? I can think of many reasons. Here are just a few of them:

Loss of Income

If you lose your job and have an amount equal to three months' salary in an emergency fund, you can live on your emergency money awhile before you are in financial bondage. Each month you would transfer the equivalent of one month's salary into your checking account, so you would have the same amount as usual for food, clothing, mortgage or rent payment, social life and even savings.

By having an emergency fund, you have provided you and your family with three or more months of *time*. In fact, if you have three months of savings, you probably can stretch this money into four or more months *if* you budget carefully. You and your family can continue the same lifestyle—only because you have planned in advance. Three months should be adequate time for you to find a new job or to come up with an alternative plan. By having an emergency fund, you relieve some of the stress that comes with a job loss.

If your present salary decreases, the emergency fund can also be used. You can transfer the difference between your normal take-home pay and the amount you are now receiving into your checking account. This can be done for several months until you can adjust your budget or find another job.

Death of a Family Member

A death in the family—a husband, wife, or child—means there will be expenses and/or loss of income. Emergency money will again help to "buy time" during this very stressful period. These funds can be used until the life insurance money arrives or other arrangements are made.

Unexpected Expenses

If unexpected medical or repair bills occur, this emergency money can become very helpful. Normally these expenses would have to be put on a credit card. However, emergency money can be used for this purpose and keep you out of debt. Naturally, this money should be replaced as soon as possible.

Ability to Avoid Debt

I view this reason as one of the most important purposes for establishing an emergency fund. Most people do not have emergency money so they have to go into debt when unexpected expenses arise.

In the Event of Disability

Disability insurance usually has a ninety-day waiting period before benefit payments begin. An emergency fund will provide for your needs through that time.

Commission-Only Job

If you are in a commission-only job and have a few lean months, your emergency fund gives you something to fall back on.

We all need to be prepared for the unexpected. Crisis planning should be one aspect of any financial plan.

In the next chapter we will look at generous giving, another habit of a smart money manager.

Review

Take a moment to review some of the most important points about insurance:

Insurance Concepts

1. A statistical analysis and probability of risk
2. A pooling of large numbers of people
3. A spreading out of the risk
4. Administration of plan

Different Types of Insurance

1. Life
2. Health
3. Disability
4. Property

Every family needs to establish an emergency fund!

GENEROUS GIVING: 11

What Are You Doing with the $20 in Your Pocket?

T*here is no trouble too great, no humiliation too deep, no suffering too severe, no love too strong, no labor too hard, no expense too large, but that it is worth it, if it is spent in the effort to win a soul"* (*The Open Bible,* Thomas Nelson Publishers, 1285).

I have been privileged to work with many churches of different denominations across the nation. During a conference, I usually have the opportunity to eat a meal with one of the ministers. Without prying for confidential information, I get around to asking, "Is the eighty-twenty rule true for your church? Do twenty percent of your members give eighty percent of the budget, while eighty percent of your members give twenty percent of the budget?"

The answer is almost always yes.

Giving is one area where most people know the right thing to do, but very few are doing it. It is common for 20 percent of any local church to be giving 80 percent of the budget. This proportion is not due to the rich giving more and the middle class and poor giving less. It is a matter of commitment to God.

One dynamic evangelical church I visited shared the following statistics:

- 20 percent of the members give more than 80 percent of the budget.
- 20 percent of the members don't give $1 to the church.
- 32 percent of the members give less than $10 a week or $520 annually.

Where has our commitment gone? Approximately 52 percent of this church's entire membership gives a token gift to their church! Something is wrong—very wrong.

Most Christians pay more money in interest on their debt than they give to the kingdom of God each year! Couples who have a $75,000 mortgage at 10 percent for thirty years pay $7,481.24 in interest during the first year of their mortgage. I wonder how much they contribute to the kingdom of God during that same one-year period.

The Bible never teaches "token" giving. Your giving is a direct reflection of your commitment to Jesus Christ. A smart money manager gives generously. It is very simple: You give little if your commitment is little. You give generously if your commitment is great. If you don't believe your church is using your money wisely or impacting the world, either work for change—or change churches. Then begin to support the work of God.

From a biblical perspective, giving should be preeminent in your financial dealings. We take the family to the movies and spend $20 but find it a struggle to drop $20 in the church offering plate on Sunday. Isn't it amazing how small a $10 bill looks in the grocery store but how large it becomes on Sunday?

> ## *The real question is not "What would you do if you had $1 million?" but "What are you doing with the $20 in your pocket?"*

Money is the acid test in a person's life. You can fake other areas of commitment to Jesus, but you cannot fake a real financial commitment to the kingdom of God.

What are your priorities in life? Just let me look at your checkbook for ten minutes and I will be able to tell you. The way a person spends his or her money is a direct reflection of what is important to him or her.

From an eternal perspective there is no better place to invest your money than in the kingdom of God! Its security is 100 percent guaranteed by God (not by your country), and its returns are out of this world!

You might be asking, What does the Bible say about giving? Good question! Let's look at seven principles we find in God's Word.

1. Give in secret.
The Sermon on the Mount, found in Matthew 5—7, has much to say about money and giving. Jesus said that when we give, we are to give in secret.

Beware of practicing your righteousness before men to be noticed by them; otherwise you have no reward with your Father who is in heaven. When therefore you give alms, do not sound a trumpet before you, as the hypocrites do in the synagogues and in the streets, that they may be honored by men. Truly I say to you, they have their reward in full. But when you give alms, do not let your left hand know what your right hand is doing that your alms may be in secret; and your Father who sees in secret will repay you. (Matt. 6:1–4 NAS)

When you give, is it for the praise of those around you? If it is, enjoy your reward now because you will have *no reward* later from your heavenly Father.

Does this mean that we should not have our names on our checks? No, this passage does not teach that at all. The key perspective is your motive. *Why* are you giving?

If I were to take my check and prop it up on the inside of the collection plate, pass it down the row and smile, I would be giving in order to seek the praise of others, and after others had praised me, I would have received my reward in full!

I appreciate the promise of the verse in the previous passage that says, "And your Father who sees in secret will repay you." We don't know *when* our Father will repay or *how* He will repay, but we are promised that one day, in His own timing, He *will* repay!

2. Give on a systematic basis.

In 1 Corinthians 16:2, Paul gave instructions to the church in Corinth as to how they should be giving:

On the first day of the week let each one of you lay something aside, storing up as he may prosper, that there be no collections when I come.

Paul set forth a principle of regular, consistent giving so that the believers would not have to be pressured to give when he arrived. There are many benefits of giving in this manner.

Wrong motives might arise for the person who wants to give a big check at the end of the year. Would it not be better to systematically give during the year as God prospers you?

Writing your check each week will help you to get in the habit of consistently giving. Giving once a year will not keep you in the "spirit" of giving on a continuous basis.

Since giving is an act of worship, it becomes simply another part of the worship service in which we are actively involved. When we give, we are acknowledging with our actions our faith and trust in God for providing our needs, and we show an attitude of thankfulness toward Him.

3. Give cheerfully.

The third principle reflects on the joy in giving; God wants us to be cheerful givers. Giving should be an act of praise and thankfulness for all God has done for us: for our lives, possessions, talents, church, and friends.

> So let each one give as he purposes in his heart, not grudgingly or of necessity; for God loves a cheerful giver. (2 Cor. 9:7)

If God *loves* a cheerful giver, can we assume He is not pleased with an uncheerful giver?

4. Give generously.

Every time I think about generous giving I am reminded of something that happened during the first year of our marriage. Janet and I were on the staff of Campus Crusade for Christ, and we were attending a meeting where we were challenged to make a "faith promise" to the Jesus Film Project.

A "faith promise" is not a pledge but a step of faith. If you receive money that you had not expected to receive during the year, you are to view it as God's fulfilling your faith promise. I had been making faith promises for several years, always in the amount of $200 each year, and God always seemed to fulfill my little faith promise. At that meeting we were given our cards, and I had put down my usual $200. I asked Janet what her faith promise was. Janet had written $2,000 on her card. I almost fell out of my chair. I gasped, "WHAT ARE YOU DOING?" She said simply, "Making a faith promise."

I had the wrong perspective of a faith promise. Each year, I had felt an obligation to fulfill my faith promise. But Janet never felt an obligation unless God provided. That year I kept my card and Janet turned in hers.

Several months later I came home from the office and Janet greeted me with a smile (as always). I changed my clothes and eventually got around to checking the mail. There was a check we hadn't been expecting, and it was for exactly $2,000! *Wow!*

Then Janet said, "Ethan, do you think that $2,000 was God providing for our faith promise?" I suddenly felt sick.

I thought, *How could she do this to me?* I immediately left the room and went off to pout. Janet knew she did not need to say another word about the faith promise. She would leave the results to God.

That night, I couldn't sleep. God convicted me that He had fulfilled our faith promise to the penny! The next day, we cheerfully mailed in our faith promise to the Jesus Film Project, convinced that due to this contribution, thousands of individuals would be able to hear the gospel for the very first time in their lives. God even returned to us numerous other financial blessings during the year—far more than the $2,000 we had given to Him.

God had used us as a channel for His blessing to others. What an awesome privilege!

In 1 Timothy, Paul teaches us about being generous and ready to share:

> Instruct them to do good, to be rich in good works, to be generous and ready to share, storing up for themselves the treasure of a good foundation for the future, so that they may take hold of that which is life indeed. (1 Tim. 6:18–19 NAS)

Are you allowing God to use you as a channel for His blessing to others?

5. Do not give out of legalism.

The fifth principle states that our giving must not be done out of legalism! It is done out of grace, obedience, and love for the Lord Jesus Christ. When you love someone, you will do anything for that person. Obedience is an essential ingredient of the Christian life, and obedience includes faithfulness and commitment to giving. There is no better use or blessing than to invest in God's kingdom.

6. Acknowledge that you can't take it with you.

I was privileged to see both of my children being born. I was right there with Janet in the delivery room when each child took his or her first breath. This is an experience that I will never forget, but there was one thing that I noticed when each one was born. They were not born with any clothes on, nor did they have any money with them. (Since that event, I have verified with my doctor friends that 100 percent of the babies come out this way!)

One day I will die. They will only put one thing in the box, and that is me. Whatever I have been able to accumulate during my brief visit on this earth will be of absolutely no value to me.

It makes no difference if you are the richest man or woman in the cemetery! At death, material things become totally insignificant.

Solomon, in Ecclesiastes, and Paul, writing to Timothy, confirmed this real-life truth: You can't take it with you!

> As he had come naked from his mother's womb, so will he return as he came. He will take nothing from the fruit of his labor that he can carry in his hand. (Eccles. 5:15 NAS)

> For we brought nothing into this world, and it is certain we can carry nothing out. (1 Tim. 6:7)

I believe it was Billy Graham who once said, "I have never seen a hearse pulling a U-Haul." No, neither have I. It just doesn't work that way. But I did hear about a man who wanted to disprove this truth. He was about to die, and he called three of his best friends to come and see him. His friends were a doctor, a pastor, and a CPA. He said, "I have accumulated $90,000 during my life, and I want to take it with me when I die. I am going to give you each an envelope with $30,000 cash in it. Promise me that when I die, right before they bury me, you will place the envelope in my coat pocket." They all agreed to honor his wish. Sure enough, the following week, the man died.

The three friends attended the funeral service together. Each one placed the envelope in his coat pocket, just as he had asked. After the service, the three men were riding together in the same car. There was silence in the car. Finally the doctor broke the silence and said, "I have a confession to make. I took $10,000 out of the envelope to pay for some new equipment we needed at the hospital." No one said a word. A few more miles down the road, the pastor spoke up and said, "I also have a confession to make. You know we are in a new building program, and I took $20,000 out of the envelope. I am indeed sorry. Please forgive me."

Immediately the CPA spoke up and said, "Men, I am ashamed of both of you. I cannot believe you did that to our good friend. I want you to know, that I took all of the cash and put in a *personal check for the entire amount!*"

No matter how hard you try, you cannot take it with you!

But you can *send it on ahead!* A transfer of equity is one result of giving. Just look at the following verses:

> But lay up for yourselves treasures in heaven, where neither moth nor rust destroys and where thieves do not break in and steal. For where your treasure is, there your heart will be also. (Matt. 6:20–21)

> Not that I seek the gift itself, but I seek for the profit which increases to your account. (Phil. 4:17 NAS)

I don't understand all the ramifications, but I do know that when I give, I am investing in eternity.

7. How much should you give?

We have finally made it to the question that everyone wants to ask: How much? Let me begin by saying that God's Word and the convictions that He gives you are very important. My prayer is that what I share in the pages that follow will guide you in this vital area of life.

I struggled with the area of "how much" for years. Most struggles in this area center directly around the principle of tithing.

What Is a Tithe?

Our study will begin by defining a tithe: It is 10 percent. To make a contribution in any amount does not mean you are tithing. A tithe is a specific amount. For example, a tithe of $1,000 is $100.

We find the first tithe recorded in the Bible in Genesis 14:18–20 when Abraham gave a tithe.

Then Melchizedek king of Salem brought out bread and wine; he was the priest of God Most High. And he blessed him and said:

> *"Blessed be Abram of God Most High,*
> *Possessor of heaven and earth;*
> *And blessed be God Most High,*
> *Who has delivered your enemies into your hand."*

And he [Abram] gave him [Melchizedek] a tithe of all.

According to the text of this passage, it does not appear that Abraham was *required* to give a tithe. It was a free-will gift. And Abraham was not the only one to do so. Jacob also promised God 10 percent:

> Then Jacob rose early in the morning, and took the stone that he had put at his head, set it up as a pillar, and poured oil on top of it. And he called the name of that place Bethel; but the name of that place had been Luz previously. Then Jacob made a vow, saying, "If God will be with me, and keep me in this way that I am going, and give me bread to eat and clothing to put on, so that I come back to my father's house in peace, then the LORD shall be my God. And this stone which I have set as a pillar shall be God's house, and of all that You give me I will surely give a *tenth* to You." (Gen. 28:18–22, emphasis mine)

Both of these examples took place before the Law was given to Moses and were therefore not "required." Later, when the Law was given to Moses for all the Israelites, they were required to give a tithe of land and livestock. Leviticus 27:30 says, "And all the tithe of the land, whether of the seed of the land or of the fruit of the tree, is the LORD's. It is holy to the LORD."

The Israelites were to give a tithe of everything the land produced. When harvesttime came, they were to give 10 percent and keep 90 percent. They were also to tithe from their herds: "And concerning the tithe of the herd or the flock, of whatever passes under the rod, the tenth one shall be holy to the LORD" (Lev. 27:32).

When ten calves were born, one of them was to be given to the Lord! The Israelites demonstrated by their obedience that God was first in their lives!

When the Lord blesses you, how do you respond? Do you desire to honor Him? By faithfully giving, we bring honor to Him. Proverbs 3:9 says, "Honor the LORD with your possessions, / And with the first-fruits of all your increase."

The Purpose of Tithing

The eleven tribes through their tithes were to provide support for the Levite tribe. Numbers 18:21 says, "Behold, I have given the children of Levi all the tithes in Israel as an inheritance in return for the work which they perform, the work of the tabernacle of meeting." (See also Num. 18:12 and Neh. 10:37–39.)

The Levites served in the sanctuary and did not "farm the land," as all the other tribes did. Therefore, the Levites were to obtain their "living" by receiving tithes from the other tribes. But even *they* were not exempt from tithing. The Lord told Moses, "Speak thus to the Levites, and say to them: 'When you take from the children of Israel the tithes which I have given you from them as your inheritance, then you shall offer up a heave offering of it to the LORD, a tenth of the tithe'" (Num. 18:26). In other words, even those who received the tithe were to give a tithe!

Is the Tithe for the Modern-Day Church?

In dealing with this issue, the Lord impressed me to go through the Bible and study every verse on giving with this question in mind. My goal was to have an open mind and heart and let God put a conviction in my heart in the area of giving. I wondered: *Is there even one verse in the Bible that models, illustrates, or gives an example of anyone giving* less *than a tithe?*

My personal conclusion was no! Nowhere in Scripture did I find one single verse that modeled, illustrated, or gave as an example anyone giving less than a tithe! The examples always began with a teaching about the tithe, or if the tithe was not mentioned the example appeared to teach us to give beyond a tithe.

Nowhere in my study did I find one verse that said, "And he gave 2 percent but loved God" or, "Conditions were hard, so he decided it would be best not to give to the Lord at that time." No, in Scripture I found a deep commitment to giving modeled by the men and women of God. In both the Old and New Testaments I sensed that they were *excited* that they were *investing* in the kingdom of God, and they were committed to being *obedient* in this area of their lives. I also noticed a commitment to go *beyond* the tithe, and I never found encouragement or instructions to give less than a tithe.

Let's look at five additional Scripture verses that influence us to at least tithe or give beyond that amount.

1. Generosity does not equal 2 percent.

The biblical teaching of generosity supports our call to tithe or give more than a tithe! God desires for you to be generous with your resources and not withhold what is justly due.

Proverbs 11:24–25 (NAS) states:

> *There is one who scatters, yet increases all the more,*
> *And there is one who withholds what is justly due,*
> *but it results only in want.*
> *The generous man will be prosperous,*
> *And he who waters will himself be watered.*

A person would have to have a wild imagination to conclude that giving or scattering 2 percent of your income could be defined as "generous." The very meaning of the word *generous* is "large, ample, big-hearted, and magnanimous." The generous (not the selfish) man is blessed of God.

2. Sacrificial giving is praised in Scripture.

To be committed to something means you are willing to give sacrificially of your time and money. God's economy is different from the world's. In God's economy, commitment and sacrifice are used as multiples! The greater your sacrifice, the greater your gift. If this is not true, how else could one individual's gift of two small copper coins be worth more than the sum total of what everyone else gave?

> And He [Jesus] sat down opposite the treasury, and began observing how the multitude were putting money into the treasury; and many rich people were putting in large sums. And a poor widow came and put in two small copper coins, which amount to a cent. And calling His disciples to Him, He said to them, "Truly I say to you, this poor widow put in more than all the contributors to the treasury; for they all put in out of their surplus, but she, out of her poverty, put in all she owned, all she had to live on." (Mark 12:41–44 NAS)

Once again, Scripture is not pointing us or encouraging us to ever give less than 10 percent.

3. You are called to give even when living in deep poverty.

Living in deep poverty would seem like a most appropriate opportunity for someone to say, "I really don't have very much. I'd better not give this time." But in God's Word this is not the *model*.

Paul described the Macedonians in 2 Corinthians 8:1–4 (TLB) this way:

Now I want to tell you what God in his grace has done for the churches in Macedonia. Though they have been going through much trouble and hard times, they have mixed their wonderful joy with their deep poverty, and the result has been an overflow of giving to others. They gave not only what they could afford, but far more; and I can testify that they did it because they wanted to, and not because of nagging on my part. They begged us to take the money so they could share in the joy of helping the Christians in Jerusalem.

They gave joyfully even when it was hard! To God be the glory! May the spirit of the Macedonians influence God's people around the world. May God find us just as faithful as the Macedonians when faced with hard times or with abundance. May we never choose to give a token gift to God, even when living in poverty!

4. You will suffer the consequences of disobedience.

The Old Testament records the story of how the Israelites were disobedient in their giving and were reaping the consequences of their hardness of heart. They were giving God offerings that not even the government would accept for taxes. In other words, God was getting the worst offering a person could possibly give. He was getting the leftovers! The 2 percent! Read carefully what the prophet Malachi told them:

> *"And when you offer the blind as a sacrifice,*
> *Is it not evil?*
> *And when you offer the lame and sick,*
> *Is it not evil?*
> *Offer it then to your governor!*
> *Would he be pleased with you?*
> *Would he accept you favorably?"*
> *Says the LORD of hosts. (Mal. 1:8)*

The Ethan Pope translation of the above verse reads, "If you tried to pay your taxes with the same thing you are offering to God, the governor would kick you out by the seat of your pants!"

Because of their lack of faith and disobedience, the Israelites were suffering hardships in life. The prophet Haggai described their condition this way:

> *"You have sown much, and bring in little;*
> *You eat, but do not have enough;*
> *You drink, but you are not filled with drink;*
> *You clothe yourselves, but no one is warm;*
> *And he who earns wages,*
> *Earns wages to put into a bag with holes."*

Thus says the Lord of hosts: "Consider your ways!"(Hag. 1:6–7)

Have you ever felt like you were earning money only to put it into a pocket with holes in it?

Do you ever feel like you never have enough?

Are you always living in need and want?

If this is true of you . . . Consider your ways!

One of the first areas I explore when doing financial counseling is the area of giving. Cheerful, generous giving is an important aspect of living in God's economy. There is no way around it.

If you violate the principle of tithing, you *will* reap the consequences.

5. The blessings of tithing.

Who in his or her right mind would intentionally rob God? Absolutely no one! Yet I am confident that millions of Christians are robbing God every day. And ultimately, they are robbing themselves of the joy that comes from giving.

Malachi explained how it's done in this passage, in which God asks:

> *Will a man rob God?*
> *Yet you have robbed Me!*
> *But you say,*
> *"In what way have we robbed You?"*
> *In tithes and offerings.*
> *You are cursed with a curse,*
> *For you have robbed Me,*
> *Even this whole nation. (Mal. 3:8–9)*

The Lord's words here refer back to the covenant in Deuteronomy 28. God told the nation of Israel if they obeyed Him, He would bless them and give them a life of prosperity. On the other hand, He told them if they disobeyed, their lives and their land would be cursed.

Could You Be Found Guilty?

If you were on trial for being a Christian, and the only piece of evidence the prosecutors could use against you was your checkbook, would there be enough evidence to convict you? Or would you be found not guilty due to lack of evidence?

Stop Robbing God

If you are not at least tithing your income, let me strongly encourage you to stop robbing God (see Mal. 3:8–10) and begin to experience the joy and blessing that results from giving.

Scripture has clearly spoken in this area. In every area of Christian life, we are called to commitment. Our money and giving are no exceptions! A life committed to Christ *will produce* revolutionary and radical giving. Now the decision is up to you. Will you be faithful and generous?

WHO SHOULD GIVE?

Now that we have covered how much to give, we need to look at *who* should give. When is it acceptable not to support God's kingdom? In the following list you will find a check next to each acceptable reason for a family not to be faithful in their giving to support God's kingdom:

_____ We have just built a new house and the payments require a large portion of our income.

_____ I just had to take a 10 percent cut in my salary.

_____ We have three children in college.

_____ We have two car payments.

_____ I'm the pastor.

_____ Our family needs new clothes.

_____ This has been an expensive year for our medical bills.

_____ Our car is six years old, and we must buy a new one.

_____ We are sending our children to Christian schools.

_____ I'm in seminary, preparing to be a pastor.

_____ It costs a lot just to live these days.

_____ I haven't received a raise in ten years.

_____ I give my time to the church. You know, time is money.

_____ The people at church are not friendly.

_____ I don't like the pastor.

_____ We only have one income now.

_____ We have not been on a vacation in three years.

_____ I have too much credit card debt.

_____ My car repairs this month were $600.

_____ The air conditioner unit was just replaced.

_____ The church is always asking for more money.

_____ My insurance premium is due next week.

_____ I must pay off my school loans.

_____ We are prepaying our mortgage and trying to become debt free.

How many checks did you find next to the list above? That's right, you did not find even one. People use every rationale in the book to convince themselves why they don't need to invest in God's kingdom! Every excuse and reason with the *exception of one* is unacceptable.

The only time that we are not called to give is when we have absolutely no income coming into our household. If you have any "increase," be faithful to give! If you do not have any income, there is no tithe because 10 percent of zero is zero.

REASONS PEOPLE DON'T GIVE MORE

1. We are constantly increasing our lifestyles. This continually robs us in the area of giving. The average American spends 93 percent, saves 5 percent, and gives 2 percent. When most people get a raise or bonus, they simply increase their lifestyles. The more we earn, the more we spend and want to buy.

2. We do not operate our lives on a budget. When there is no budget, the checkbook becomes the bottom line. We pay our bills, buy the groceries, have fun, save, and give God what's left over, if anything. A budget helps us have giving as a priority.

3. We have to stay ahead of the Joneses. The Joneses buy a new house; we have to buy a bigger one. The Joneses buy a used second car; we have to have a new car. The Joneses go on a ski trip; we have to go on a cruise.

4. We are self-centered.

5. We are deep in debt—therefore in financial bondage. We have so many debts to repay that we never have money to give generously. We are earning money simply to give it to someone else.

6. We think we have given enough. These persons have the mine-versus-God's attitude: *We have paid God off; therefore, the rest belongs to us.* The truth is, it all belongs to God . . . 100 percent of it! We owe it all to Him.

7. Money brings false security, so we hoard and save more and more. We are basically more committed to saving than to giving.

8. We have the attitude, "I'll start giving more when . . ." It might be "after I finish college," "after I get married," "after we have our baby," "after the kids finish college," "after we pay off MasterCard and Visa." It's always later, never today.

9. We have bought into the philosophy of the world and do not have an eternal perspective. If we have an eternal perspective, we realize that giving is the best option for using our money; we lay up treasures in heaven for eternity. Without an eternal perspective, we are more consumed with laying up treasures on earth.

10. Because we are not committed to Christ, we are not committed to His calling to be cheerful and generous givers.

Supporting the Kingdom of God

You have a need to give more than God needs your money. Jesus predicted tribulation for His followers, and whether or not you have noticed, that tribulation is all around us. The world is attacking every principle we Christians believe in. We are being laughed at, mocked, and literally ripped apart by the media. Call it conflict, call it difference of opinion, or call it war. The battle lines are clearly being drawn, and we need to support our side as we help fulfill the Great Commission.

MONEY MYTHS: 12

"I Can Write It Off on My Taxes" and Other Misconceptions

Amyth is something you perceive to be true but in reality is false. A smart money manager recognizes money myths and rejects them. John 8:32 says, "And you shall know the truth, and the truth shall make you free."

Let's look at some myths that many people accept all too easily.

Myth One: Money brings happiness.

Benjamin Franklin said it best: "Money never made a happy man yet, nor will it. There is nothing in its nature to produce happiness. The more a man has, the more he wants. Instead of it filling a vacuum, it makes one. If it satisfies one want, it doubles another."

Franklin's thought is not new. Ecclesiastes 5:10 (NAS) says essentially the same thing: "He who loves money will not be satisfied with money, nor he who loves abundance with its income. This too is vanity."

I am not saying that money can never bring us any happiness in life. Using money to buy an ice-cream cone will bring a smile to any child's face. Eating out, going to a football game, or spending a day at an amusement park can bring happiness to our lives, and it takes money to do all these things. Money can and does bring much circumstantial happiness to our lives. It is true that the more money a family has, the more "things" they can do in life.

However, if money brings the ultimate happiness in life, why are some very wealthy people so unhappy in life? I have known many people with very little financial means who never spoke a word of complaint. These are the people who can be found humming a song while they work; they always seem to have a smile on their face. It is possible that they are bitter on the inside, but if that is true, they're better actors than anyone I know. No amount of money can give a person inner peace with self or God.

Myth Two: Money brings security.

It was October 19, 1987, the day that has been labeled "Black Monday" in the history books. The Dow Jones Industrial Average fell more than 500 points in a single day, the largest single-day drop in history. Stocks and mutual fund shares were being sold by the millions. People were in a panic to sell before the Dow dropped even lower the following day. It has been reported that more than $500 billion "vanished" from the marketplace on that single day—$500 billion dollars lost, gone forever! This event brings to mind the advice in Proverbs 23:4–5 (NAS):

> *Do not weary yourself to gain wealth,*
> *Cease from your consideration of it.*

> *When you set your eyes on it, it is gone.*
> *For wealth certainly make itself wings,*
> *Like an eagle that flies toward the heavens.*

"Ultimate" security cannot be found in money! The Bible makes this very clear:

> Instruct those who are rich in this present world not to be conceited or to fix their hope on the uncertainty of riches, but on God, who richly supplies us with all things to enjoy. (1 Tim. 6:17 NAS)

Pull out a bill or a coin from your wallet. Does it say anything about God on it? It sure does! Our security and trust should be in God. We are reminded of this truth on every piece of currency we have. It says, "In God we trust." It does not say, "In this money we trust."

An interesting story lies behind this saying. In 1861, during the dreadful Civil War, the secretary of the United States Treasury wrote a letter to the director of the mint at Philadelphia. He said: "No nation can be strong except in the strength of God or safe except in His defense." The trust of the people in God should be declared on their coins, he said. Accordingly, orders were given to prepare a motto to express national recognition and trust in God. At first this read, "God, our trust." Later it was changed to, "In God we trust."

There is absolutely nothing wrong with having investments, owning stocks, and planning for future financial needs. However, we have no assurance that our money and financial institutions will be secure tomorrow. Nations rise, and nations fall. America, which is still a young nation, is not exempt. What would happen to the value of our money if we began to have hyperinflation? The buying power of the dollar would quickly vanish.

We must acknowledge that our ultimate security in this life comes from God and God alone.

Myth Three: The Bible does not have much to say about money.

Not true! The Bible has a lot to say about money. In fact, Jesus had more to say about money and possessions than about heaven and hell combined!

Following are just a few examples of passages in which the Bible specifically addresses financial issues:

Bribes	Exodus 23:8
Contentment	Philippians 4:11–12
Coveting	Exodus 20:17
Debt	Proverbs 22:7
Financial setbacks	Job 1:1—2:10
Fraud	Leviticus 19:11
Greed	Luke 12:15
Giving	2 Corinthians 8—9
Poverty	Matthew 26:11
Riches	1 Timothy 6:7–19
Taxes	Mark 12:13–17
Tithing	Malachi 3:9–10
Wealth	Deuteronomy 8:11–19

Myth Four: Money is the root of all evil.

How often have you heard someone say, "Money is the root of all evil"? This is probably one of the most misquoted verses in the Bible. Let's set the record straight by quoting 1 Timothy 6:10, the verse from which this saying is derived. First Timothy says, "For the love of money is a root of all kinds of evil." Note the focus is on the "love of money," not on money itself. Money, in itself, is just paper or metal; in people's hands it is sometimes used for evil purposes.

Myth Five: It's 10 percent God's and 90 percent mine.

It is very common for people to believe the portion of their income they give to God already belongs to Him; therefore, they say, 10 percent is God's and 90 percent is theirs. However, this is not what the Bible teaches.

The Bible clearly teaches that 100 percent of everything we have belongs to God. Psalm 24:1 (NAS) says, "The earth is the LORD's, and all it contains, / The world, and those who dwell in it."

It all belongs to God; we are simply stewards of His possessions. He has entrusted the earth's resources to us to oversee. It is our responsibility to properly manage them during our brief stay on earth.

Myth Six: If I give enough money, it will help me get to heaven.

It is absolutely, positively impossible for us to "buy" our salvation by our giving or works. Ephesians 2:8–9 says, "For by grace you have been saved through faith, and that not of yourselves; it is the gift of God, not of works, lest anyone should boast."

If you trust in your own good works to get you to heaven, you will not make it. Salvation is a free gift from God. We can't work for it; we must simply receive it. The only thing you can put your trust in to obtain salvation is Jesus!

If you have never trusted Jesus as your Savior, there would be no better time than right now. All you have to do by faith is to repent of your sins and invite Him to come into your life. You might pray this simple prayer:

Lord Jesus, I invite You to come into my life. Please forgive me of all my sins. Take control of my life from this very day. Thank You for coming into my life. Amen.

If you pray that prayer, Jesus will come into your life, and He will never leave you (see John 1:12 and Acts 16:30–33).

Myth Seven: It is difficult . . . but we can serve God and mammon.

Many people are fence straddlers. We have never fully committed ourselves to live in God's economy or in the world's economy. Our feet are firmly planted in both economies. God says we cannot do this; Jesus made this very clear in the Sermon on the Mount:

> No one can serve two masters; for either he will hate the one and love the other, or else he will be loyal to the one and despise the other. You cannot serve God and mammon. (Matt. 6:24)

Myth Eight: We should not pay taxes to an ungodly government.

If we follow the teaching of Jesus and the instructions of Paul, we should pay our taxes. Jesus made this clear in Mark 12:17 when He said, "Render to Caesar the things that are Caesar's, and to God the things that are God's." And Paul tells us in Romans 13:7, "Render therefore to all their due: taxes to whom taxes are due, customs to whom customs, fear to whom fear, honor to whom honor."

Yet there is absolutely nothing wrong with taking every legal deduction available to reduce our tax obligation. That's why the laws are in place.

Myth Nine: The rich in this world are those who make more than I do.

When we read the warnings in the Bible to the rich, we often think, _That doesn't apply to me because I'm not rich._ We classify everyone who has more than we do as the "rich."

Has it ever occurred to you that there are billions of people in the world who have less than you do—and they think you are rich? I believe all the warning verses in the Bible apply to 99 percent of

Americans. Compared to the world, *you* are probably rich. Keep that in mind the next time you read those verses to the rich!

Myth Ten: I can write it off on my taxes.

Many people see interest payments as a plus. They think, *I can write it off on my taxes.* Please note, *the majority of your interest is not tax deductible.* This includes the interest you pay on your home. Only a portion of your interest is written off. Yes, you do list the entire amount of your interest on your tax return, but this is not a direct dollar-for-dollar tax reduction. What this does is lower the amount of your "taxable" income. If you are in a 28 percent tax bracket, 72 percent of your interest is *not* written off. Don't become too excited or comfortable with the fact that "you can write it off" on your taxes.

Myth Eleven: As long as I'm making my monthly payment, I'm really not in debt.

One day while I was in the process of signing some legal papers, I began to express my views on why it is best to eliminate all debt as quickly as possible. The man I was talking with smiled and said, "If you make your monthly mortgage payment on time, you're really not in debt." I said, "Yes, you are." He said, "No, you're not."

Then I said, "Well, if you're not in debt, why are you sending the bank money *every month?* Are you doing it out of the goodness of your heart? I don't think so! I think you are doing it because you are in debt; you have a financial and legal obligation to send the bank money!"

Yes, even when you are up-to-date on your monthly payments, *you are still in debt;* you are "indebted," and you make monthly payments. Another fact that proves this is the lien the lender usually has against your property, *until* you pay the debt in full.

Myth Twelve: If I tithe, I will receive a financial blessing.

God does promise you a blessing if you tithe (Mal. 3:10), but His blessings are not always what you had in mind. For example, when we think *blessing,* we immediately begin to think of financial or material wealth. However, God's blessing might come in the form of good health, contentment, spiritual blessings, good family relationships, or joy that will come in eternity!

Myth Thirteen: If you are spiritual, you will never have any financial problems.

The apostle Paul was deeply spiritual, and God allowed him to pen more books in the New Testament than anyone else. Yet God did not spare him from financial hardships. Consider just two of the statements he made:

> [I have been] in weariness and toil, in sleeplessness often, in hunger and thirst, in fastings often, in cold and nakedness. (2 Cor. 11:27)

> Not that I speak from want; for I have learned to be content in whatever circumstances I am. I know how to get along with humble means, and I also know how to live in prosperity; in any and every circumstance I have learned the secret of being filled and going hungry, both of having abundance and suffering need. I can do all things through Him who strengthens me. (Phil. 4:11–13 NAS)

I rest my case!

Myth Fourteen: So what if I get a thirty-year mortgage? I only plan to live in each house five to ten years!

We discussed thirty-year and fifteen-year mortgages in Chapter 5. In case you are still in doubt about which mortgage is best for you, let me give you some added information.

Let's assume the following:

1. You will buy five homes during your lifetime.
2. You will obtain a new thirty-year loan each time.
3. Since you will be buying a larger, more expensive home each time, you will apply all the money you earned on the home due to inflation to the next home, slightly increasing your mortgage each time you buy a new home.

The following table shows how much of your money is going to interest and how little is going to reduce the principal for the loans on your first four homes. If you sell your home every five years and obtain another thirty-year mortgage, the majority of your money goes toward interest.

WHAT HAPPENS WHEN YOU BUY FOUR SUCCESSIVE HOMES WITH THIRTY-YEAR MORTGAGES IN TWENTY-FIVE YEARS

At age twenty-five you buy your first home and keep it for five years.

Mortgage:	$75,000
Interest rate:	10 percent
Monthly payment:	$658.18
Total amount paid out of checkbook during five years:	$39,490.80 ($658.18 × 12 × 5)
Total amount paid in interest during five years:	*$36,921.47*
Amount still owed on mortgage after five years:	$72,430.74

At age thirty you buy your second home and keep it for ten years.

Mortgage:	$80,000
Interest rate:	10 percent
Monthly payment:	$702.06

Total amount paid out of checkbook
during ten years: $84,247.20 ($702.06 × 12 × 10 years)

Total amount paid in interest during
ten years: *$76,997.30*

Amount still owed on mortgage after
ten years: $72,750.42

Total amount you have paid in interest
for your first two homes: *$113,918.77*

At age forty you buy your third home and keep it for four years.

Mortgage:	$95,000
Interest rate:	10 percent
Monthly payment:	$833.69

Total amount paid out of checkbook
during four years: $40,017.12 ($833.69 × 12 × 4 years)

Total amount paid in interest during
four years   *$37,549.37*

Amount still owed on mortgage after
four years: $92,532.11

Total amount you have paid in interest
for your first three homes: *$151,468.14*

At age forty-four you buy your fourth home and keep it for six years.

Mortgage:	$110,000
Interest rate:	10 percent
Monthly payment:	$965.33

Total amount paid out of checkbook
during six years: $69,503.76 ($965.33 × 12 × 6 years)

Total amount paid in interest during
six years: *$64,729.37*

Amount still owed on mortgage after
six years: $105,225.70

Total amount you have paid in interest
for your first four homes: *$216,197.51*

At age fifty you buy your fifth home and have no intentions of buying another home.

Mortgage:	$130,000
Interest rate:	10 percent
Monthly payment:	$1,140.84
Total amount paid out of checkbook during thirty years:	$410,702.40 ($1,140.84 × 12 × 30 years)
Total amount paid in interest during thirty years:	*$280,730.49*
Amount still owed on mortgage after thirty years:	$ NONE
Total amount you have paid in interest for your five homes over fifty-five years.	*$496,928.00*

Look at the financial cost of keeping a mortgage during your working life: a half a million dollars! Look at the financial waste of obtaining a new thirty-year mortgage each time you buy a new home.

Having a mortgage is the American way. However, the American way is not always the best way. Every person should have a goal to become debt free as soon as possible. Stop thinking you will "always" have a mortgage! This attitude is destructive to your financial life!

Myth Fifteen: Insurance is gambling.

Some people would like to view insurance as gambling. Someone might say, "You are wagering the insurance company your $500 against their $250,000 that you might die this year." Or they say, "You are wagering the insurance company $300 against their $70,000 that your house will burn down this year."

Look at it from this perspective: Gambling creates a risk. If I never bet on a football game, there is 0 percent risk that I will win or lose money. If I do bet on a football game, there is 100 percent chance that I will win or lose money. You see, gambling *creates* a risk. This is totally different from insurance, which protects against a preexisting risk.

Whether or not I have life insurance, there is a risk that I might die this year. Whether or not I have fire insurance, there is a risk that my home might burn down this year. By buying insurance, I am not creating the risk; I am protecting against a risk that is already there.

Gambling creates risk, while insurance protects you from risk.

Myth Sixteen: Sweepstakes are gambling.

I'll say it again: To gamble, you must create risk, which involves making a wager. By filling out a sweepstakes form you are not wagering or creating the potential for loss, so you are not gambling.

But you say, "The stamp costs money and the amount of your wager makes no difference. Gambling with a twenty-nine-cent stamp is the same as gambling with $25,000."

But wait a minute. Have your ever thought about the fact that the money you spent on the stamp did not go to the sweepstakes people, but to the United States Postal Service? Therefore, you did not make a wager, even of twenty-nine cents.

No, entering a sweepstakes is not gambling unless you have to send money specifically to the sponsor in order to enter the sweepstakes.

**Myth Seventeen: Social security is supposed
                  to support my needs fully.**

It is common for people to believe that social security benefits will fully support their family during their retirement years. I have researched the initial purpose of social security, and it is clear that this program was never supposed to fully support Americans during their retirement. It was to be *a supplement* in addition to personal or corporate pensions!

Somewhere along the way, the purpose of social security payments has been forgotten. Now far too many people *depend totally* on their social security.

Myth Eighteen: Renting is a waste of money.

Renting is not a total waste of your money. Owning a home does have its advantages, but renting also has many advantages. Your money is not wasted. If you've been renting during the past year, think about the following questions:

- Did you have a place to sleep during the past year?
- Did you have a place to use for entertaining your friends?
- Did you have a place to store your personal belongings?
- Did you have a place to cook your meals?
- Did you have a place to do your work away from the office?

Get the point? You did receive something for your money!

A big benefit of renting over ownership is flexibility. When your six-month or one-year lease ends, you have the freedom to stay or move. This is not true when you own a home. When the housing market is down and homes are not selling, some home owners are unable to move as easily as they wish.

Also, when you consider that you accumulate minimal equity during the first years of a mortgage, you might be wiser to rent until the timing is right. After paying the first year of payments on a thirty-year, $75,000 mortgage at 10 percent, you have only obtained an additional .5 percent equity (ownership) in your home.

Did you catch that? After making twelve monthly payments of $658.18 during the first year ($7,898.16) on your $75,000 mortgage, you have increased your equity (or ownership) in your home by approximately only *½ of one percent!*

You paid in more than 10 percent of the original loan balance, but you sill owe 99.4 percent on your loan.

Myth Nineteen: My money will compound faster if I keep it in one investment rather than spread it out in several investment accounts.

Which is the better plan?

Plan A: Invest $10,000 in one investment that will earn 7 percent for the next ten years.

Plan B: Invest $1,000 in ten separate investments with each earning 7 percent for the next ten years.

After ten years Plan A and Plan B will have *exactly* the same amount of the total investment: $19,671.51. It is very common for people to think it is better to have all their money together so it will take advantage of the compounding-interest effect. However, this is just another myth! It will grow the same whether it is divided or together.

Now that we've looked at these myths, let's consider the money allocation plan, the budget that allows a smart money manager to stay on the right track.

THE MONEY ALLOCATION PLAN:

Your Map to Success

I did not marry Janet directly out of college. In fact, I purchased a house in Dallas, Texas, as a single and lived there for three years with two roommates who worked in the same office with me. Every day at about 5 P.M. we would meet to decide who would cook the meal that night. The "chosen" person would leave the office, stop by the grocery store, buy the food, and then cook the meal. We lived day by day.

When I married Janet, she moved in and the guys moved out. One of the first things she checked out was the kitchen. She quickly realized the cupboards were almost bare. Sure, we had salt, pepper, and lemon pepper, but that was the extent of our spices. I think there were even a few cans of baked beans that had been hanging around for a few months.

"I think we need to go grocery shopping," she immediately said.

"Great!" I agreed. I could picture us holding hands as we walked through the aisles together. I enjoyed being with Janet, no matter what we were doing.

Janet selected a very large grocery cart once we entered the store, and we began going up and down each and every aisle. Eventually, the top part of the cart was full and overflowing, and so was the bottom; in addition, I was holding items in both hands. (I was holding hands with a bag of potatoes, not Janet.)

Finally, we made it to the checkout counter, and the clerk began to ring up the items. The total was almost $200! I turned to Janet and said something like, "Janet, I buy groceries by the day, not by the year."

Well, she didn't appreciate that very much. So we went home and "discussed" it some more.

Before we were married, Janet and I had a great financial relationship, we decided. She had her checkbook and spent money exactly like she wanted to. I had my checkbook and spent money exactly like I wanted to. It was an amiable relationship. Then, the two checkbooks became one. *Our* checkbook. Every time either of us wanted to buy something, we felt an obligation to talk to the other person.

Finally, Janet came to me and said, "Ethan, I think we need a budget." I answered, "I think you are right." That was the beginning of the first money allocation plan (MAP).

The first thing we did was to decide how much money we projected to come in that year. Then we asked the question, "Where do we need to allocate it?" After several hours we had determined how we would give, save, and spend our money.

The MAP helps to take the financial stress out of a marriage. If there is money in the clothing allocation, go spend it. No talking, no discussion necessary. If there is no money in the furniture account, you wait until the money builds back up. There is no need to pout or to scheme or to even talk about it.

Without a MAP, some families have to discuss *every* spending decision. Or if they don't discuss it, they end up fighting over every item purchased. Or even worse, one spouse hides a purchase from the other to avoid a confrontation, and the other spouse hides money in a secret account so it won't all be spent.

A smart money manager has a money allocation plan. We highly recommend it to everyone who is trying to find some freedom in managing his or her money.

Your Financial Map:
The Money Allocation Plan

I have personally been using and teaching people how to use a money allocation plan since 1982. It is a simple, easy budgeting system. There are three quick benefits to this plan:

It's easy to use!

All you need is one MAP per month (twelve per year). You don't need anything complex, or a notebook full of tabs and paper.

It provides the big picture!

The MAP helps you to focus on the big picture, not on the insignificant details. On twelve pieces of paper, you will have your entire financial life documented. You will have a record of all your income and expenses for the year, and you will quickly be able to see where the money came from and where it went.

You will now be able to oversee your finances with a simple and easy-to-use resource.

You'll waste less money!

It's a fact, if you live on a MAP you will waste less money. Why? Because now you have a plan, and you can maximize your resources. The MAP brings freedom, not bondage.

Don't be fooled by three prevalent budget myths:

- Budgets are bondage.

- Budgets take all the fun out of life.

- Budgets are too complex.

A Sample MAP

Take a look at the sample MAP on pages 239–242. Immediately following the sample MAP you will find detailed explanations.

Let me begin by explaining the big picture of how the money allocation plan works; then I will move to the specific details. In using a MAP, you determine ahead of time how your money (income) will be allocated into numerous budget categories. Before you begin, understanding the word *allocation* is very important in using a MAP.

Think of using a MAP in this way: Picture yourself working in a post office. There are numerous boxes on the wall with little doors on the other side, and your job is to "allocate" the mail into the proper boxes. Some mailboxes have lots of mail while others have a little or none. Later on in the day, people come along and take the mail out of the boxes. If you have not put any mail in a particular box, they cannot take anything out of the box.

The MAP is very similar. Every time you receive a paycheck you take this money and allocate it into various money boxes. When you write a check or spend money, you are taking money out of the box. Before you go shopping, you might want to look on your MAP to see how much money (if any) is remaining in a particular category or box.

MONEY ALLOCATION PLAN

DATE	SOURCE OF INCOME	BUDGETED	NON-BUDGETED	TOTAL DEPOSIT
3-1	ABC Comapny	1,500		1,500
3-15	ABC Company	1,700		1,700
TOTALS FOR MONTH		**$3,200**	**$**	**$3,200**

	ALLOCATION WORKSHEET								
	BUDGET $	DEPOSIT AMOUNTS FROM INCOME CHART ABOVE							
MAP CATEGORY	$ 3,200	$1,500	$1,700	$	$	$	$	$	$	$
Mortgage	600	600								
Insurance	120		120							
Taxes	75		75							
Debt Repayment	100	100								
Car Pay/Savings	200		200							
Car Expenses	170		170							
S. Term Savings	150	150								
L. Term Savings	150		150							
Utilities	150	150								
Home Repair	75		75							
Food	350	350								
Children	50		50							
Giving	320	150	170							
Social	50		50							
Clothing	130		130							
Medical	100		100							
Household	50		50							
Gifts	60		60							
Allowance (H)	100		100							
Allowance (W)	100		100							
Misc.	100		100							

Mortgage

D/#	+	−	=
BB			0
3-1	600		600
501		600	0

Car Pay/Savings

D/#	+	−	=
BB			2000
3-15	200		2200

Taxes

D/#	+	−	=
BB			150
3-15	75		225

Car Expenses

D/#	+	−	=
BB			140
3-15	170		310
512		80	230
513		160	70
CC		20	50

Household

D/#	+	−	=
BB			40
508		12	28
3-15	50		78
529		18	60

Clothing

D/#	+	−	=
BB			100
3-15	130		230
514		80	150
CC		90	60

Children

D/#	+	−	=
BB			60
509		25	35
3-15	50		85
538		25	60

Gifts

D/#	+	−	=
BB			80
3-15	60		140
527		20	120

House Repair

D/#	+	−	=
BB			80
3-15	75		155
527		45	110

Allowance H

D/#	+	−	=
BB			68
504		50	18
3-15	100		118
528		20	98
534		50	48
Food	20		68

Allowance W

D/#	+	−	=
BB			93
507		50	43
3-15	100		143
520		50	93
537		20	73

Social

D/#	+	−	=
BB			37
503		10	27
3-15	50		77
519		50	27
CC		25	2

Utilities

D/#	+	−	=
BB			92
3-1	150		242
516		19	223
517		82	141
518		47	94

Food

D/#	+	-	=
BB			21
3-1	350		371
505		60	311
510		19	292
511		37	255
515		97	158
522		53	105
526		60	45
532		19	26
A(H)		20	6

Misc.

D/#	ITEM	+	-	=
BB				5
3-15		100		105
523	Cleaners		15	90
531	Cash		20	70
540	Postage		10	60
	Bal. Budget	2		62

Insurance

D/#	ITEM	+	-	=
BB				240
3-15			120	360
541	Life		90	270

Giving

D/#	ITEM	+	-	=
BB				0
3-1		150		150
502	Church		75	75
3-15		170		245
521	Church		75	170
530	ABC Min.		50	120
535	Church		75	45

Short Term Saving

D/#	+	-	=	D/#	+	-	=	D/#	+	-	=
BB			300	BB				BB			
3-1	150		450								

CREDIT CARDS

D/#	ITEM	Transfer From	CARD	PD	+	-	=
BB							100
3-17	Gas	Car Expense	MC		20		120
3-19	Mr. Steak	Social	MC		25		145
3-24	Fashion Tree	Clothing	MC		90		235
536	Payment for Last Month		MC			100	135
3-26	Hotel-Boston	Business Reimb.	Visa		120		255

Long Term Savings

D/#	+	−	=	D/#	+	−	=	D/#	ITEM	+	−	=
BB				BB				BB				850
								3-1		150		1000
								3-10	Transfer to IRA		1000	0

Debt Repay

D/#	+	−	=	D/#	+	−	=	D/#	ITEM	+	−	=
BB				BB				BB				0
								3-1		100		100
								506	School Loan		50	50
								525	Visa		50	0

Medical

D/#	+	−	=	D/#	+	−	=	D/#	ITEM	+	−	=
BB				BB				BB				94
								3-15		100		194
								524	Mary		35	159
								533	John		35	124

Business Reimbursement

D/#	+	−	=	D/#	+	−	=	D/#	ITEM	+	−	=
BB				BB				BB				250
								CC	Hotel-Boston		120	130

If the allocation box in your MAP is empty, you cannot spend money in that category. If there is money in that category, it will be fine to spend it. That is why it is there!

Now let's go back and look at the first page of the sample MAP. As you read the following notes flip back to look at what we are discussing.

Front Page

The box on the top of the page is where you record all the income you receive for your family. Examples of things you would record in this income box would be:

- Paychecks

- Bonus check

- Interest income for checking account

- Dividend income

- Gift money

- Hobby income

- Tax refund money

- All the income you ever put into your checking account!

Notice how this section has a place for the date, source, and income amount.

Date. You always need to record the date you received the income and deposited it in your checking account.

Source of Income. In this space you list where the income came from. If you work for ABC Company, that is exactly what you would write here. If you received a dividend check from Jones & Co., you would list "Jones & Co." in this space. Write down the source of all your income!

Budgeted or Nonbudgeted. Did you plan, or budget, for this money? Is this money to be used as a part of your regular household budget money? If the answer is yes, it is "budgeted income." Examples of budgeted income usually include your salary and any other sources of income you expect to receive and use for your regular household expenses. If the answer is no, you call it nonbudgeted income. Examples of nonbudgeted income include gift money, bonus checks, and business reimbursements. Put the amount in the proper budgeted or nonbudgeted column.

Total Deposit. This column is used for the total dollar amount for *each individual deposit* made during the current month. Some deposits will only have one check while other deposits will have two or more checks. If you only have one check to deposit, the total deposit column will be the same as the amount you either put in the budgeted or nonbudgeted column. If you have several checks, the grand total for budgeted and nonbudgeted will equal the amount in the total deposit column.

Immediately below the income chart at the top of the front page is the *allocation worksheet.*

Category. The first column on this worksheet is where you will list all your budget categories for your family. There is no set list of categories because your list should include categories that *your* family needs, not what my family needs.

Here are some of the most common budget categories most families will use. Your family will not need to use every category I have listed.

Allowance: husband
Allowance: wife
Auto expenses: gasoline, oil, tires, repairs
Auto insurance

Car payment/savings
Children: allowances, toys, sports
Clothing: husband
Clothing: children
Clothing: wife
Debt repayment: for all past debts you have incurred
Food
Gifts: birthday, anniversary, baby, Christmas
Giving: local church and other ministries
Home repair
Household: furniture, appliances, supplies
Life insurance
Medical: insurance, doctor bills, prescriptions
Miscellaneous
Mortgage/rent
Savings, retirement
Savings, short-term
Savings, college
Savings, emergency fund
School expense
Social: eating out, vacations
Telephone
Utilities: gas, electric, water

Budget $. This is where you put the amount you are going to allocate for the month *into* the specific category. This is your planned budget for the month. The sample MAP plans to have $3,200 in income, so the total of all the amounts in this column for all the allocations equals this amount.

By allocating your money this way, this is what you are saying: "I plan to receive $3,200 in income this month, and I plan to allocate/distribute this money into the following twenty-one budget categories."

Determining how much you need to allocate into each category is one of your biggest challenges. The first time you do this will be your most time consuming. In determining how much you need for each category, consider the following points.

For MAP categories that are fixed amounts, such as mortgage or rent, the process is easy; just fill in the amount you need for the month. For example, if your mortgage payment is $600, this is the amount you must allocate into that category.

Next, you need to deal with expenses that are not monthly but are quarterly, semiannual, or annual expenses. For example, if your car insurance premium of $600 is due once every six months, you will need to allocate $100 each month into an insurance MAP category. In six months, when the premium is due, you will have all the needed money in your MAP insurance category.

If you plan to spend $300 for Christmas, why not allocate $25 each month into a Christmas category during the year? The same would be true for an annual life insurance premium. If the premium is $500, allocate $42 each month into your life insurance category.

Examples of nonmonthly expenses may include: auto insurance, life insurance, disability insurance, vacations, and Christmas expenses.

By taking a major expense and allocating funds into your MAP category, or money box, *each month,* you will take away the stress of major expenses and find that life is a lot easier when you have money in your category to cover this major expense.

You will definitely need to put more thought and planning into how much you will allocate for MAP categories such as food, clothing, savings, and social, but once again you are looking at the financial needs for one month.

The first time you do this may take some time, but for future months, all the work is done and you simply use the same amounts each month!

Deposit Amounts from Chart Above. Each time you make a deposit, record it in the first available deposit column in the chart. Our illustration shows a family receiving $1,500 in income on March 1. This amount from the income chart on the top of the page is transferred to the deposit column on the bottom of the page. Your next job is to decide how you want to allocate this income. Notice, in our example, this $1,500 was allocated into the mortgage, debt repayment, short-term savings, utilities, food, and giving categories. You will do this for each deposit you make in your checking account. The first few months will take more time because the whole process is new. However, over time, if you follow a regular routine for how each paycheck will be distributed in which categories, the process will become much faster and easier.

Notice how the total for all the allocations equals the total deposit!

Inside and Back Pages

The two inside pages and the back page are used for all your different MAP categories, or money boxes. The first thing you notice is that the boxes are all different sizes; different-size categories are to be used for different purposes. The larger ones are to be used for categories with frequent use, such as food. I don't know about your family, but we write more checks to the grocery store than anywhere else.

The small ones are to be used for budget categories that usually have one or two entries each month. Examples are categories such as mortgage, insurance, or long-term savings.

Your next job is to "transfer" each allocated amount (from the allocation worksheet, or front page) to the appropriate MAP category on the inside and back pages of the MAP. Notice how the $600 allocated for mortgage was transferred to the mortgage category on the inside page of the MAP; the $600 was put into the + column. This makes $600 available in the mortgage money box. Until now, the box was empty and you had no money available to use for a mortgage payment! The same transfers are made for the remaining categories: You will transfer $100 into the debt repayment category (or money box), $150 into the short-term savings category, $150 into the utilities category, $350 into the food category, and $150 into the giving category!

Now you have received income, allocated it, and transferred it to the proper category. Your money boxes, or categories, now have $1,500 more money in them for you to use during the coming days, weeks, and months. Let's look at how those categories and columns work.

D/# Column. Notice how each category has a variety of columns. The first column is the "D/#" column. This is to be used for either the *date* or the *check number.* I recommend you use dates for " + transactions" (allocations) and check numbers for " − transactions" (expenses) in each category. (BB stands for beginning balance.)

+ Column. Use the + column when you are allocating money *into* a budget category. For example, look at the food category. In the D/# column, you see "3-1," representing March 1, and $350 in the + column. This tells you that on March 1, you allocated $350 into your food category.

Now is a good time for a MAP tip: When using the MAP categories, round your entry to the nearest whole dollar. Notice how this has been done on the sample MAP. Rounding will save you hours every month. You do not need to keep your MAP to the penny! However, be sure to keep your checkbook register to the penny.

− Column. Use the − column when you spend money in this particular category. Look again at the food category. In the D/# column we see 505. We also see $60 in the − column and $311 in the = column. This tells us we wrote check number 505 for $60 and we have $311 remaining dollars to be spent for food this month.

If for some reason you wanted to find out what store you wrote the check to and when it was dated, you could go to your checkbook register and look up check number 505.

= Column. The first entry in the = column shows the beginning balance (BB) for the month. For example, in the food category, we had $21 left over in the food category when February ended. Therefore, we simply transfer the ending food balance of $21 to the beginning balance for the food category for March. This column tells you how much money you have remaining in your category. If it has a balance, you have money available to spend. If this column is empty, you do not have any money to spend in this category until you allocate some more money into it.

Item Column. Notice how some categories have an additional column that says "item." These categories are used for expense categories where it would be helpful to have some additional data in the MAP. I recommend you use these for categories for giving, miscellaneous, medical, savings, insurance, and reimbursement. Study the sample MAP to see how this is done. For example, in the giving category, you can list in the item column who you gave to, or in the reimbursement category you can list what you bought; this information can help you fill out a reimbursement form at a later date. This is done because it might be helpful to have a more detailed information for your giving, medical, or insurance expenditures. But most people really do not need detailed information about purchases for food and clothing.

Credit Cards. As you can imagine, the credit card category is very important. Look at the credit card category in the sample MAP, and let's discuss the first transaction.

On March 17, you filled up your car with gasoline and charged the gas on your MasterCard. When you update the budget at the end of the week, you record this charge and budget the expense in the following way:

You put the date "3/17" in the D/# column of the credit card category. This records the date you actually made the purchase. It is very helpful to have the purchase date when your bill arrives in the mail.

Next, you put "gas" or the store name in the item column. This tells you what you purchased, and/or from whom.

Then, in the "Transfer From" column you put the category you are spending money out of. In our example our purchase was for gas, so it will come out of our car expense category. Think about it; even though this is a credit card purchase, you have still spent money! Money must be immediately taken out of the car expense category and put into your credit card category.

Now look at the last entry in the car expense category. You will find the letters "CC" in the D/# column. This indicates a credit card transfer. Notice the 20 in the – column. We are taking $20 out of car expenses and putting $20 into the credit card category. Now we have $50 remaining in our car expense category.

Now your MAP shows that you have less money in your car expenses category to be spent, and you have more money in your credit card category, so when the bill arrives you already have money in your credit card category to use to pay it!

Next, put the name of the card (MC) in the "Card" column. This will help you when it comes time to pay all the MasterCard charges.

Now, put the charge amount ($20) in the " + " column of the credit card category. This might seem strange, putting what you just charged in the + column, but this is exactly what you need to do. Remember, we just took $20 out of the car expense category and now we are putting it into the credit card category until the bill comes and we need to take it out!

Now the ending balance in the credit card category is $120. In our illustration, $100 was the beginning balance brought forward from last month. In other words we already had $100 in our credit card money box from charges last month. This money will be used to pay the credit card bill that will arrive this month. When the bill comes, go back to last month's budget and place a check in the paid column beside each entry that is being paid; then write the check to Master-Card.

Find where we wrote check number 536 in the credit card category. Note that this amount ($100) is recorded in the " – " column, and the new balance of $135 is recorded in the " = " column. The $135 balance in the credit card category represents the total of all outstanding credit card charges we have made this month.

It is best if you update your credit card charges weekly to keep your budget categories current. If you did not reflect your credit card charges immediately, it would be easy to overspend because it takes most credit card bills twenty-five to thirty-five days to arrive in your mailbox. By updating the credit card expenses weekly, you know exactly how much you actually have to spend in each category.

Balancing and Updating the MAP Weekly

Either Janet or I will update our MAP once a week. We sit down with our checkbook, the MAP, a pencil, and a calculator. This is when we record on our MAP all the financial activities that took place in our checkbook during the week.

The updating must take place at least weekly to let you know how you are doing in all your MAP categories. In my opinion, if you only update your MAP once a month you are simply wasting your time. You are not budgeting but spending a lot of time tracking where all the money went to!

That's right, each week you sit down with your checkbook and update the budget categories. Put a check next to each entry in your checkbook documenting that the expense item has been recorded in the MAP. Next week when you update the budget again, you will know where to begin.

Balancing the Budget Each Week

Now here is an important aspect of making the MAP work. The total balances of all the MAP categories should equal the balance in your checkbook.

If we added the ending balances of every category in our sample MAP they would equal $4,212.00. This should be the same amount in your checkbook. You see, as money goes into your checkbook, you are putting money into all the MAP categories. As you spend money out of your checkbook, you are taking money out of your MAP categories.

Let's look once again at our example: If you look at the sample MAP you will find the following ending balances:

Mortgage	$ 0
Car payment/savings	2,200
Taxes	225
Car expenses	50
Household	60
Clothing	60
Children	60
Gifts	120
House repair	110
Allowance (H)	68
Allowance (W)	73
Social	2
Utilities	94
Food	6
Miscellaneous	62
Insurance	270
Giving	45
Short-term savings	450
Credit cards	255
Debt repayment	0

Medical	$ 124
Business reimbursement	130
Long-term savings	0
Total for all categories	$4,464

When I add them all up each week, the grand total should equal the balance in my checkbook. However, due to rounding, you might have a difference of a few dollars (+) or (−). This is what you do to correct this small difference between your checkbook and your MAP.

If the MAP total is *less* than your checkbook balance, *add* the difference to your miscellaneous category. Look at the miscellaneous category on our sample MAP. Notice the "Item" column says, "Bal. Budget" and the " + " column has a 2 in it. This is where I adjusted the MAP to equal the balance in my checkbook.

If the MAP total is *more* than your checkbook, *subtract* the difference from your miscellaneous category. If the difference is more than $5, you have probably made an error in recording somewhere. The simplest way to find the error is to go back through your checkbook and double-check each transfer of information from checkbook to MAP.

A New MAP Each Month

You will use a new MAP each month, transferring all the ending balances from last month's MAP to the "BB" (beginning balances) column of the current month's MAP.

Another important perspective in using your MAP is how you handle your income when it arrives.

All Income Goes into the Checkbook

Record 100 percent of your income on your *MAP.* Do not cash a paycheck and put $100 in your pocket, then deposit the rest in your checking account. Deposit the entire paycheck and then, if needed, write a check for $100 and cash it. By following this procedure, you have established a clear "paper trail" to document your income and expense activities.

Pay All Expenses Out of the Checkbook

Try to pay for everything by check with the exception of "small personal expenses." These should be paid for out of your personal allowance money you carry in your pocket. This is the money you use for lunch, sports, haircuts, and personal items.

Since we are on the topic of personal allowance money, let me explain why it is so important for every MAP to have these categories.

Personal allowance categories are required for your family to find *freedom!*

I do not recommend you walk around with three-by-five cards recording every penny you spend. *Your personal allowance should be a minimum of $50 to $100 per month for each spouse.* In my opinion, this is a minimum, nonnegotiable budget item. You must allow some personal money! You should be free to spend for small things without having to record every dollar.

Your personal allowance money is the *cash* you will keep in your wallet. When you need personal allowance money, you should write a check and cash it at the bank. This cashed check is recorded in the " – " column of the personal allowance category on the MAP.

Find the "Allowance (H)" category on our sample MAP. Notice that check number 504 was written for $50. This means this husband went to the bank, cashed a check for $50, and put the money in his pocket. This money can now be spent for personal expenses during the week or month.

However, if you do have a large personal allowance expense, it is fine to write a check. This check will then be recorded later in your personal allowance category. But remember, *always* try to use checks when you spend money for nonpersonal expenses such as groceries, monthly bills, clothing, and gifts.

Now, I feel the need to get really personal at this point. From my years of helping people in money management, I must make a few comments to men or women who are tightwads.

A Personal Note to Tightwads

I have observed that some spouses like to keep a real "tight" budget. Everyone in the family is instructed to record every penny he or she spends on a three-by-five card to be turned in each day (or some other modification of this plan).

If that is true of you, loosen up! These plans very seldom work, especially if you demand that it be done *your* way. Give your spouse freedom! It is not your money. It's his or her money too! The allowance account is intended to give each spouse freedom to make his or her own choices. Don't fight over how every penny was or will be spent. In my opinion, this is one sure way to take all the fun out of a marriage.

Spend Based Upon the MAP Category, Not the Checkbook Balance

If you are operating on a MAP, your checkbook balance will grow because you are allocating on a monthly basis for Christmas, car insurance premiums, and future things like vacations. *You must not spend based upon the checkbook balance but upon each individual budget category balance.* Your checkbook balance has been allocated into many different categories. Spend according to what your MAP says you have to spend.

MAP Account "Paper Transfers"

You can do budget account transfers any time you like. For example, if I go by the grocery store and do not have the checkbook but spend $20 of my personal allowance money, I can put the grocery store bill in my billfold and, at the end of the week when I update the budget, transfer $20 from the food category to my personal allowance category.

Look at the food and husband's allowance categories on the sample MAP. You will see $20 was taken out of the food MAP category and $20 was put into the husband's allowance MAP category.

When a Category Becomes a Minus

When you run out of money in a category, stop spending money in that category! Next, decide from which positive-balance category you want to transfer funds. If you continually run negative balances in your MAP, you are wasting your time and the system has lost all its integrity. It is not helping you. You must work at keeping all categories in a positive or zero balance.

Debt Repayment Category

If you have outstanding debts you are paying off monthly (not including your home or car) you need to have a debt repayment category on your MAP. For example, this category would be used if you have outstanding credit card debt *when you first begin using the MAP.* You do not pay "old credit card debt" out of the credit card category. Other items that might fall in this category are old school loans, furniture or appliance loans, and medical bills. You need to allocate money into your debt repayment category just like you allocate money into the food category. *If you have debt, then debt repayment should be a high priority in any budget!*

All *future* credit card purchases should go in the credit card category so you can pay each month's bill in full.

People sometimes ask me, "Should I keep all the budget money in a checking account?"

Should I Keep All the Budget Money in a Checking Account?

The first rule for your checking account should be to find one that pays interest.

Second, as a general rule of thumb, I recommend you keep the equivalent of one month's salary in your checking account. If your checking account balance consistently is more than the equivalent of one month's salary, you should transfer the surplus into a money market account where it will earn more than it does in your checking account. Most money market accounts allow you to write *only* three to five checks per month. However, some allow you to transfer funds between your checking and money market account several times each month.

When you need funds to pay for a large expense such as an annual life insurance premium, Christmas, or semiannual car insurance premium, you simply transfer funds out of your money market account into your checking account. After the funds have been transferred, you write the check out of your checkbook.

By using this plan, you are able to earn additional interest while having the money available for your use.

Note: If you are using a checking account and money market account, the formula to balance the budget is as follows:

Total of all MAP categories =
total of checking account balance + money market account balance

Investments

Except for short-term savings and emergency funds, investments are not kept "within" the MAP system. For example, if you are saving for retirement and put your money into an IRA, these funds are not a part of the MAP system anymore. In the long-term savings category of the sample MAP you will notice transfer on 3-10 was for $1,000, which was taken out and put into an IRA. IRAs and other investments should be accounted for on a personal balance sheet. Savings for college, if kept in a mutual fund, would also be accounted for outside the MAP system. Investment money just "flows through" the MAP; you initially put the funds in the MAP but later remove them from the system once the investment is purchased.

Now, for one of the most important questions: How do I begin my MAP for the first time?

How to Begin Your MAP

To begin, you will need a blank MAP (see pages 263–266).

1. On the first page, fill in the MAP categories and the amounts you have decided to budget for each one. It's easiest if you begin at the first of the month so you don't have to determine partial amounts to budget in each category.

2. Fill in all the category headings (food, clothes, giving, etc.) on the inside and back pages of your MAP.

3. Next, allocate your present checkbook balance into the MAP, allocating these funds into the various categories in the budget. You choose where you want to allocate the funds. You might choose to put a portion of these funds in food, giving, saving, clothing, or social.

4. Now the total of your checkbook balance should equal the total of all your MAP budget categories.

5. Finally, begin using the MAP as you make deposits and write checks, following the previous instructions.

How Should Flexible Income or Commissioned People Budget?

While speaking at my seminars I frequently hear, "But I don't receive the same income every month!" Those people who have an inconsistent income or income based upon commissions particularly need to budget! Base your MAP on an average month's income. During months of an income surplus, put away the surplus into short-term savings and during lesser months withdraw the difference from that same savings account.

For anyone, discipline is the key to budgeting. When your income for the month is high, put aside a portion of the income to supplement the income when it is low. The goal is to obtain a *consistent level of lifestyle* from month to month. If you have been incorrectly basing your budget on $2,500 in monthly income but only $2,000 is actually coming in, *change your lifestyle!*

Study the following example:

Determine the average monthly income you received during the prior year:

Jan	$3000	Feb	$2000	Mar	$2500
Apr	1000	May	1500	Jun	1700
Jul	2700	Aug	2400	Sep	4000
Oct	2000	Nov	500	Dec	2200

The average equals the total income divided by twelve: $2,125 per month. I would recommend that this family budget their giving, saving, and spending on $2,000 every month. Be very conservative when you operate on inconsistent income. It is easier to deal with a surplus each month than a shortfall!

The graph below shows why an inconsistent lifestyle can easily lead to *stress and depression* when the actual income drops below the budgeted income. One month you eat steak and lobster, the next hot dogs and chips.

CONSISTENT LIFESTYLE
Or, Emotional Roller Coaster

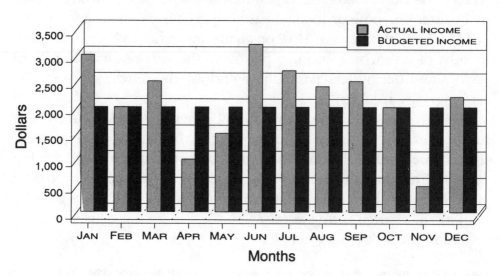

You need to have a money market account to store your surplus income.

How to Use a Money Market Account and a Checking Account

When more than $2,000 is earned, be faithful to deposit the excess earnings in a money market account.

When less than $2,000 is earned: Determine the shortfall. If you only earned $1,500 this month, the shortfall is $500. Therefore you will need to transfer $500 from the money market account into your checking account. The $1,500 in earnings plus the $500 from the money market account will equal your budgeted need of $2,000.

Study the chart on pages 261–262 and note that when income exceeds $2,000 for the month, we save the excess in a money market account. When the income is less than $2,000 we transfer money out of the money market account and put it into the checking account. First, let me explain what the various columns represent:

Income Column. Income received for the current month.

MM + Column. This is the amount of money to be deposited in the money market account. Determine this figure by taking the income for the month (i.e., $3,000 in January) and subtracting the planned budget amount ($2,000): $3,000 – $2,000 = $1,000.

MM – Column. This amount of money was transferred out of the money market and *into* the checking account to make up for the income shortfall for the month.

MM Bal. The current balance in the money market account each month is shown in this column. This money is available to be transferred into checking when income is less than $2,000 per month.

Checking Deposit. The total funds deposited into the checking account each month are shown here. This amount is either 100 percent of the income for the month or a combination of income and the money transferred from the money market. Notice the amount is *consistently* $2,000 every month.

	Income	MM +	MM –	MM Bal	Checking Deposit
Jan	$3000	$1000	$ 0	$1000	$2000
Feb	2000	0	0	1000	2000
Mar	2500	500	0	1500	2000
Apr	1000	0	1000	500	2000

	Income	MM +	MM −	MM Bal	Checking Deposit
May	$1500	$ 0	$ 500	$ 0	$2000
Jun	3200	1200	0	1200	2000
Jul	2700	700	0	1900	2000
Aug	2400	400	0	2300	2000
Sep	2500	500	0	2800	2000
Oct	2000	0	0	2800	2000
Nov	500	0	1500	1300	2000
Dec	2200	200	0	1500	2000

What If I Don't Have a Money Market Account?

If you don't have a money market account to fall back on, you have only one option. Allocate exactly what came in! Ask yourself, based upon the money I do have, how do I want to allocate it? *Don't use debt to live beyond your means!*

If this is your situation for more than three months, lower your planned budget allocations until the circumstances change!

Be faithful to be a good steward over the resources God has entrusted to you at this time. It is better to lower your standard of living and be realistic than to foolishly keep living at a level of income you are not presently earning. If and when your income increases, *then* you have the freedom to raise your budget allocations.

Your Own MAP Budget

On pages 263–266 you will find blank MAPS for your personal use. Due to the size of this book, the MAP charts are smaller than normal. The regular size is 8½ x 11. You can order a one-year supply of full-size MAPS by writing us at the address in the back of this book. We will send you an order form with current prices and information.

MONEY ALLOCATION PLAN

DATE	SOURCE OF INCOME	BUDGETED	NON-BUDGETED	TOTAL DEPOSIT
	TOTALS FOR MONTH	$	$	$

	ALLOCATION WORKSHEET									
	BUDGET $	DEPOSIT AMOUNTS FROM INCOME CHART ABOVE								
MAP CATEGORY	$	$	$	$	$	$	$	$	$	$

D / #	+	−	=	D / #	+	−	=	D / #	+	−	=	D / #	+	−	=
BB				BB				BB				BB			

D / #	+	−	=	D / #	+	−	=	D / #	+	−	=	D / #	+	−	=
BB				BB				BB				BB			

D / #	+	−	=	D / #	+	−	=	D / #	+	−	=	D / #	+	−	=
BB				BB				BB				BB			

D / #	+	−	=	D / #	+	−	=	D / #	+	−	=	D / #	+	−	=
BB				BB				BB				BB			

D / #	+	−	=	D / #	ITEM	+	−	=	D / #	ITEM	+	−	=
BB				BB					BB				
									D / #	ITEM	+	−	=
									BB				

	D / #	+	−	=	D / #	+	−	=	D / #	+	−	=
	BB				BB				BB			

C R E D I T   C A R D S

D / #	ITEM	Transfer From	CARD	PD	+	−	=
BB							

D / #	+	−	=	D / #	+	−	=	D / #	ITEM			+	−	=
BB				BB				BB						

D / #	+	−	=	D / #	+	−	=	D / #	ITEM			+	−	=
BB				BB				BB						

D / #	+	−	=	D / #	+	−	=	D / #	ITEM			+	−	=
BB				BB				BB						

D / #	+	−	=	D / #	+	−	=	D / #	ITEM			+	−	=
BB				BB				BB						

Remember, a MAP is intended to help you to accomplish three objectives:

1. Allow you to be generous in your giving.
2. Allow you to be consistent in your saving.
3. Allow you to find freedom in your spending.

The final habit of a smart money manager is having an eternal perspective. We'll look at that perspective and the war between the two economies in the world today in Chapter 14.

THE TWO ECONOMIES:
Which Will You Choose?

14

Two economies are prevalent in our world: God's economy and the world's economy. Two kinds of people also live in our world: those who know Jesus as Savior and those who do not (the Bible often calls a person like this a natural man).

The world's economy is based upon the world's wisdom, tradition, philosophy, and elementary principles. God's economy is based on the principles found in His Word, the Bible.

In 1 Corinthians 2:14 the apostle Paul tells us that the natural man believes the things of God are foolish. A "natural man" literally does not have the ability to understand the things of God. If you don't know Jesus as your Savior, you will think this chapter is foolish.

What is God's perspective on the "wisdom" this world has to

offer? We find our answer in 1 Corinthians 3:19: "For the wisdom of this world is foolishness with God."

So the natural man believes the things of God are foolish, and God states the wisdom of the world is foolish. The best way to illustrate this biblical truth is with the chart on page 271.

We all must ask ourselves the question, Am I living in God's economy or the world's economy? I believe there are seven reasons smart money managers choose to live in God's economy.

Seven Reasons to Live in God's Economy

1. God Owns It All

Psalm 24:1 clearly states the biblical perspective of ownership: "The earth is the LORD's, and all it contains, / The world, and those who dwell in it" (NAS).

Acknowledging that God owns it all is the foundational point in Christian money management and of living in God's economy. It all begins here. We cannot continue on until we totally accept this position.

Specifically, I am convinced that Christians cannot mature and become all that God wants them to become until they believe in their hearts that God owns it all and that they are stewards. They will remain spiritually and financially immature until they begin to apply this principle to their lives.

I remember when this truth became a reality in my life. Within one week's time, our dishwasher and washing machine were in need of repair. I called the repair man, and he came to fix our appliances. After I wrote a check for a rather large amount, I thought to myself, _It all belongs to God. If He wants to take His money to repair His dishwasher and washing machine, that's okay with me!_

TWO ECONOMIES

	God's Economy	World's Economy
Natural Man	Foolish	Wise
Christian	Wise	Foolish

2. Life Is Short

Just look at how the Word of God describes man's brief condition while on earth:

> *For He knows our frame;*
> *He remembers that we are dust.*
>
> *As for man, his days are like grass;*
> *As a flower of the field, so he flourishes.*
> *For the wind passes over it, and it is gone,*
> *And its place remembers it no more. (Ps. 103:14–16)*

"You do not know what will happen tomorrow. For what is your life? It is even a vapor that appears for a little time and then vanishes away" (James 4:14).

Have you ever considered how short life is compared to eternity? Imagine a line that extends from eternity past to eternity future. Now take a sharp pencil and put a dot on the line:

The line stands for eternity, and the dot represents our time here on earth. Stand back and take a good look at the line and the dot, then ask yourself the question: "What am I living for—the line or the dot?"

In reality, our time on earth—even if we live to be one hundred years old—is like a flash compared with eternity. The question we all need to ask is, "How am I using every day between my first and last breath?"

Several years ago, after teaching this concept in a seminar, a CPA came up to me and said this truth had literally changed his life! He commented that he had been a faithful church member and committed Christian, but he had never been challenged to live his daily life with an eternal perspective.

If you believe there is a God and an eternity, then live your life accordingly. This should affect how you give, save, and use your money. An individual without an eternal perspective will not be as excited about investing financially in the kingdom of God as someone who lives for eternity. The reason is quite obvious. We are indeed just sojourners on this earth, passing through on our way to our eternal home.

3. *You Can't Take It with You*

When you die, your brief life on this earth has vanished away. At that point, it makes absolutely no difference how much any of us has accumulated. We exit without anything (see 1 Tim. 6:7). All of our hard-earned possessions are left behind. Solomon had an interesting perspective on the topic of leaving our possessions behind:

Then I hated all my labor in which I had toiled under the sun, because I must leave it to the man who will come after me. And who knows whether he will be wise or a fool? Yet he will rule over all my labor in which I toiled and in which I have shown myself wise under the sun. This also is vanity. (Eccles. 2:18–19)

Jesus reminds us, "For what profit is it to a man if he gains the whole world, and loses his own soul?" (Matt. 16:26).

So what if you owned the entire world but did not know Jesus as your Savior? From an eternal perspective, owning everything is insignificant compared with knowing Jesus (see Phil. 3:8).

Now, I am not saying that operating a business, being a surgeon, or a schoolteacher, or any other kind of honest worker is not important. These roles are very important in God's economy! And I am not saying that having investments and owning a home are not important in God's economy. They are! The goal is to keep them in the right perspective!

When Howard Hughes died, someone asked his accountant, "How much money did he leave?" The response was, "All of it!"

You've probably seen the bumper sticker that states, "He who dies with the most toys wins." My question is "Wins what?"

Earthly kingdoms have come and gone for centuries. Nations rise and fall. Family names and wealth come and go as history marches on. Our little kingdom that we are building in one corner of the world will be no different . . . unless we choose to make it different by investing our lives in eternity.

4. *Our Citizenship Is in Heaven*

Another reason to live for eternity is that our true citizenship, our real home, is in heaven (see Phil. 3:20). In Hebrews 11 the author reminded the early Christians of their great forefathers—Enoch, Noah, and Abraham, to name a few—and then he said:

> These all died in faith, not having received the promises, but having seen them afar off were assured of them, embraced them and confessed that they were strangers and pilgrims on the earth. For those who say such things declare plainly that they seek a homeland. And truly if they had called to mind that country from which they had come out, they would have had opportunity to return. But now they desire a better, that is, a heavenly country. Therefore God is not ashamed to be called their God, for He has prepared a city for them. (Heb. 11:13–16)

I don't know about you, but I'm ready to claim my citizenship in the city God has prepared for me.

5. We Are Commanded to Have an Eternal Perspective

The apostle Paul taught the Colossians to set their minds on things above:

> If then you were raised with Christ, seek those things which are above, where Christ is, sitting at the right hand of God. Set your mind on things above, not on things on the earth. (Col. 3:1–2)

A smart money manager has this eternal perspective.

6. One Day We Will Give an Accounting

One day every person will stand before the Lord and give an accounting of his or her life! The apostle Paul warned the Corinthian

Christians, "For we must all appear before the judgment seat of Christ" (2 Cor. 5:10).

And he also told the early Roman Christians, "So then each of us shall give account of himself to God" (Rom. 14:12). When you give an accounting, what will you say? Did you live for God every day of your life? Did you honor God in your business and ministry? Did you faithfully live in God's economy?

7. The Great Commission

Being involved in helping fulfill the Great Commission is one aspect of living in God's economy. Jesus said,

> Go therefore and make disciples of all the nations, baptizing them in the name of the Father and of the Son and of the Holy Spirit, teaching them to observe all things that I have commanded you; and lo, I am with you always, even to the end of the age. (Matt. 28:19–20)

It will take people and money to fulfill this Great Commission. Yet there is ample wealth in the world today to do so. Just think what would happen if every Christian began to faithfully support the fulfillment of Jesus' Great Commission. If the money were available, we have the know-how and strategies to take the gospel to everyone in the world. The *only* thing holding us back is the money. Living in God's economy involves a commitment to help fulfill the Great Commission with your financial support!

Does this mean we should be doing everything different from the world? No, it just means that our perspective may be different. For a Christian to live in the world's economy is foolish. Our goal is to be living in God's economy.

Study the chart below to develop a better understanding of how the two economies are different. You will find a variety of areas to compare.

TWO ECONOMIES: THE WORLD'S AND GOD'S

Area	World's Economy	God's Economy	Scripture
Provision	Financial independence	God is provider	Philippians 4:19
Financial security	Comes from accumulation	Comes from God	1 Timothy 6:17
Mind-set	Earthly things	Heavenly things	Colossians 3:2
Possessions	100 percent mine	100 percent God's	Psalm 24:1
Problems/anxiety	Keep/all mine	Give to God	Philippians 4:6–8
Financial freedom	External circumstances	Internal	John 8:32
Store treasures	On earth	In heaven	Matthew 6:19–20
Treasures	Will rot/can be stolen	Safe/do not rot	Matthew 6:19–20
Body	Belongs to self	Belongs to God	1 Corinthians 3:16
Citizenship	Country	In heaven	Philippians 3:20
Who to serve?	Self/mammon	God	Matthew 6:24
View of debt	Get all you can	Avoid/be careful	Proverbs 22:7
Life spent	Acquiring things	Serving God	Matthew 16:26
Perspective	Worldly	Eternal	Philippians 3:7–14
Standards	Set by others/world	Word of God	2 Timothy 3:16–17
Death	Not prepared	Prepared	Hebrews 9:27–28
Goals	Short-range/100 years	Long-range/eternal	Hebrews 11:13–16
Giving	Token/2 percent	Generous	2 Corinthians 8–9
Hope	False hope	Real security	Proverbs 23:4–5

As you can see, one economy offers false hope while the other offers real security. One offers frustration while the other offers a peace that can only come from God. One is temporal while the other is eternal.

As Christians, we have a choice in how we live. If we choose to live in the world's economy as Christians, we will be frustrated every day of our lives. We will never be content and never find the abundant life Jesus promised in John 10:10.

Which Will You Choose?

I challenge you to hesitate no longer. Elijah's challenge to the people concerning Baal is equally relevant to each of us today: "How long will you hesitate between two opinions? If the LORD is God, follow Him; but if Baal, follow him" (1 Kings 18:21 NAS).

The issue in life is not the size of your investment portfolio or your position within the company. The real issue is: In whom are you placing your trust? Solomon said, "For who can eat or enjoy apart from him?" (Eccles. 2:25 TLB). It is Jesus who brings meaning and enjoyment to life.

Where are your real priorities in life? Remember, God does not condemn wealth itself. It is the misuse of wealth and the wrong attitude toward it that displeases God.

Look at the following lists of attitudes and character qualities of Christians living in the world's economy compared with those of Christians living in God's economy:

Christians living in the world's economy . . .

- Find ultimate security in money and possessions.
- Abuse the use of debt and credit.
- Live beyond their means.
- Are financially frustrated due to lack of direction.
- Never seem to have enough . . . always want more.
- Look for quick solutions or get-rich-quick schemes.
- Have little desire to give to the Lord's work.
- Have no savings, or hoard money.
- Suffer guilt feelings.
- Live in bondage to their money or their possessions.

Now compare these attitudes with Christians living in God's economy:

Christians living in God's economy . . .

- Find ultimate security in God alone.
- Control or avoid credit/debt.
- Live within their means.
- Have clearly established goals.
- Are content.
- Are generous givers.
- Save consistently.
- Suffer no guilt feelings for how money is managed.
- Live in freedom.

I am fully convinced that people who are actively seeking to live in God's economy will give, save, and spend their money in a different manner. Their eternal perspective has to affect the way they view life on this earth and how they view money.

Life is too short and eternity too long not to be making the right decisions today.

Secret Service agents are trained to spot counterfeit currency by spending hundreds of hours studying authentic bills. Why? They know if they study the real thing, they will be able to easily spot a fake! Be ready to see through the philosophy, deception, tradition, and elementary principles the world has to offer you (see Col. 2:8).

If you have never been challenged to live for eternity, let me challenge you today. Make your life count for Christ! It does not matter if you are a businessperson, physician, pianist, professor, police officer, president, politician, or preacher. Be committed to make every day count for Christ.

Not everyone is called to work in a ministry vocation. But you can still serve God effectively every day of your life. Your service to God will be in the way you treat people, in the way you make decisions, in your honesty in dealing with people, and in your faithfulness to support the kingdom of God financially.

Do you believe there really is a God? If you do, then live every day like you believe it.

Life is too short and eternity too long not to be making the right decisions today. Press on, my friend, because smart people make smart decisions!

YOUR PERSONAL FINANCIAL PLAN:

An Accurate Forecast of Your Future

15

Here is where you begin to pull it all together. You have read, you have learned many new financial concepts, you have processed the information, and now you are ready to roll up your sleeves and get to work on your own personal financial plan.

It is possible that you already worked through many of the worksheets included in this chapter when they appeared earlier in this book. However, you will also find some *new information* here—worksheets or questions you have not seen up to this point. On the other hand, you cannot just work through this chapter alone and obtain all the concepts presented in this book. I have provided all the worksheets here, but you must read the expanded instructions in the appropriate chapters to fully understand how to use them.

I have included this chapter for two primary reasons. First, I want to put all the worksheets in one location so they are convenient for you to use. You will need them as you work on your complete financial plan now and in years to come. Next year and for years after that, you can turn to this chapter and review your financial plan.

Second, financial planning is not a once-in-a-lifetime event. It is a process you set into motion at some point and evaluate repeatedly throughout your entire life. The earlier in life you begin the process, the more success you will have.

This chapter will help you evaluate what you have done in the past, determine exactly where you are today, and then decide where you want to be in the future. It is one thing to know how to manage your money; it is another thing to apply your knowledge.

For couples, this planning time gets you involved in the communication process.

On the pages that follow you will find an eleven-step financial planning process. When you finish the last step, you will have completed a basic financial plan for your family. As mentioned earlier, you should work through this planning process at least once every year.

Before we begin, let's look at all eleven steps, the "big picture" of financial planning, most of which are reflected by the Biblical Financial Planning Concept chart on page 283.

The Biblical Financial Planning Concept

Let's begin at the bottom of the chart and work through the steps, one by one.

1. Know the Word of God

This is the foundation to the entire plan. The Word of God is our ultimate standard and authority in life. Any other foundation will crumble (see Matt. 7:24–28).

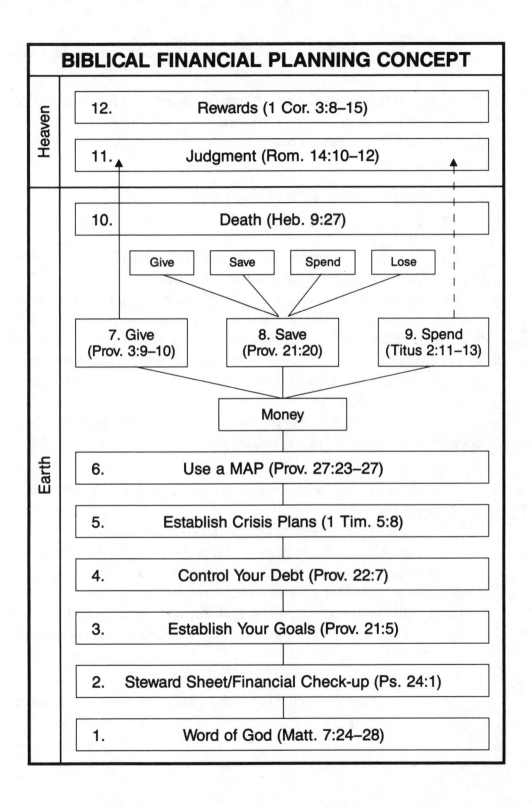

Begin your planning time with prayer, asking God for His wisdom. Financial planning depends on making wise decisions, and true wisdom is found in the Bible (James 1:5–8).

2. *Your Steward Sheet (Your Personal Balance Sheet)*

The second step involves putting together what I call a "steward sheet." (The accounting name for this is a balance sheet.)

I see this step as gathering the facts. You are trying to pull together your overall financial picture, which is a snapshot of your present financial condition. Here you list your assets (the things you own). Your liabilities (what you owe). And you list your equity/net worth (what you're worth). Listing these items helps you determine exactly what you have to manage.

Balance Sheet Benefits. Your balance sheet can be very beneficial to you as you develop your financial plan:

1. It shows you how much debt you have incurred, compared to what you own.
2. It helps you establish financial trends in your life.
3. It can help you make giving, saving, and purchasing decisions.
4. It helps you view your situation in a realistic way.
5. It helps you find potential problems.
6. It helps you find assets you had forgotten you owned.
7. It can be used to summarize your financial condition for your spouse.

Look through the following list to determine your assets and liabilities:

Assets: What You Own.

____ Cash and cash equivalents: Cash, savings accounts, money market funds, checking accounts.

____ Invested assets: CDs, stocks, mutual funds, IRAs, real estate, corporate bonds, U.S. savings bonds, silver, gold, stamp collections.

____ Use assets: Home, car, furniture, clothes, personal property, jewelry.

Use the current market value for your assets. Do not use what you paid for them.

I am often asked, "Should I list my life insurance as an asset?" If it is whole life or universal life, list the present cash value. Term life insurance has no cash value and therefore should not be listed.

Now look through the list of liabilities to determine what you owe.

Liabilities: What You Owe.

____ Short-term: Payable in full in less than one year—credit cards, personal notes.

____ Long-term: Payable in full in more than one year—home mortgage, business debt, personal debt.

Use the principal balance. What do you owe today?

Equity: What You Are Worth.

(Assets − Liabilities = Equity/net worth.)

If you sold all your assets and paid off all your debt, what would you have left?

I am often asked, "How often should a person prepare a balance sheet?" I always reply, "At the minimum, once a year, and preferably semiannually or quarterly, depending upon your financial situation."

YOUR PERSONAL BALANCE SHEET

_____

_____

ASSETS (what you own)

Cash and Cash Equivalents:

Cash in pocket $_____
Checkbook(s)   _____
Money market(s)   _____
Savings account(s)   _____
Other: _____   _____

Total cash and cash equivalents $_____(A1)

Invested Assets:

CDs $_____
Stocks   _____
Real estate   _____
Mutual funds   _____
IRAs   _____
Coin collection   _____
Business interest   _____
Life insurance   _____
Savings bonds   _____
Pensions   _____
Notes receivable   _____
Antiques   _____
Bonds   _____
Gold/silver   _____
Other: _____   _____

Total invested assets $_____(A2)

Use Assets:

Residence	$_____
Automobile(s)	_____
Personal items	_____
Misc. inventory	_____
Furniture	_____
Total use assets	$_____ (A3)

TOTAL ASSETS (A1 + A2 + A3) $_____ (A4)

LIABILITIES (what you owe)

Short-Term:

Credit cards	$_____
Personal loans	_____
School loans	_____
Total short-term liabilities	$_____ (L1)

Long-Term:

Home mortgage(s)	$_____
Car loan(s)	_____
Personal loan(s)	_____
School loan(s)	_____
Business loan(s)	_____
Total long-term liabilities	$_____ (L2)

TOTAL LIABILITIES (L1 + L2) $_____ (L3)

EQUITY (what you are worth)

Total Assets − Total Liabilities = Equity (A4 − L3) $_____ (E1)

Once you have filled out your balance sheet, proceed to the Balance Sheet Ratios chart on page 288, which will help you determine how you are presently doing. In my opinion it is best to be debt free, but if you do have debt, this chart will help you see if it is too much.

For example, let me show you how to analyze an individual's ratio of total assets to total debts. First, divide your total assets by your total debt. For example, if you have $200,000 in assets and $125,000 in debt your ratio would be 1.6 ($200,000 ÷ $125,000 = 1.6).

Looking at the chart, you would find this is "okay." If you have a ratio less than 1.0, the chart will tell you, "You are in danger."

You can also use the chart to analyze your short-term debt.

BALANCE SHEET RATIOS

Total Asset to Total Debt Ratio:

Total Assets $_____(A4) ÷ Total Debt $_____(L3) = _____

Ratio	Result
Less than 1	DANGER!
1.00–2.00	okay
2.01–5.00	good
More than 5	best

Liquid Cash (cash and cash equivalents) to Short-Term Debt Ratio:

Cash and Cash Equivalents $_____(A1) ÷ Short-Term Debt $_____(L1) = _____

Ratio	Result
Less than 1	DANGER!
1.00	okay
1.01–2.00	good
More than 2	great

What is your total asset to total debt ratio? _____

What is your cash and cash equivalent to short-term debt ratio? _____

What changes are necessary?

Next, give yourself a financial checkup. For a detailed explanation of the financial checkup, refer to Chapter 1.

By giving yourself this checkup you will have a good feel for the basic ingredients that are in place—and those that are still missing. The bottom line: It will tell you how you are doing overall.

Don't be discouraged if you don't score high right now. However, after several months or a year, you should be making good progress.

FINANCIAL CHECKUP

_____ I have the equivalent of one month's salary in savings available for a crisis. (10 points for more, 5 points for one month, and 0 points for no savings)

_____ I have no outstanding *past-due* bills. (5 points for a yes)

_____ I save money each month to pay for major expenses like Christmas or car insurance. (5 points for a yes)

_____ I have written financial goals for my life. (5 points for a yes)

_____ I am prepaying on my mortgage to quickly reduce the debt and save on interest. Or my house is completely debt free. (5 points for a yes)

_____ I have insurance on my car(s). (5 points for a yes)

_____ I have insurance on my home or apartment. (5 points for a yes)

_____ I have health insurance. (5 points for a yes)

_____ I have disability insurance. (5 points for a yes)

_____ If you are earning income, do you have life insurance coverage equivalent to at least five times your annual income? (5 points for a yes)

_____ I have filled out a personal balance sheet within the last twelve months. (5 points for a yes)

_____ I have a written budget that I use every week/month. (5 points for a yes)

_____ There is no tension or stress in our family over money issues. (5 points for a yes, 3 points for some, 0 points for much tension)

_____ I have a legal will. (If married, both the husband and wife have wills.) (5 points for a yes)

_____ I have a regular savings plan for salary income. Do not consider company pension plans in answering this question. (1 point for each percent of salary saved, with a maximum of 10 points)

_____ I am involved and take advantage of my company pension savings plan. (5 for yes or company offers no plan, 3 for one spouse involved, 0 for no involvement in an offered plan)

_____ I make charitable contributions. (5 points for 10 percent, 2 points for 5 percent, 0 points for less)

_____ I pay all my credit card bills in full every month. (5 points for a yes, 0 points for a no)

_____ Write your total here, then mark your score below:

0	10	20	30	40	50	60	70	80	90	100

Critical Condition   Danger   Poor   Fair   Good   Excellent

What areas do you need to work on in order to receive a 90 + score on your financial checkup? List them below:

☐ _____

☐ _____

☐ _____
☐ _____
☐ _____

It is only after compiling your steward sheet and taking a financial checkup that you can even think about moving to the next step in your financial plan: establishing your financial goals.

3. Establish Your Goals

Next to having the Word of God as our foundation, I consider this step one of the most important aspects of the entire plan. We begin this step with the Husband and Wife's Goal-Setting Exercises (refer to Chapter 2). If you are married, each spouse should do this exercise. Two forms have been provided. Do not let your spouse see your answers until you both have finished. Once you finish, compare your lists.

HUSBAND'S GOAL-SETTING EXERCISE

Establish your priorities (from 1 to 17) on the following list, making your highest priority number 1. You cannot use a number more than once. You must rank all 17!

1. _____ Pay for college expenses for our children.

2. _____ Pay off all credit card debt.

3. _____ Pay off home mortgage.

4. _____ Pay off business debt.

5. _____ Leave our children an inheritance.

6. _____ Plan for retirement financial needs.

7. _____ Increase our giving.

8. _____ Major purchase of _____ (home, furniture, etc.).

9. _____ Buy a car or van.

10. _____ Send our children to Christian school.

11. _____ Move to a new home.

12. _____ Start a new business.

13. _____ Have more children.

14. _____ Operate our family finances on a budget.

15. _____ Accumulate a specific amount of money.

16. _____ Take annual family vacations.

17. _____ Enjoy an annual getaway as a couple.

WIFE'S GOAL-SETTING EXERCISE

Establish your priorities (from 1 to 17) on the following list, making your highest priority number 1. You cannot use a number more than once. You must rank all 17!

1. _____ Pay for college expenses for our children.

2. _____ Pay off all credit card debt.

3. _____ Pay off home mortgage.

4. _____ Pay off business debt.

5. _____ Leave our children an inheritance.

6. _____ Plan for retirement financial needs.

7. ___ Increase our giving.

8. ___ Major purchase of _____ (home, furniture, etc.).

9. ___ Buy a car or van.

10. ___ Send our children to Christian school.

11. ___ Move to a new home.

12. ___ Start a new business.

13. ___ Have more children.

14. ___ Operate our family finances on a budget.

15. ___ Accumulate a specific amount of money.

16. ___ Take annual family vacations.

17. ___ Enjoy an annual getaway as a couple.

Now look at your answer sheets together. Do you have the same priorities?   Yes ___   No ___

What did you learn from this exercise? _____
_____
_____
_____
_____
_____
_____
_____
_____

CAR WORKSHEET 1
CARS-FOR-CASH WHILE
ACCUMULATING SAVINGS

Many factors could enter into this decision, such as present loan rates and what your savings will be able to earn each year, but by using the calculations below, you will be headed in the right direction.

First, determine how often you would like to buy your new cars. Will it be once every three, four, five, or six years? Second, determine the general price of the cars you plan to purchase each time. Once you know these two factors, you can determine the amount you need to *pay yourself* each month.

CAR SAVINGS
CALCULATION CHART

Years	Factor
Three-year plan	32.27
Four-year plan	25.37
Five-year plan	21.25
Six-year plan	18.53

Let's work a sample problem to show how to use this chart. Suppose you want to buy a $14,000 car on the four-year plan.

1. Price of Car : *$14,000 ÷ 1,000 = $14.00* (a)

2. Multiply (a) (which, in this case, is *$14.00*) × the appropriate factor from the Car Savings Calculation Chart (in this case, *25.37*) = *$355.18,* the amount you need to save each month.

Now work this calculation for your own car:

1. Price of Car : $_____ ÷ 1,000 = $_____ (a)

2. Multiply (a) _____ × the appropriate factor from the Car Savings Calculation Chart _____ = $_____, the amount you need to save each month.

To establish accurate financial goals, you will need to complete these financial planning worksheets: a car worksheet, a college funding worksheet, and a retirement planning worksheet.

Details for completing the car worksheet are found in Chapter 6; the other worksheets are self-explanatory.

CAR WORKSHEET 2
CARS-FOR-CASH WITHOUT
ACCUMULATING SAVINGS

But what if you don't want a savings program built into your car-purchasing savings plan? If not, here is another car-for-cash plan that allows you to save enough money on a monthly basis to buy your next car for cash. This worksheet *does not allow for any buildup of savings.* You will simply have enough money to purchase your next car for cash.

CARS-FOR-CASH WITHOUT
ACCUMULATING SAVINGS

Step One: Selling price of a new or used car $ 8,000 (1)

Step Two: Trade-in or selling price of your present car $ 2,500 (2)

Step Three: Dollars needed to buy car (line 1 minus line 2) $ 5,500 (3)

Step Four: Number of years until purchase   4 (4)

Step Five: Interest rate you can earn on money   8 (5)

Step Six: Use the Monthly Savings Table (page 296) to find the appropriate division factor by using information in lines 4 and 5: Factor: 56.26 (6)

Step Seven: Divide the dollars needed to buy the car (line 3) by the factor from the Monthly Savings Table (line 6) to determine how much you need to save each month to buy a car for cash: $ 97.76 (7)

$5,500 ÷ 56.26 = $97.76, the amount you need to save each month.

TABLE A
MONTHLY SAVINGS TABLE

(This is a condensed chart of interest rates and years;
see Table A in Appendix A for more interest rates and years.)

Years Until Purchase	Projected Interest Rate				
	6%	8%	9%	10%	12%
1	12.34	12.45	12.51	12.56	12.68
2	25.43	25.91	26.19	26.44	26.97
3	39.34	40.49	41.15	41.76	43.08
4	54.10	56.26	57.52	58.67	61.22
5	68.77	73.32	75.42	77.36	81.67
6	86.41	91.79	95.01	97.98	104.71
7	104.07	111.78	116.43	120.77	130.67
8	122.83	133.40	139.86	145.92	159.93
9	142.74	156.81	165.48	173.70	192.89
10	163.88	182.13	193.51	204.38	230.04

Now fill in your own car worksheet.

Step One: Selling price of a new/used car $_____(1)

Step Two: Trade-in or selling price of your current car $_____(2)

Step Three: Dollars needed to buy car (line 1 minus line 2) $_____(3)

Step Four: Number of years until purchase   _____(4)

Step Five: Interest rate you can earn on money   ____%__(5)

Step Six: Division factor from Monthly Savings Table (use information in lines 4 and 5) Factor: _____(6)

Step Seven: Divide the dollars needed to buy the car (line 3) by the factor from the Monthly Savings Table (line 6) to determine how much you need to save each month to buy a car for cash.

Savings needed each month: $_____(7)

Do you need to plan for college expenses?

COLLEGE FUNDING WORKSHEET

This worksheet must be calculated annually to account for increasing expenses due to inflation. Use one worksheet for each child.

Step One:	Child's current age:	_____
Step Two:	Number of years until college (18 − child's age):	_____
Step Three:	Annual college costs:	$_____
Step Four:	Total cost of college (Step 3 × 4 years):	$_____
Step Five:	Percent of college expenses to be paid by parents:	_____%
Step Six:	Total savings needed (Step 4 × percentage in Step 5):	$_____
Step Seven:	Present college savings:	$_____
Step Eight:	Value of current savings when college begins (multiply Step 7 × appropriate projected interest rate from Table D on page 299):	$_____
Step Nine:	Additional savings needed (Step 6 − Step 8):	$_____
Step Ten:	Find monthly savings factor in Table A on page 298:	$_____
Step Eleven:	Monthly savings needed to fund college expenses (Divide Step 9 by factor found in Step 10):	$_____
Step Twelve:	Total monthly savings needed for all children:	$_____

TABLE A
MONTHLY SAVINGS FACTORS
FOR PROJECTED INTEREST RATES

(Note: A more in-depth version of Table A can
be found in Appendix A.)

Yrs. Till College	8%	10%	12%
1	12.45	12.56	12.68
2	25.91	26.44	26.97
3	40.49	41.76	43.08
4	56.26	58.67	61.22
5	73.32	77.36	81.67
6	91.79	97.98	104.71
7	111.78	120.77	130.67
8	133.40	145.92	159.93
9	156.81	173.70	192.89
10	182.13	204.38	230.04
11	209.54	238.25	271.90
12	239.19	275.66	319.06
13	271.29	316.97	372.21
14	306.01	362.58	432.10
15	343.59	412.95	499.58
16	384.56	468.57	575.62
17	428.27	530.00	661.31

TABLE D
FUTURE VALUE FACTORS

(Note: A more in-depth version of Table D can
be found in Appendix A.)

Yrs. Till College	8%	10%	12%
1	1.08	1.10	1.12
2	1.17	1.21	1.25
3	1.26	1.33	1.40
4	1.36	1.46	1.57
5	1.47	1.61	1.76
6	1.59	1.77	1.97
7	1.71	1.95	2.21
8	1.85	2.14	2.48
9	2.00	2.36	2.77
10	2.16	2.59	3.11
11	2.33	2.85	3.48
12	2.52	3.14	3.90
13	2.72	3.45	4.36
14	2.94	3.80	4.89
15	3.17	4.18	5.47
16	3.43	4.59	6.13
17	3.70	5.05	6.87

RETIREMENT PLANNING WORKSHEET

*To account for inflation and investment returns, this worksheet needs to be calculated
each year to account for inflation, current return on investments, and salary trends.*

1. Present salary $_____(1)

2. Multiply line 1 times .8 (or 80 percent) $_____(2)

3. Total retirement income expected (in today's dollars)
   Estimated annual pension plan $_____

Estimated annual social security $_____

Total $_____(3)

4. Income gap (line 2 minus line 3) $_____(4)

5. Lump sum needed at beginning of retirement to fund annual cash needs (Multiply line 4 times 19.60) $_____(5)

6. Current assets available/assigned for retirement (IRA, 401k) $_____(6)

7. Value of current assets when retirement begins (Multiply line 6 times Factor found in Table D on the following page (301). $_____(7)

8. Capital gap at beginning of retirement (line 5 minus line 7) $_____(8)

9. MONTHLY savings needed to make up for gap found in line 8 (Divide line 8 by Factor found in Table A on page 301.) (Use years till retirement on Table A.) $_____(9)

10. Multiply line 9 times 12 to determine ANNUAL savings needed $_____(10)

NOTES:

Line 2: You will need less income because you should have no mortgage, the kids have finished college, etc.

Line 3: Ask your employer for pension plan projections. Call 1-800-772-1213 for social security projections.

Line 5: This is the amount you need at the beginning of retirement in order to withdraw annually the amount calculated on line 4. We are assuming an 8 percent return on investment, 5 percent inflation, and thirty years of withdrawals (from age sixty-five to ninety-five). Use Table C in Appendix A to adjust any of these assumptions.

Line 7: At a growth rate of 8 percent, this is the future value of your present investments allocated for retirement. (Use Table D in the Appendix to change the growth rate.)

Line 8: This amount represents the difference between what you will have (line 7) and what you will need (line 5).

Line 9: This calculation tells you how much you need to save each month in order to make up the "gap."

Years Till Retirement	Table A 8%	Table D 8%
10	$ 182.13	$ 2.16
15	343.59	3.17
20	583.20	4.66
25	938.75	6.85
30	1,466.38	10.06
35	2,249.33	14.79
40	3,411.20	21.72

What are some other specific financial goals (in addition to cars, college, and retirement) that you would like to accomplish? How much do you need to be saving each month in order to accomplish them?

See Chapter 3 for establishing goals using the time value of money tables.

Goal 1. _____

Which table will you use?
____ Monthly Savings Table
____ Inflation Table
____ Annual Outflow Table
____ Future Value Table
____ Present Value Table
____ Annual Savings Table

Answer: _____

Goal 2. _____

Which table will you use?
____ Monthly Savings Table
____ Inflation Table
____ Annual Outflow Table

_____ Future Value Table
_____ Present Value Table
_____ Annual Savings Table

Answer: _____

Goal 3. _____

Which table will you use?
_____ Monthly Savings Table
_____ Inflation Table
_____ Annual Outflow Table
_____ Future Value Table
_____ Present Value Table
_____ Annual Savings Table

Answer: _____

Goal 4. _____

Which table will you use?
_____ Monthly Savings Table
_____ Inflation Table
_____ Annual Outflow Table
_____ Future Value Table
_____ Present Value Table
_____ Annual Savings Table

Answer: _____

Goal 5. _____

Which table will you use?
_____ Monthly Savings Table
_____ Inflation Table
_____ Annual Outflow Table

_____ Future Value Table
_____ Present Value Table
_____ Annual Savings Table

Answer: _____

So far you know what you have (the Steward Sheet) and you know where you are going (Goals). Your next step is to be sure you are controlling your debt or getting out of debt as soon as possible.

4. Debt Analysis

My advice concerning debt is simple and straightforward: Control your present debt, and if you are in debt, get out as fast as possible. Refer to the following chapters concerning debt: Chapter 4 (credit cards); Chapter 5 (mortgages); Chapter 6 (cars); Chapter 7 (living debt free). Now you have an opportunity to analyze your own debt.

Calculate the total cost of your present mortgage.

$_____	×	12	×	_____	=	$_____
Monthly Payment				# Years of Mortgage		Total Cost

Calculate the total cost of your car loan(s).

$_____	×	12	×	_____	=	$_____
Monthly Payment				# Years of Car Loan		Total Cost
$_____	×	12	×	_____	=	$_____
Monthly Payment				# Years of Car Loan		Total Cost

My debt-free goal date: _____

Begin a prepayment schedule on your mortgage.

How much can I increase my payment each month? $_____

When will I begin? _____

What is my total credit card debt?

Name	Amount Due
_____	$_____
_____	_____
_____	_____
_____	_____
_____	_____
_____	_____
_____	_____
TOTAL	$_____

Summary of credit card debt history:

19____ $_____
19____   _____
19____   _____
19____   _____
19____   _____

Is my credit card debt increasing or decreasing each year?

How much can I allocate each month to pay off my credit card debt?
$_____

What item(s) do we plan to use credit cards for?

What item(s) are not acceptable for us to use them for?

DEBT ANALYSIS WORKSHEET

Monthly net income: $_____(a)

Consumer debt payments:

_____ $_____

_____ $_____

_____ $_____

_____ $_____

_____ $_____

     Total $_____(b)

Mortgage debt payment:

_____ $_____

_____ $_____

     Total mortgage debt $_____(c)

Total consumer and mortgage debt: $_____(d)

How are you doing with consumer debt?

(Total consumer debt ÷ net income)

$_____(b) ÷ $_____(a) = _____ OR _____%

(Check Debt Guideline Chart on page 306 for answer.)

Answer: _____

How are you doing in mortgage debt?

(Total mortgage ÷ net income)

$_____(c) ÷ $_____(a) = _____ OR _____%

(Check Debt Guideline Chart on page 306 for answer.)

Answer: _____

How are you doing in your combined debt?

(Consumer and mortgage debt ÷ net income)

$_____(d) ÷ $_____(a) = _____ OR _____%

(Check Debt Guideline Chart below for answer.)

Answer: _____

DEBT GUIDELINE CHART

	Best	Good	OK	Danger
Consumer	0%	1–6%	7–14%	15 + %
Mortgage	0%	1–19%	20–28%	29 + %
Combined	0%	1–21%	22–35%	37 + %

The following notes should be helpful as you use the Debt Guideline Chart.

1. Percentages should be based on your net income (take-home pay).
2. Consumer debt includes things such as cars, appliances, and furniture purchased on credit.
3. Mortgage debt is what you owe for the home you are living in. How much is your mortgage payment each month?
4. Use this chart as a general guideline, not as an absolute rule.
5. If you receive a high "OK" or "Danger" signal, changes are in order.

MORTGAGE MONTHLY PAYMENT WORKSHEET

1. Amount of loan: $_____ ÷ 1,000 = _____(a)

2. On the chart on page 307, find the factor corresponding to your interest rate and term. Your interest rate is _____% and the term (years for the loan) is _____, so your factor is _____(b).

3. Multiply (a) _____ × (b) _____ = $_____ monthly payment.

MORTGAGE MONTHLY PAYMENT CHART

Interest Rate	Years of Loan		Interest Rate	Years of Loan	
	15 Factor	30 Factor		15 Factor	30 Factor
4.00	7.40	4.77	11.00	11.37	9.52
4.25	7.52	4.92	11.25	11.52	9.71
4.50	7.65	5.07	11.50	11.68	9.90
4.75	7.78	5.22	11.75	11.84	10.09
5.00	7.91	5.37	12.00	12.00	10.29
5.25	8.04	5.52	12.25	12.16	10.48
5.50	8.17	5.68	12.50	12.33	10.67
5.75	8.30	5.84	12.75	12.49	10.87
6.00	8.44	6.00	13.00	12.65	11.06
6.25	8.57	6.16	13.25	12.82	11.26
6.50	8.71	6.32	13.50	12.98	11.45
6.75	8.85	6.49	13.75	13.15	11.65
7.00	8.99	6.65	14.00	13.32	11.85
7.25	9.13	6.82	14.25	13.49	12.05
7.50	9.27	6.99	14.50	13.66	12.25
7.75	9.41	7.16	14.75	13.83	12.45
8.00	9.56	7.34	15.00	14.00	12.64
8.25	9.70	7.51	15.25	14.17	12.85
8.50	9.85	7.69	15.50	14.34	13.05
8.75	9.99	7.87	15.75	14.51	13.25
9.00	10.14	8.05	16.00	14.69	13.45
9.25	10.29	8.23	16.25	14.86	13.65
9.50	10.44	8.41	16.50	15.04	13.85
9.75	10.59	8.59	16.75	15.21	14.05
10.00	10.75	8.78	17.00	15.39	14.26
10.25	10.90	8.96	17.25	15.57	14.46
10.50	11.05	9.15	17.50	15.75	14.66
10.75	11.21	9.33	17.75	15.92	14.87

HOW MUCH MORTGAGE CAN I AFFORD?

1. What is your total monthly gross (before taxes) income? $_____(1)

2. Total monthly payment of all present loans (car, school, credit cards) $_____(2)

3. Maximum monthly payments for your mortgage, taxes, and insurance is the larger of the two calculations below:

    A. Gross income $_____ × .28 = $_____(3a)

    B. Gross Income $_____ × .36 = $_____

         Minus line 2 $_____

         Equals $_____(3b)

4. Price of the home you plan to purchase: $_____(4a)

    Add: Estimated closing expenses (2 percent to 4 percent of line 4) $_____(4b)

    Total (4a) + (4b) $_____(4c)

5. Assets or cash available for down payment. $_____(5a)

    Minus 2.5 percent of (4a) to be used for house repairs $_____(5b)

    Subtract 5b from 5a $_____(5c)

6. Amount of loan you need to obtain (4c) − (5c) = $_____(6a)

7. Calculate your monthly mortgage payment: (Use Mortgage Monthly Payment Chart on page 307: _____ years @ _____ percent) $_____(7a)

    Add: Projected monthly insurance premium $_____(7b)

    Add: Projected monthly real estate taxes $_____(7c)

    Equals total payment for mortgage, taxes, and insurance $_____(7d)

8. Is (7d) less than the amount calculated in either steps (3a) or (3b)?

   If yes, you are within your limits. If no, the amount of the price of home (4a) needs to be lowered. Reduce (4a) and recalculate.

5. Establish Your Crisis Plan

Now you will establish your own crisis plan (refer to Chapter 10). I believe that there are three crisis areas we need to plan for:

- Emergency expenses
- Insurance
- Death

CRISIS PLANNING WORKSHEET

Emergency expenses

1. Calculate how much you need in your emergency fund:

   Your minimum amount: 1 × $_____ (Your monthly take-home pay) = $_____

   Your maximum amount: 3 × $_____ (Your monthly take-home pay) = $_____

2. Do you have this much available in an emergency fund? YES NO
   If not, what are some creative things you can do to jump-start your fund?

   1. _____

   2. _____

   3. _____

Next, you need to plan your insurance program. Begin by filling in the life insurance worksheet (see Chapter 10).

LIFE INSURANCE WORKSHEET

*Be sure to recalculate each year due to changing income,
investments, debt, and needs.*

1. Current annual income needs for
   entire family $_____ × 80 percent = $_____(1)

2. Continued or new income to be received after death:

Income of living spouse	$_____
Social Security	$_____
Other income	$_____
Total	$_____(2)

3. Net annual income needs after death of spouse (line 1 minus
   line 2) $_____(3)

4. Lump sum needed to fund annual cash needs determined in
   line 3 $_____(4)

   Multiply line 3 times the factor below. (This assumes 8 percent
   interest and 5 percent inflation.)

Number of Years Income Needed	Factor
5	4.58
10	8.53
15	11.94
20	14.88
25	17.41
35	21.49

5. College funding needs $_____(5)

6. Outstanding debt to be paid $_____(6)

7. Medical and burial expenses (estimate $5,000 to $10,000) $_____(7)

8. Emergency fund (line 1 divided by 12 multiplied by 3) $_____(8)

9. Total needs (add lines 4 + 5 + 6 + 7 + 8) $_____(9)

10. Liquid assets/investments available to offset total needs $_____(10)

11. Face value of all life insurance coverage you presently have on $_____(11)
    yourself.

12. Total funds available at death (add lines 10 + 11) $_____(12)

13. Additional life insurance needs (if any) (subtract line 9 minus 12) $_____(13)

NOTES:

Line 2:   Call 1-800-234-5772 for Social Security information and projections.

Line 4:   Will you need additional income until (1) You can go to work, (2) The children
          finish college, (3) Retirement income begins? Use Table C in Appendix A if you
          want to change the assumptions of 8 percent interest and 5 percent inflation.
          These factors come from the 3 percent column of Table C (8 percent − 5 percent
          = 3 percent).

Line 5:   The college funds will need to be invested and earn at least 6 percent to keep
          up with college inflation costs.

Line 6:   Do you want to pay off credit card debt, mortgage, personal loans?

Line 10: Investments, CDs, stocks, mutual funds.

Now, you need to evaluate your health insurance (see Chapter 10).

WORKSHEET FOR ASSESSING HEALTH
INSURANCE OPTIONS

Option 1

Amount of monthly premium:	$_____
Amount of deductible:	$_____
Coinsurance	_____ / _____
Stop-Loss	$_____
Maximum	$_____

Your Personal Financial Plan:

1 Name	2 Amount of Medical Bills	3 Amount You Pay for Deductible	4 Amount You Pay for Coinsurance	5 Total Amount You Will Be Paying
_____	$_____	$_____	$_____	$_____
_____	_____	_____	_____	_____
_____	_____	_____	_____	_____
_____	_____	_____	_____	_____
_____	_____	_____	_____	_____
_____	_____	_____	_____	_____
_____	_____	_____	_____	_____

Monthly insurance premium _____ × 12 months = $_____

Total Out-of-Pocket
Cost to You: $_____

WORKSHEET FOR ASSESSING HEALTH INSURANCE OPTIONS

Option 2

Amount of monthly premium: $_____
Amount of deductible: $_____
Coinsurance   _____ / _____
Stop-Loss $_____
Maximum $_____

1 Name	2 Amount of Medical Bills	3 Amount You Pay for Deductible	4 Amount You Pay for Coinsurance	5 Total Amount You Will Be Paying
_____	$_____	$_____	$_____	$_____
_____	_____	_____	_____	_____
_____	_____	_____	_____	_____
_____	_____	_____	_____	_____

1 Name	2 Amount of Medical Bills	3 Amount You Pay for Deductible	4 Amount You Pay for Coinsurance	5 Total Amount You Will Be Paying
_____	$_____	$_____	$_____	$_____
_____	_____	_____	_____	_____
_____	_____	_____	_____	_____

Monthly insurance premium _____ × 12 months = ... $_____

Total Out-of-Pocket Cost to You: $_____

WORKSHEET FOR ASSESSING HEALTH INSURANCE OPTIONS
Option 3

Amount of monthly premium: $_____
Amount of deductible: $_____
Coinsurance _____ / _____
Stop-Loss $_____
Maximum $_____

1 Name	2 Amount of Medical Bills	3 Amount You Pay for Deductible	4 Amount You Pay for Coinsurance	5 Total Amount You Will Be Paying
_____	$_____	$_____	$_____	$_____
_____	_____	_____	_____	_____
_____	_____	_____	_____	_____
_____	_____	_____	_____	_____
_____	_____	_____	_____	_____
_____	_____	_____	_____	_____
_____	_____	_____	_____	_____

Monthly insurance premium _____ × 12 months = ... $_____

Total Out-of-Pocket Cost to You: $_____

Next, you need to review your other insurance needs. Meet with your agent and confirm that you have adequate insurance. Ask about ways to lower your premium if possible.

_____ Home or Renters
_____ Car
_____ Health
_____ Disability
_____ Life

Suggested insurance changes to consider making:

1. _____

2. _____

3. _____

4. _____

Families will find the next chart helpful, especially when there is an unexpected death in the family. Just because one spouse knows where all the important papers are located does not mean the other spouse does. By taking the time to fill out this sheet now, you could save months of frustration for your spouse and other family members.

IMPORTANT RECORDS

Date filled out: _____

Name: _____

Social Security #_____ - _____ - _____

Address: _____ City_____ State_____ Zip_____

If information is not on this sheet, you will find it attached.

An Accurate Forecast of Your Future _____

Location of:

____ Safe-deposit box: _____

____ Birth certificates: _____

____ Will: _____

____ Car title: _____

____ Marriage license: _____

____ House deed: _____

____ Past tax records: _____

____ Current-year tax records: _____

____ Home insurance policy: _____

____ Auto insurance policy: _____

____ Life insurance policy: _____

____ Most recent copy of steward sheet (personal balance sheet) listing all our assets and liabilities. This balance sheet should also include a detailed list of investments owned and debts owed and when due.

____ Retirement information (list of IRAs and company retirement benefit plan).

Bills due: List to whom and approximately how much is due.

The bills to be paid monthly are:

1. _____
2. _____
3. _____

4. _____

5. _____

6. _____

The bills to be paid semiannually are:

1. _____

2. _____

3. _____

4. _____

5. _____

6. _____

The bills to be paid annually are:

1. _____

2. _____

3. _____

4. _____

5. _____

6. _____

Key people you should know about and seek help from:

Life insurance agent:

Name: _____ Address _____

Phone Number _____

Attorney:

Name: _____ Address _____

Phone Number _____

Accountant/CPA/Tax Adviser:

Name: _____ Address _____

Phone Number _____

Financial Adviser/Investor:

Name: _____ Address _____

Phone Number _____

Banker:

Name: _____ Address _____

Phone Number _____

Seek overall advice concerning financial matters from:

Name: _____ Address _____

Phone Number _____

Burial Information:

Name of Funeral Home: _____

Location _____

Phone Number _____

Preference of Pastor/Speaker:

Name: _____ Address _____

Phone Number _____

6. *Develop and Use a Money Allocation Plan*

Begin using your money allocation plan to help you accomplish your goals! The money allocation plan is the key tool that will keep you headed in the right direction with your financial plan! If you haven't already done so, use the MAP form on pages 319 to 322 to begin your allocation system *now.*

Once you have established your goals and personal budgeting, you are ready to begin implementing your plan. The first active step in dispersing your income should be to have "giving" as your highest financial priority.

7. Give Generously

We discussed the importance of generous giving in Chapter 11. Now work through your own contributions below:

ANALYSIS OF CHARITABLE CONTRIBUTIONS

Total income last year: $_____(a)

Total given last year: $_____(b)

Total given last year as a percentage
(b) ÷ (a): _____%

Are you satisfied with this percentage? Yes   No

Total income expected this year: $_____

Percent to be given _____%

Amount to be given this year: $_____

To whom	**How much**
_____	$_____
_____	_____
_____	_____
_____	_____
_____	_____
_____	_____

MONEY ALLOCATION PLAN

DATE	SOURCE OF INCOME	BUDGETED	NON-BUDGETED	TOTAL DEPOSIT
TOTALS FOR MONTH	$	$	$

	ALLOCATION WORKSHEET									
	BUDGET $	DEPOSIT AMOUNTS FROM INCOME CHART ABOVE								
MAP CATEGORY	$	$	$	$	$	$	$	$	$	$

D / #	+	−	=	D / #	+	−	=	D / #	+	−	=	D / #	+	−	=
BB				BB				BB				BB			

D / #	+	−	=	D / #	+	−	=	D / #	+	−	=	D / #	+	−	=
BB				BB				BB				BB			

D / #	+	−	=	D / #	+	−	=	D / #	+	−	=	D / #	+	−	=
BB				BB				BB				BB			

D / #	+	−	=	D / #	+	−	=	D / #	+	−	=	D / #	+	−	=
BB				BB				BB				BB			

D / #	+	−	=	D / #	Item	+	−	=	D / #	Item	+	−	=
BB				BB					BB				
									D / #	Item	+	−	=
									BB				
				D / #	+	−	=	D / #	+	−	=	D / #	+	−	=
				BB				BB				BB			

C R E D I T   C A R D S

D / #	Item	Transfer From	Card	PD	+	−	=
BB							

D / #	+	−	=	D / #	+	−	=	D / #	ITEM	+	−	=
BB				BB				BB				

D / #	+	−	=	D / #	+	−	=	D / #	ITEM	+	−	=
BB				BB				BB				

D / #	+	−	=	D / #	+	−	=	D / #	ITEM	+	−	=
BB				BB				BB				

D / #	+	−	=	D / #	+	−	=	D / #	ITEM	+	−	=
BB				BB				BB				

8. Saving/Investing

Review Chapter 9 for additional information.

When someone finds out I am a financial counselor, one of the most common questions I receive is: "Where should I invest my money?"

I always hold up my hands and say, "Wait just a minute. Have you earned the right to invest? Before we can talk about where you ought to invest your money, we need to discuss seven preliminary steps."

Then I go through the first seven steps in biblical financial planning, which we have discussed throughout this chapter. Very few have earned the right to invest! That comes at the end of our plan, not at the beginning.

Now that *you* have completed these first seven steps, you are ready to consider investing.

SETTING UP YOUR SAVINGS PLAN

Total income last year: $_____(a)

Total saved last year: $_____(b)

Total saved last year as a percentage
   (b) ÷ (a):   _____%

Are you satisfied with this percentage?   _____ yes _____ no

Savings Analysis

1. What percent of your income do you plan to save this year? _____

2. Are you satisfied with this percent? _____ yes _____ no

3. If you are not satisfied with the percent you plan to save, what changes can you make that will help you to save more?

4. Are you taking advantage of any company savings or investment plans?

Investment Analysis

Investment	Amount	Return of Investment This Year (%)
_____	$_____	_____%
_____	_____	_____%
_____	_____	_____%
_____	_____	_____%
_____	_____	_____%
_____	_____	_____%
_____	_____	_____%
_____	_____	_____%

1. Review each investment in your portfolio.

2. Are you satisfied with the performance of your investments?
   _____ yes _____ no

3. Are any changes needed at this time?

Now look at your daily spending.

9. Spending

Answer the following questions and consider whether you are using your money as wisely as possible.

1. Do you need to make any changes in your spending habits?
    _____ yes _____ no

2. Are you using a MAP?
    _____ yes _____ no

3. Are you satisfied with how your financial resources are being spent?
    _____ yes _____ no

Before we finish, it's important to keep an eternal perspective.

10. Maintain an Eternal Perspective

Our eternal perspective is covered in Chapter 14. Now is the time to decide which economy is guiding you.

1. Are you prepared to give an accounting of your life here on earth?

2. What things can you do in your life, that will help you to become a better steward?

Finally, the last step reemphasizes that financial planning is a continuous process.

11. Consistently Analyze Your Financial Condition

1. Evaluate and update your MAP weekly.

2. Evaluate your investments at least monthly.

3. Evaluate your overall plan at least annually.

Conclusion

If I had to use one word to summarize the advice I've shared in this book, I would use the word *faithful*. Be *faithful* in the small things of life. *Faithful* in the big things in life. *Faithful* to your family and faithful to your God.

You don't have to be intelligent to be faithful. You don't have to be rich to be faithful. Anyone, young or old, rich or poor, can be faithful. Are you being a faithful steward and smart money manager?

One day, when you meet the Lord face-to-face, will He find you faithful? Will you hear Him say, "Well done, good and faithful servant"? (see Matt. 25:21). The answer to this question rests totally with you.

What will be your answer?

APPENDIX A:
Financial Tables

The six financial tables in this appendix are designed to help you project how various interest rates will affect your savings plans. The tables are:

- **Table A: Monthly Savings Factors.** This table helps you determine the dollar amount you need to save each month to accomplish a specific financial goal.

- **Table B: Inflation Factors.** This table will help you determine what a dollar today will be equivalent to in a specific number of years with various inflation rates.

- **Table C: Annual Outflow Factors.** Using this table, you can determine the "lump sum" you need to fund a specific cash flow over a specified period of time.

- **Table D: Future Value Factors.** Determine the future value of a single sum using the information in this table.

- **Table E: Present Value Factors.** What lump-sum dollar value do you need to invest today in order to accomplish a specific goal? This table will help you determine how much you need to invest.

- **Table F: Annual Savings Factors.** This table will help you determine how much your investment account will be worth in a specified number of years when you consistently save a specified amount each year.

Table A: Monthly Savings

Table A will help you determine the dollar amount you need to save each month to accomplish a specific dollar goal. One way to use this is in saving money so you can buy a car for cash (see Chapter 6).

How Table A Works

Let's say you have established a savings goal of $10,000, and you need to accomplish your goal in five years. How much do you need to save each month to do this? In using this table, three known factors are needed: the dollar amount of the goal, the projected rate the investment will earn, and the number of years until you reach the goal. In this example, we plan to invest our money in an investment returning 8 percent.

First, find 8 percent and five years on the table. The factor given is 73.32.

Second, divide the goal amount ($10,000) by the factor (73.32), which equals $136.39. Therefore, you need to save $136.39 each month for five years earning 8 percent to accomplish your goal of $10,000.

Summary

$ Goal ÷ factor = Amount to be saved each month

TABLE A
MONTHLY SAVINGS FACTORS

How much do I need to save each month in order
to have $_____?*

PROJECTED RATE

Years	2%	4%	6%	8%	9%	10%	12%
1	12.11	12.22	12.34	12.45	12.51	12.56	12.68
2	24.48	24.93	25.43	25.91	26.19	26.44	26.97
3	37.09	38.16	39.34	40.49	41.15	41.76	43.08
4	49.97	51.92	54.10	56.26	57.52	58.67	61.22
5	63.11	66.23	68.77	73.32	75.42	77.36	81.67
6	76.52	81.12	86.41	91.79	95.01	97.98	104.71
7	90.21	96.61	104.07	111.78	116.43	120.77	130.67
8	104.18	112.73	122.83	133.40	139.86	145.92	159.93
9	118.44	129.50	142.74	156.81	165.48	173.70	192.89
10	132.99	146.94	163.88	182.13	193.51	204.38	230.04
11	147.84	165.09	186.32	209.54	224.17	238.25	271.90
12	163.00	183.96	210.15	239.19	257.71	275.66	319.06
13	187.64	203.60	235.44	271.29	294.39	316.97	372.21
14	194.26	224.03	262.30	306.01	334.52	362.58	432.10
15	210.37	245.29	290.82	343.59	378.41	412.95	499.58
16	226.82	267.40	321.09	384.56	426.41	468.57	575.62
17	243.60	290.40	353.23	428.27	478.92	530.00	661.31
18	260.73	314.33	387.35	475.90	536.35	597.83	757.86
19	278.21	339.23	423.58	527.43	599.17	672.73	866.66
20	296.05	365.13	462.04	583.20	667.89	755.44	989.26
21	314.26	392.08	502.87	643.55	743.05	846.78	1127.40
22	332.84	420.11	546.23	708.85	825.26	947.64	1283.07
23	351.81	449.27	592.25	779.52	915.18	1059.02	1458.47
24	371.81	479.61	641.12	856.00	1013.54	1182.01	1656.13
25	390.92	485.43	692.99	938.75	1121.21	1317.83	1879.85
26	411.09	544.00	748.07	1028.31	1238.90	1467.81	2129.81
27	431.06	578.16	806.55	1125.22	1367.51	1433.42	2412.61

PROJECTED RATE—*Cont'd*

Years	2%	4%	6%	8%	9%	10%	12%
28	452.67	613.69	868.63	1230.09	1508.30	1816.31	2731.27
29	474.10	650.66	934.54	1343.57	1662.30	2018.27	3090.35
30	495.98	689.12	1004.52	1466.38	1830.74	2241.29	3494.96
31	518.30	729.13	1078.81	1599.27	2014.99	2487.56	3950.90
32	541.09	770.76	1157.68	1743.08	2216.51	2759.52	4464.65
33	564.34	814.06	1241.42	1898.70	2436.95	3059.83	5043.56
34	588.08	859.11	1330.32	2067.10	2678.06	3391.46	5695.90
35	612.30	905.97	1424.71	2249.33	2941.78	3757.66	6430.96
36	637.02	954.73	1524.92	2446.54	3230.25	4162.06	7259.25
37	662.25	1005.45	1631.31	2659.94	3545.78	4608.62	8192.59
38	688.00	1058.22	1744.26	2890.87	3890.90	5101.74	9244.29
39	714.28	1113.11	1864.18	3140.77	4268.41	5646.29	10429.38
40	741.10	1170.22	1991.49	3411.20	4681.32	6247.62	11764.77
41	768.47	1229.63	2126.66	3703.83	5132.97	6911.65	13269.52
42	796.41	1291.44	2270.16	4020.51	5626.98	7644.93	14965.11
43	824.92	1355.74	2422.51	4363.19	6167.34	8454.57	16875.75
44	854.02	1422.63	2584.26	4734.03	6758.39	9348.84	19028.70
45	883.72	1492.22	2755.99	5135.32	7404.88	10336.35	21454.69

*$ Goal ÷ factor = the monthly savings needed to accomplish dollar goal

Table B: Inflation Factors

Table B will help you determine what a dollar amount today will be equivalent to in a specific number of years with various inflation rates.

How Table B Works

If you want to determine what $30,000 in today's dollars will be equivalent to in thirty years due to inflation, use this table along with three known factors: The present amount in today's dollars ($30,000), the projected inflation rate (in our example, 4 percent), and the number of years (in this example, thirty).

First, find 4 percent and thirty years on the table. The factor given is 3.24.

Second, multiply 3.24 × $30,000, which equals $97,200. Therefore, $30,000 in today's dollars with an inflation rate of 4 percent is equivalent to $97,200 in thirty years.

TABLE B
INFLATION FACTORS

PROJECTED INFLATION RATE

Years	3%	4%	5%	6%	7%	8%	9%	10%
1	1.03	1.04	1.05	1.06	1.07	1.08	1.09	1.10
2	1.06	1.08	1.10	1.12	1.14	1.17	1.19	1.21
3	1.09	1.12	1.16	1.19	1.23	1.26	1.30	1.33
4	1.13	1.17	1.22	1.26	1.31	1.36	1.41	1.46
5	1.16	1.22	1.28	1.34	1.40	1.47	1.54	1.61
6	1.19	1.27	1.34	1.42	1.50	1.59	1.68	1.77
7	1.23	1.32	1.41	1.50	1.61	1.71	1.83	1.95
8	1.27	1.37	1.48	1.59	1.72	1.85	1.99	2.14
9	1.30	1.42	1.55	1.69	1.84	2.00	2.17	2.36
10	1.34	1.48	1.63	1.79	1.97	2.16	2.37	2.59
11	1.38	1.54	1.71	1.90	2.10	2.33	2.58	2.85
12	1.43	1.60	1.80	2.01	2.25	2.52	2.81	3.14
13	1.47	1.67	1.89	2.13	2.41	2.72	3.07	3.45
14	1.51	1.73	1.98	2.26	2.58	2.94	3.34	3.80
15	1.56	1.80	2.08	2.40	2.76	3.17	3.64	4.18
16	1.60	1.87	2.18	2.54	2.95	3.43	3.97	4.59
17	1.65	1.95	2.29	2.69	3.16	3.70	4.33	5.05
18	1.70	2.03	2.41	2.85	3.38	4.00	4.72	5.56
19	1.75	2.11	2.53	3.03	3.62	4.32	5.14	6.12
20	1.81	2.19	2.65	3.21	3.87	4.66	5.60	6.73

PROJECTED INFLATION RATE—*Cont'd*

Years	3%	4%	5%	6%	7%	8%	9%	10%
21	1.86	2.28	2.79	3.40	4.14	5.03	6.11	7.40
22	1.92	2.37	2.93	3.60	4.43	5.44	6.66	8.14
23	1.97	2.46	3.07	3.82	4.74	5.87	7.26	8.95
24	2.03	2.56	3.23	4.05	5.07	6.34	7.91	9.85
25	2.09	2.67	3.39	4.29	5.43	6.85	8.62	10.83
26	2.16	2.77	3.56	4.55	5.81	7.40	9.40	11.92
27	2.22	2.88	3.73	4.82	6.21	7.99	10.25	12.11
28	2.29	3.00	3.92	5.11	6.65	8.63	11.17	14.42
29	2.36	3.12	4.12	5.42	7.11	9.32	12.17	15.86
30	2.43	3.24	4.32	5.74	7.61	10.06	13.27	17.45
31	2.50	3.37	4.54	6.09	8.15	10.87	14.46	19.19
32	2.58	3.51	4.76	6.45	8.72	11.74	15.76	21.11
33	2.65	3.65	5.00	6.84	9.33	12.68	17.18	23.23
34	2.73	3.79	5.25	7.25	9.98	13.68	18.73	25.55
35	2.81	3.95	5.52	7.69	10.68	14.79	20.41	28.10
36	2.90	4.10	5.79	8.15	11.42	15.97	22.25	30.91
37	2.99	4.27	6.08	8.64	12.22	17.25	24.25	34.00
38	3.07	4.44	6.39	9.15	13.08	18.63	26.44	37.40
39	3.17	4.62	6.70	9.70	13.99	20.12	28.82	41.14
40	3.26	4.80	7.04	10.29	14.97	21.72	31.41	45.26
41	3.36	4.99	7.39	10.90	16.02	23.46	34.24	49.79
42	3.46	5.19	7.76	11.56	17.14	25.34	37.32	54.76
43	3.56	5.40	8.15	12.25	18.34	27.37	40.68	60.24
44	3.67	5.62	8.56	12.99	19.63	29.56	44.34	66.26
45	3.78	5.84	8.99	13.76	21.00	31.92	48.33	72.86

© 1989 Ethan Pope

Table C: Annual Outflow

Table C will help you determine the "lump sum" needed to fund a specific cash flow over a certain period of time. This is useful in deciding how much money you need to have when you retire.

How Table C Works

Let's say you are planning for retirement and decide you need an annual income of $30,000 each year for a total of twenty-five years. How much do you need in an investment account when you retire at age sixty-five to fully fund your annual income needs?

To use this table, three known factors are needed: the dollar amount of the annual income needed (in this case, $30,000), the projected rate the investment will earn (let's say 8 percent), and the number of years money will be paid out of the fund (let's say twenty-five).

First, find 8 and 25 years on Table C. The factor given is 10.67.

Second, multiply 10.67 × $30,000, which equals $320,100. Therefore, $320,100 is needed in an investment account to fully fund an annual payout of $30,000 for twenty-five years.

Note: After the last payout is made in twenty-five years, you will have $0 in your investment account. During those twenty-five years you will be using both principal and interest money.

TABLE C
ANNUAL OUTFLOW FACTORS

How much do I need in a fund to have an annual outflow
of $_____ for _____ years?

PROJECTED RATE

Years	2%	3%	4%	5%	6%	7%	8%	9%	10%
1	.980	.971	.962	.952	.943	.935	.926	.917	.909
2	1.94	1.91	1.89	1.86	1.83	1.81	1.78	1.76	1.74
3	2.88	2.83	2.78	2.72	2.67	2.62	2.58	2.53	2.49
4	3.81	3.72	3.63	3.55	3.47	3.39	3.31	3.24	3.17

PROJECTED RATE—Cont'd

Years	2%	3%	4%	5%	6%	7%	8%	9%	10%
5	4.71	4.58	4.54	4.33	4.21	4.10	3.99	3.89	3.79
6	5.60	5.42	5.24	5.08	4.92	4.77	4.62	4.49	4.36
7	6.47	6.23	6.00	5.79	5.58	5.39	5.21	5.03	4.87
8	7.33	7.02	6.73	6.46	6.21	5.97	5.75	5.53	5.33
9	8.16	7.79	7.44	7.11	6.80	6.52	6.25	5.99	5.76
10	8.98	8.53	8.11	7.72	7.36	7.02	6.71	6.42	6.14
11	9.79	9.25	8.76	8.31	7.89	7.50	7.14	6.81	6.50
12	10.58	9.95	9.39	8.86	8.38	7.94	7.54	7.16	6.81
13	11.35	10.63	9.98	9.39	8.85	8.36	7.90	7.49	7.10
14	12.11	11.30	10.56	9.90	9.29	8.75	8.24	7.79	7.37
15	12.85	11.94	11.12	10.38	9.71	9.11	8.56	8.06	7.61
16	13.58	12.56	11.65	10.84	10.11	9.45	8.85	8.31	7.82
17	14.29	13.17	12.17	11.27	10.48	9.76	9.12	8.54	8.02
18	14.99	13.75	12.66	11.69	10.83	10.06	9.37	8.76	8.20
19	15.68	14.33	13.13	12.09	11.16	10.34	9.60	8.95	8.36
20	16.35	14.88	13.59	12.46	11.47	10.59	9.82	9.13	8.51
21	17.01	15.42	14.03	12.82	11.76	10.84	10.02	9.29	8.65
22	17.66	15.94	14.45	13.16	12.04	11.06	10.20	9.44	8.77
23	18.29	16.44	14.86	13.49	12.30	11.27	10.37	9.58	8.88
24	18.91	16.94	15.25	13.80	12.55	11.45	10.53	9.71	8.98
25	19.52	17.41	15.62	14.09	12.78	11.65	10.67	9.82	9.08
26	20.12	17.88	15.98	14.37	13.00	11.83	10.81	9.93	9.16
27	20.71	18.33	16.33	14.64	13.21	11.99	10.94	10.03	9.24
28	21.28	18.76	16.66	14.90	13.41	12.14	11.05	10.12	9.31
29	21.84	19.19	16.98	15.14	13.59	12.28	11.16	10.20	9.37
30	22.40	19.60	17.29	15.37	13.76	12.41	11.26	10.27	9.43
31	22.94	20.00	17.59	15.59	13.93	12.53	11.35	10.34	9.48
32	23.47	20.39	17.87	15.80	14.08	12.65	11.43	10.41	9.53
33	23.99	20.77	18.15	16.00	14.23	12.75	11.51	10.46	9.57
34	24.50	21.13	18.41	16.19	14.37	12.85	11.59	10.51	9.61
35	25.00	21.49	18.66	16.37	14.50	12.95	11.65	10.57	9.64
36	25.49	21.83	18.91	16.55	14.62	13.04	11.72	10.61	9.68

Years	2%	3%	4%	5%	6%	7%	8%	9%	10%
37	25.97	22.17	19.14	16.71	14.74	13.12	11.78	10.65	9.71
38	26.44	22.49	19.37	16.87	14.85	13.19	11.83	10.69	9.73
39	26.93	22.81	19.58	17.02	14.95	13.26	11.88	10.73	9.76
40	27.36	23.11	19.79	17.16	15.05	13.33	11.92	10.76	9.78
41	27.80	23.41	19.99	17.29	15.14	13.39	11.97	10.79	9.80
42	28.23	23.70	20.19	17.42	15.22	13.45	12.01	10.81	9.82
43	28.66	23.98	20.37	17.55	15.31	13.51	12.04	10.84	9.83
44	29.08	24.25	20.55	17.66	15.38	13.56	12.08	10.86	9.85
45	29.49	24.52	20.72	17.77	15.46	13.61	12.11	10.88	9.86

Table D: Future Value

This table will help you determine the future value of a single sum.

How Table D Works

You presently have $10,000 in an investment earning 8 percent compounded annually, and you want to know how much your investment will be worth in thirty years if you do not invest any additional money in the account. To use this table, you need three known factors: the present dollar amount of the investment (in our example, $10,000), the projected rate on your investment (in this case, 8 percent), and the number of years to be compounded (thirty).

First, find 8 percent and thirty years on the table. The factor given is 10.06.

Second, multiply 10.06 × $10,000, which equals $100,600. Therefore, your investment of $10,000 will be worth $100,600 if it earns 8 percent, compounded annually for thirty years.

TABLE D
FUTURE VALUE FACTORS

PROJECTED RATE

Years	3%	4%	5%	6%	7%	8%	9%	10%	12%
1	1.03	1.04	1.05	1.06	1.07	1.08	1.09	1.10	1.12
2	1.06	1.08	1.10	1.12	1.14	1.17	1.19	1.21	1.25
3	1.09	1.12	1.16	1.19	1.23	1.26	1.30	1.33	1.40
4	1.13	1.17	1.22	1.26	1.31	1.36	1.41	1.46	1.57
5	1.16	1.22	1.28	1.34	1.40	1.47	1.54	1.61	1.76
6	1.19	1.27	1.34	1.42	1.50	1.59	1.68	1.77	1.97
7	1.23	1.32	1.41	1.50	1.61	1.71	1.83	1.95	2.21
8	1.27	1.37	1.48	1.59	1.72	1.85	1.99	2.14	2.48
9	1.30	1.42	1.55	1.69	1.84	2.00	2.17	2.36	2.77
10	1.34	1.48	1.63	1.79	1.97	2.16	2.37	2.59	3.11
11	1.38	1.54	1.71	1.90	2.10	2.33	2.58	2.85	3.48
12	1.43	1.60	1.80	2.01	2.25	2.52	2.81	3.14	3.90
13	1.47	1.67	1.89	2.13	2.41	2.72	3.07	3.45	4.36
14	1.51	1.73	1.98	2.26	2.58	2.94	3.34	3.80	4.89
15	1.56	1.80	2.08	2.40	2.76	3.17	3.64	4.18	5.47
16	1.60	1.87	2.18	2.54	2.95	3.43	3.97	4.59	6.13
17	1.65	1.95	2.29	2.69	3.16	3.70	4.33	5.05	6.87
18	1.70	2.03	2.41	2.85	3.38	4.00	4.72	5.56	7.69
19	1.75	2.11	2.53	3.03	3.62	4.32	5.14	6.12	8.61
20	1.81	2.19	2.65	3.21	3.87	4.66	5.60	6.73	9.65
21	1.86	2.28	2.79	3.40	4.14	5.03	6.11	7.40	10.80
22	1.92	2.37	2.93	3.60	4.43	5.44	6.66	8.14	12.10
23	1.97	2.46	3.07	3.82	4.74	5.87	7.26	8.95	13.55
24	2.03	2.56	3.23	4.05	5.07	6.34	7.91	9.85	15.18
25	2.09	2.67	3.39	4.29	5.43	6.85	8.62	10.83	17.00
26	2.16	2.77	3.56	4.55	5.81	7.40	9.40	11.92	19.04
27	2.22	2.88	3.73	4.82	6.21	7.99	10.25	12.11	21.32
28	2.29	3.00	3.92	5.11	6.65	8.63	11.17	14.42	23.88
29	2.36	3.12	4.12	5.42	7.11	9.32	12.17	15.86	26.75

Years	3%	4%	5%	6%	7%	8%	9%	10%	12%
30	2.43	3.24	4.32	5.74	7.61	10.06	13.27	17.45	29.96
31	2.50	3.37	4.54	6.09	8.15	10.87	14.46	19.19	33.58
32	2.58	3.51	4.76	6.45	8.72	11.74	15.76	21.11	37.58
33	2.65	3.65	5.00	6.84	9.33	12.68	17.18	23.23	42.09
34	2.73	3.79	5.25	7.25	9.98	13.68	18.73	25.55	47.14
35	2.81	3.95	5.52	7.69	10.68	14.79	20.41	28.10	52.80
36	2.90	4.10	5.79	8.15	11.42	15.97	22.25	30.91	59.14
37	2.99	4.27	6.08	8.64	12.22	17.25	24.25	34.00	66.23
38	3.07	4.44	6.39	9.15	13.08	18.63	26.44	37.40	74.18
39	3.17	4.62	6.70	9.70	13.99	20.12	28.82	41.14	83.08
40	3.26	4.80	7.04	10.29	14.97	21.72	31.41	45.26	93.05
41	3.36	4.99	7.39	10.90	16.02	23.46	34.24	49.79	104.22
42	3.46	5.19	7.76	11.56	17.14	25.34	37.32	54.76	116.72
43	3.56	5.40	8.15	12.25	18.34	27.37	40.68	60.24	130.73
44	3.67	5.62	8.56	12.99	19.63	29.56	44.34	66.26	146.42
45	3.78	5.84	8.99	13.76	21.00	31.92	48.33	72.86	163.99

Table E: Present Value

How Table E Works

You estimate that you will need $75,000 in fifteen years. What lump sum dollar value do we need to invest today in order to accomplish our goal?

In using this table, three known factors are needed: the dollar amount needed (in our example, $75,000), the projected rate the investment will earn (10 percent), and the number of years the investment will earn interest (fifteen).

First, find 10 percent and fifteen years on the table. The factor given is .23939.

Second, multiply $75,000 by .23939, which equals $17,954.25. Therefore, you need to invest a lump sum of $17,954.25 earning 10 percent to accomplish your goal of $75,000 in fifteen years.

TABLE E
PRESENT VALUE FACTORS

How much do I need in a fund today to accomplish
a $_____ goal in the future?

PROJECTED RATE

Years	4%	6%	8%	9%	10%	12%	14%
1	.96154	.94339	.92592	.91743	.90909	.89285	.87719
2	.92455	.88999	.85734	.84168	.82644	.79719	.76964
3	.88899	.83962	.79383	.77183	.75131	.71178	.67497
4	.85480	.79093	.73503	.70842	.68301	.63552	.59208
5	.82192	.74726	.68058	.64993	.62092	.56742	.51937
6	.79031	.70496	.63017	.59626	.56447	.50663	.45558
7	.75991	.66505	.58349	.54703	.51316	.45235	.39963
8	.73069	.62741	.54027	.50186	.46650	.40388	.35056
9	.70258	.59190	.50025	.46042	.42409	.36061	.30750
10	.67556	.55839	.46319	.42241	.38554	.32197	.26974
11	.64958	.52678	.42888	.38753	.35049	.28747	.23661
12	.62459	.49697	.39711	.35553	.31863	.25667	.20756
13	.60057	.46884	.36769	.32618	.28966	.22917	.18207
14	.57747	.44230	.34046	.29924	.26333	.20462	.15971
15	.55526	.41726	.31524	.27454	.23939	.18269	.14009
16	.53391	.39364	.29189	.25187	.21763	.16312	.12289
17	.51337	.37136	.27027	.23107	.19784	.14564	.10780
18	.49363	.35034	.25025	.21199	.17986	.13004	.09456
19	.47464	.33051	.23171	.19449	.16350	.11610	.08295
20	.45638	.31180	.21455	.17843	.14864	.10366	.07276

Years	4%	6%	8%	9%	10%	12%	14%
21	.43883	.29415	.19865	.16370	.13513	.09256	.06382
22	.42195	.27750	.18394	.15018	.12284	.08264	.05598
23	.40572	.26179	.17031	.13778	.11678	.07378	.04911
24	.39012	.24698	.15770	.12640	.10152	.06588	.04308
25	.37511	.23300	.14601	.11596	.09229	.05882	.03779
26	.36069	.21981	.13520	.10639	.08390	.05252	.03315
27	.34681	.20736	.12518	.09760	.07627	.04689	.02908
28	.33347	.19563	.11591	.08955	.06934	.04187	.02550
29	.32065	.18455	.10732	.08215	.06303	.03738	.02237
30	.30832	.17411	.09937	.07537	.05731	.03337	.01962
31	.29646	.16425	.09201	.06914	.05210	.02980	.01721
32	.28506	.15495	.08520	.06344	.04736	.02661	.01510
33	.27409	.14618	.07888	.05820	.04305	.02375	.01324
34	.26355	.13791	.07304	.05339	.03914	.02121	.01162
35	.25341	.13010	.06763	.04898	.03558	.01894	.01019
36	.24367	.12274	.06262	.04494	.03235	.01691	.00894
37	.23429	.11579	.05798	.04123	.02941	.01510	.00784
38	.22528	.10924	.05369	.03782	.02673	.01348	.00688
39	.21662	.10305	.04971	.03470	.02430	.01203	.00603
40	.20829	.09722	.04603	.03183	.02209	.01074	.00529
41	.20027	.09172	.04262	.02920	.02008	.00959	.00464
42	.19257	.08652	.03946	.02679	.01826	.00856	.00407
43	.18517	.08163	.03654	.02458	.01660	.00765	.00357
44	.17804	.07701	.03383	.02255	.01509	.00683	.00313
45	.17120	.07265	.03132	.02069	.01372	.00610	.00275

Table F: Annual Savings

This table will help you determine how much your investment account will be worth if you are annually saving $_____ each year.

How Table F Works

You consistently save $1,500 in a mutual fund account each year for ten years. You project you can earn 10 percent on your investment each year. How much will it be worth in ten years?

In using this table, three known factors are needed: The dollar amount to be invested annually ($1,500 in our example), the projected rate on investment (10 percent), and the number of years it's to be compounded (in this case, ten years).

First, find 10 percent and ten years on the table. The factor given is 15.94.

Second, multiply 15.94 × $1,500, which equals $23,910. Therefore, your investment of $1,500 each year for ten years would be worth $23,910 if it earns 10 percent compounded annually.

TABLE F
ANNUAL SAVINGS FACTORS

I'm saving $_____ annually. What will it be worth at _____% in _____ years?

PROJECTED RATE

Years	5%	6%	8%	9%	10%	12%	14%
1	1.00	1.00	1.00	1.00	1.00	1.00	1.00
2	2.05	2.06	2.08	2.09	2.10	2.12	2.14
3	3.15	3.18	3.25	3.28	3.31	3.37	3.44
4	4.31	4.38	5.51	4.57	4.64	4.78	4.92
5	5.53	5.64	5.87	5.99	6.11	6.35	6.61
6	6.80	6.98	7.34	7.52	7.72	8.12	8.54
7	8.14	8.39	8.92	9.20	9.49	10.09	10.73
8	9.55	9.90	10.64	11.03	11.44	12.30	13.23
9	11.03	11.49	12.49	13.02	13.58	14.75	16.09
10	12.58	13.18	14.49	15.19	15.94	17.55	19.34

Financial Tables

Years	5%	6%	8%	9%	10%	12%	14%
11	14.21	14.97	16.65	17.56	18.53	20.66	23.05
12	15.92	16.87	18.98	20.14	21.38	24.13	27.27
13	17.71	18.88	21.50	22.95	24.52	28.03	32.09
14	19.60	21.02	24.22	26.02	27.98	32.39	37.58
15	21.58	23.28	27.15	29.36	31.77	37.28	43.84
16	23.66	25.67	30.32	33.00	35.95	42.75	50.98
17	25.84	28.21	33.75	36.97	40.55	48.88	59.12
18	28.13	30.91	37.45	41.30	45.60	55.75	68.39
19	30.54	33.76	41.45	46.02	51.16	63.44	78.97
20	33.07	36.79	45.76	51.16	57.28	72.05	91.03
21	35.72	39.99	50.42	56.77	64.00	81.70	104.77
22	38.51	43.59	55.46	62.87	71.40	92.50	120.44
23	41.43	46.99	60.89	69.53	79.54	104.60	138.30
24	44.50	50.82	66.77	76.79	88.50	118.16	188.66
25	47.73	54.87	63.11	84.70	98.35	133.33	181.87
26	51.11	59.16	79.95	93.32	109.18	150.33	208.33
27	54.67	63.71	87.35	102.72	121.10	169.37	238.50
28	58.40	68.53	95.34	112.97	134.21	190.70	272.89
29	62.32	73.64	103.97	124.14	148.63	214.58	312.09
30	66.44	79.06	113.28	136.31	164.49	241.33	356.79
31	70.76	84.80	123.35	149.58	181.94	271.29	407.74
32	75.30	90.89	134.21	164.04	201.14	304.85	465.82
33	80.06	97.34	145.95	179.80	222.25	342.43	532.04
34	85.07	104.18	158.63	196.98	245.48	384.52	607.52
35	90.32	111.44	172.32	215.71	271.02	431.66	693.57
36	95.84	119.12	187.10	236.13	299.13	484.46	791.67
37	101.63	127.27	203.07	258.38	330.04	543.60	903.51
38	107.71	135.90	220.32	282.63	364.04	609.83	1031.00
39	114.10	145.06	238.94	309.07	401.45	684.01	1176.34
40	120.80	154.76	259.06	337.88	442.59	767.09	1342.02
41	127.84	165.05	280.78	369.29	487.85	860.14	1530.91
42	135.23	175.95	304.24	403.53	537.64	964.36	1746.24
43	142.99	187.51	329.58	440.85	592.40	1081.08	1991.71
44	151.14	199.76	356.95	481.52	652.64	1211.81	2271.55
45	159.70	212.74	386.51	525.86	718.91	1358.23	2590.57

APPENDIX B:
Discussion Questions for Groups

The following questions are intended to prompt discussion in study groups.

Chapter 1

1. How much did you learn about money management in school?

2. What is the most important money management lesson you have ever learned? Why?

3. What causes you to be the most anxious about money matters?

4. Were your parents good role models in managing money? In what ways were they good or not so good?

5. What do you hope to learn from this book/study?

Chapter 2

1. What has been your personal experience in setting goals? Do you have written goals? Why or why not?

2. Have you ever had a "successful failure" you would like to share?

3. List three good reasons why goals and plans are so helpful in financial planning.

4. Do you and your spouse discuss your goals?

5. Who would you like to tell about the "Save 10 Percent Plan" (your child, a college student, a relative)?

6. How does a person find a way to literally save 10 percent of his or her income?

Chapter 3

1. There are many "potential" financial goals for every single or family. What financial goals do you believe that *every family* should establish? Be specific!

2. Do you have these goals for your family?

3. In what way(s) did you find the tables showing the time value of money helpful?

Chapter 4

1. What is the first sign of credit card trouble?

2. How do most people get into credit card trouble?

3. What are three rules or guidelines every family should put into practice concerning the use of credit cards?

4. Make a list of ten adjectives that best describe how a person feels when he or she is in credit card debt.

5. What are the steps to get out of credit card debt?

Chapter 5

1. What surprised you the most in this chapter about home mortgages?

2. Were you amazed to see how much debt really costs?

3. Did you realize that for most mortgages you will repay approximately 10 percent of the original loan amount after one year? What does that tell you about the "cost" of debt?

4. For a thirty-year mortgage, when does more of your monthly check start being applied to principal reduction than to pay interest? (Hint: It is more than twenty years.)

5. If a thirty-year mortgage payment is $750 per month, what will the total cost be?

6. Give three reasons everyone should be motivated to prepay on a mortgage.

Chapter 6

1. How can you make the car purchase plan work for you?

2. What steps can you take to faithfully pay yourself each month?

3. Explain why the "buy four cars and get the fifth one free" plan really works.

Chapter 7

1. Review the advantages of being debt free covered in the book.

2. Can you think of five additional advantages of being debt free?

3. What is the key for anyone to become debt free?

4. Why is debt such a part of our culture?

5. Why is being debt free so uncommon?

Chapter 8

1. List five pressures that force families to live beyond their means.

2. Come up with a solution for each pressure. How can we deal with this pressure?

3. What biblical perspective helps with this pressure?

Chapter 9

   1. Which principle was the most interesting to you?

   2. Why do so many people respond to financial scams?

   3. What is the best investment you have ever made?

   4. What is the most important concept you learned from this chapter?

   5. Reread concept number one about Johnny and Dan. What principles did you learn from this concept?

   6. Discuss the six most common investment mistakes.

Chapter 10

   1. What were your thoughts as you read the opening story about the two families, one with $25,000 in life insurance coverage and the other with $500,000?

   2. What is the number one objective in buying life insurance?

   3. Has your understanding increased about how insurance works? What have you learned?

   4. When was the last time you evaluated your life insurance coverage? Do you have enough?

   5. In your opinion, what are the most important aspects of having an emergency fund?

Chapter 11

   1. Review the statistics given at the beginning of the chapter. What do they tell you?

   2. How would you motivate God's people to be more generous in their giving?

   3. Review and briefly discuss the seven principles of giving.

Chapter 12

1. Which myth do you personally believe is the most common?

2. Name the three you think are next most common and discuss them.

3. Is there a myth we did not cover in the book that you would like to discuss?

Chapter 13

1. Discuss the importance of budgeting.

2. Why do most people fail to budget?

3. List as many benefits of budgeting as you can.

Chapter 14

1. Spend time discussing the basic differences in God's economy and the world's economy.

2. Can you draw the two-people/two-economy diagram?

3. List and discuss the seven reasons to live in God's economy.

ABOUT THE AUTHOR

Ethan Pope has trained thousands of people across America in his financial conferences and seminars.

Ethan is a Certified Financial Planner and a graduate of Dallas Theological Seminary. Ethan speaks and writes with simplicity and authority as he combines years of research, counseling, and personal experience.

For over ten years Ethan worked with Campus Crusade for Christ and the Josh McDowell Ministry. In 1988 he became the founder and president of Financial Foundations for Living Ministry.

Ethan and his wife, Janet, have two children, Natalie and Austin.

For information on:

- *Inviting Ethan Pope to speak to your church or other group*
- *Receiving a catalog of resources from Financial Foundations for Living*
- *Ordering a one-year supply of full-size (8½ by 11) MAP forms*
- *Scheduling conferences*
- *Receiving Financial Foundations for Living publications*

write to: **Ethan Pope**
Financial Foundations for Living
P.O. Box 15356
Hattiesburg, MS 39404